ZEN PIONEER

ZEN PIONEER

THE LIFE
& WORKS OF RUTH FULLER SASAKI

by Isabel Stirling

Foreword by Gary Snyder

SHOEMAKER & HOARD

Library of Congress Cataloging-in-Publication Data

Stirling, Isabel.
Zen pioneer : the life & works of Ruth Fuller Sasaki /
by Isabel Stirling ; foreword by Gary Snyder.
p. cm.
Includes bibliographical references and index.
Hardcover: ISBN-13 978-1-59376-110-3 (alk. paper)
            ISBN-10 1-59376-110-4 (alk. paper)
Paperback: ISBN-13 978-1-59376-170-3
            ISBN-10 1-59376-170-8
1. Sasaki, Ruth Fuller, 1893–1967. 2. Zen Buddhists—United States—
Biography. I. Title.
BQ984.A6757S75 2006
294.3'927092—dc22   2006008565

Book design by Gopa & Ted2, Inc.
Printed in the United States of America

Shoemaker Hoard
www.shoemakerhoard.com

Hardcover: 10 9 8 7 6 5 4 3 2
Paperback: 10 9 8 7 6 5 4 3 2 1

To Haru Yoshida and
Gary Snyder

Contents

Foreword by Gary Snyder   ix

Preface   xv

PART ONE: HER LIFE

1. The Chicago Years, 1892–1929   3

2. First Trips to Asia, 1930–1940   11

3. New York, 1941–1948   37

4. Kyoto Beginnings, 1949–1955   47

5. Rebuilding Ryosen-an, 1955–1960   71

6. Research and Translation, 1960–1967   109

7. Epilogue: Beyond 1967   131

PART TWO: HER WORK

Zen: A Religion   137

Zen: A Method for Religious Awakening   159

Rinzai Zen Study for Foreigners in Japan   179

Acknowledgments   247

Chronology   251

Endnotes	259
Glossary	271
Bibliography	275
Index	291

Foreword

WE HAVE TO FACE IT, Zen Buddhism is pretty elite. From T'ang dynasty China on, it seems that the monks and masters started out as youthful genius readers and memorizers of the Confucian classics. This means they were of the gentry class, that their parents afforded tutors, and that they were on the path toward a lifetime job in the government. One of the few exceptions seems to have been Hui-neng, the Sixth Patriarch, who by some accounts was a tribal person from the mountains of the south, what today we would call a Hmong or a Miao. He could not read or write.

But the traditional Zen biographies tell the story over and over of a young man expert first at the Chinese classics, then mastering quite swiftly all of the Buddhist texts to become a priest, skilled at lecturing and presenting esoteric doctrinal points. This educated and exceptional person via some critical event realizes that he (or occasionally she) has not yet had a deep and personal experience of Buddhist awakening and is mouthing intellectual abstractions. He finds a Zen master, who bangs on him, shouts at him, exposes his shallowness to him, and puts him onto a path of spiritual practice.

That leads into a yet further elite—the Ch'an and Zen Buddhist lineages of those who saw through self-serving rationalizations and speculative philosophies. The strength of their personal insights is not to be doubted. The role they played out for the rest of their lives is one of remarkable creativity, subtlety, ingenuity, compassion, and elegance. From time to time even emperors envied them.

But a lore of discarding books and letters, of teaching with shouts and blows, and sticking to weeding the garden and cutting firewood—as real as it was—did not disguise the special quality of this small and highly literate group. Over the centuries they developed a formidable culture of spiritual teaching texts, impenetrable anecdotes, poems, paintings, iconic carvings, sublime rituals, and fine-honed organization.

Ruth Fuller Everett did not become interested in Zen Buddhism because she was a bohemian, an artist, or any sort of cultural revolutionary. She entered onto this path because she was more than just very smart: she was smart enough to realize that her own power and drive and capacity were a little too much, and she deeply intuited that she needed another direction. From her teenage years she set herself against the assumptions of theistic religions and their language of heaven and hell, evil and sin.

Ruth Fuller Sasaki was a Lady. A Zen Lady, a title she would never shrink from. She was to become an ordained Zen priest with her own temple in Kyoto. As much as any neo-Confucian gentleman of Sung China or Tokugawa, Japan, she realized the needs and difficulties of governance. From her youthful first marriage she learned to manage a large household of cooks, servants, nannies, and gardeners. If a Tokugawa warrior was swift to draw his sword, R. F. S. was equally swift to deploy a team of lawyers, to have multiple letters out, to call meetings, and to get decisions made. She designed houses, renovated Manhattan buildings, restored a Japanese temple. Her entrance into Zen proper was facilitated by Daisetz T. Suzuki, virtual single-handed founder of an English-language literature on this school of Buddhist meditation. She had visited him in Kyoto on the return trip from a business tour of Manchuria and China with her husband, Edward Everett, in 1930. Edward played golf in China among the Imperial tombs. In 1931 Ruth sailed back to Kyoto and with Suzuki's help was allowed to sit *sesshin* at the Nanzen-ji Monastery under one of the toughest Zen masters of that time, Nanshinken Roshi. She made two later trips to Kyoto to continue her studies.

After Mr. Everett's health declined, Ruth was introduced to Sasaki Shigetsu Roshi (his teaching name was Sokei-an), who was living and working in New York City. She joined his group and improved his quarters. Mr. Everett died, and three years later Ruth and Shigetsu were married. (Mutually in love, Alan Watts said, but Shigetsu's long illness and wartime internment were also part of it.) Sasaki Shigetsu Roshi died shortly thereafter. Once the postwar Occupation began to allow Americans back into Japan, Ruth Sasaki was in Kyoto trying to locate a new Zen master to carry on the teaching work that Shigetsu Roshi had started.

This turned out to be no easy task, and she ended up staying in Japan and continuing koan work with Shigetsu's dharma-brother Goto Zuigan Roshi. She restored Ryosen-an—Dragon Springs Hermitage—a tiny dilapidated branch-temple of Daitoku-ji. She improved her Chinese and Japanese and launched the translation of those poems and koans that formal Zen students must use. She learned to allow for the vagaries of people not of her class, and she opened the Kyoto temple and library to a constant flow of younger foreign people.

Ruth Sasaki was my benefactor. Even though aware of my youthful labor union activities and FBI record, and in spite of my frank declarations of dubiousness in regard to the whole Occidental proj-ect, she still invited me to accept a paid boat ride to Japan and soon put me to work on Chinese Zen translations in her research center. I was able to begin my own formal Zen practice with the roshi of the Daitoku-ji Training Hall, Oda Sesso.

Ruth Sasaki was in her sixties when I started working with her. She spent her days in elegant casual wear—many cashmere sweat-ers. Her hair and grooming were perfect, finished with pearl earrings. She started the mornings with a walk and sometimes an interview with her roshi. Then she might go to her study and review her literary Chinese-language readings, addressing translation problems from the text at hand. Much of the time it was the *Rinzai-roku*, or *The Record of Lin-chi*. She carried herself with imperious and matronly grace, and during her workday spoke with the cheerful and mannerly confidence that brooks little dissent. On issues of meaning in medieval Chinese, she was particularly stubborn but would eventually defer to the grand expert Dr. Iriya Yoshitaka, who came every Saturday morning.

Her young kitchen staff, two women from the countryside, had been personally trained by Ruth to do the traditional Ameri-can cooking she loved. Ruth had guests for dinner several nights a week. Dining was in a tatami room. Ruth poured martinis. She loved conversation, and after work hours enjoyed joining in a free-flowing debate. She had read widely in philosophy and literature and could hold her own with almost anyone. Still, on some issues she was (I thought) extremely conservative and would not give way. One time she commented that most of the modern world's prob-lems started with Woodrow Wilson's idea of "the self-determina-tion of nations."

Illustrious Americans and Europeans were often at the dining table of this small and perfectly outfitted Zen temple. Ruth Sasaki was hard to work for, but I found her to be good company after hours, and I am grateful for how much I learned on many levels. She held women to much higher standards than men, and treated many of us almost like family. Family has, as someone said, "the benefit of exposing you to people you ordinarily wouldn't meet." Her own roshi, Goto Zuigan, and my roshi (who was his dharma-heir) never once accepted an invitation to her famous American-style meals.

She labored as though her vision held the only possible path that could take genuine Zen to the West. By the mid-sixties, though, she could see that the Rinzai Zen lineage of which she was part (coming from the earlier masters Soyen and Sokatsu, through Sasaki Shigetsu and Goto Zuigan) would be but one of many streams. She came to realize that her ambitious plans for translation and publishing would have to be scaled back. Her little booklets, in particular *Zen: A Religion*, were written in response to those who might hope to set aside "Buddhism" and treat Zen as a secular psychological method of aesthetics, or self-help. Her writings from the sixties were ahead of their time and remain accurate and relevant. I am glad to see them made available again in this book.

She thought of herself as a scholar-translator-facilitator and apparently never aspired to be a formal master. Her task was to prepare the way for those non-Asians who would eventually do full-scale traditional Rinzai-style koan study. She died, still at her temple in Kyoto, of a sudden heart attack in October 1967.

Suzuki Daitsetsu first opened the gate of Zen for her, but it was Sasaki Shigetsu—a tough teacher and a free spirit—who charmed and inspired her for her life work. His given name was Yeita. As a youthful art student in Tokyo he lived a while as an itinerant woodcarver.

Buddhism and Zen were spreading west in the late 1960s and early 1970s. The Soto school of Zen sent warmhearted teacher

Suzuki Shunryu to set up in San Francisco. The rigorous and adventurous Tibetan schools with their Born Again boy leaders—the calm, gentle Vipassana Bhikkus—and the supremely humble and confident Pure Land teachers (who were in California all along)—each found a place in this West that lies east of Asia.

The core Zen practices of long-term sitting meditation and koan study are now available for a few hardy Americans, and those who are on that path know the value of Ruth Sasaki's great publishing achievement, *Zen Dust*. They in turn can also appreciate Victor Sogen Hori's extension of *Zen Dust* in his grandly scholarly book of Zen phrase translations called *Zen Sand*. The "dust" and "sand" that are nourishing to the Zen few will ultimately become tasty food for hungry spirits and our own culture's spiritual hungers.

A deep bow to Ruth *Eryu* Sasaki, a Lady Teacher Scholar Bodhisattva, whose unspoken model might be Tara herself. And our gratitude to Isabel Stirling, who saw that this story needed to be told, and though already a fully engaged science librarian at a major research university, made it her own practice for a number of years.

Gary Snyder

Preface

I STOOD IN THE SMALL, quiet library of a temple called Ryosen-an. Here, in the midst of the Daitoku-ji Temple complex in Kyoto, Japan, I first encountered the remarkable life of Ruth Fuller Sasaki.

Ryosen-an has well over a thousand books and journals in English, Japanese, Chinese, French, German, and some Sanskrit, covering Buddhism, philosophy, literature, Eastern religions, and Japanese culture. The library, although open, ceased acquisitions in the late 1960s. Still, there was much to discover and learn here. Shelves full of the ancient, the rare, the classic.

I stood there in Japan and realized that Ruth Fuller Sasaki was a pivotal figure in the emergence and development of Zen Buddhism in America. Ruth was a wealthy, upper-middle-class society matron of Chicago at the turn of the century, merging her Christian, Victorian upbringing with a new life of Zen Buddhism when she began studying in Japan in the early 1930s. By luck, coincidence—and some may say karma—on her first trip to Asia in 1930 (a three-month vacation with her husband, daughter, and governess), she was introduced to Dr. Daisetz T. Suzuki by William T. McGovern, an old family friend from Chicago. On her second trip to Japan in 1932, Suzuki introduced her to a Japanese Zen master in Kyoto, Nanshinken Roshi, who accepted her as a student.

Under Nanshinken Roshi, Ruth became one of the first foreigners to be immersed in Zen study in Japan. She studied at the Nanzen-ji Monastery in Kyoto in two periods, 1932 and again in 1933. During her stays at Nanzen-ji, she made friends with several of the monks, notably Miura Isshu, who years later would become a colleague and coauthor of *Zen Dust*, a classic in Western Zen literature. Ruth left Japan in 1932 and returned to Chicago. There, she continued developing her role in Buddhist circles. She became friends with Dwight Goddard, who had started the ZEN Hermitage in Vermont in the early 1930s after studying in Japan.

Ruth's life changed even more fundamentally in 1933 when she first met Sasaki Sokei-an Roshi after her return from her first experience at Nanzen-ji. A Zen disciple when he first came to the United States in 1906, Sokei-an stayed at the request of his teacher, Shaku Soyatsu Roshi, to study the English language and American culture, making trips back to Japan to meet with his teacher.

After receiving *inka*, the transmission from his teacher in 1928, Sokei-an began to teach Zen to students in New York in 1928, at what was first called the Buddhist Society of America in 1930 (later the First Zen Institute). After meeting him in 1933, Ruth began studying Zen with Sokei-an in 1938 while still married to Edward Warren Everett, then in a sanitarium. Edward died in 1940 after a long mental illness.

Ruth and Edward's only child, Eleanor, had accompanied Ruth on her trips to Japan, and while Ruth studied Zen with Nanshinken Roshi at Nanzen-ji, Eleanor, a teenager, spent her days learning Japanese culture, taking flower arranging, tea ceremony, and Japanese language classes. When Ruth took Eleanor, then eighteen, to London to enroll her in advanced piano study (Ruth had done the same in her teenage years in Switzerland with Rudolf Ganz), they spent time with Christmas Humphreys, head of the Buddhist Society of London. While there, Eleanor was introduced to the young Alan Watts, already a known name in the Buddhist Society of London and beyond for his essays on Zen and Buddhism. In 1938, Ruth became Alan's mother-in-law, when Alan and Eleanor married. Alan continued publishing essays on Zen, Buddhism, and Eastern philosophy, later paralleling the popular D. T. Suzuki in achieving wide recognition for interpreting Zen Buddhist thought, history, and culture to English-speaking people.

By then Ruth was a senior student of Sokei-an and began using her already accomplished social and organizational skills to strengthen and enhance the infrastructure for his study group. She bought a brownstone in New York and helped design the interior with the idea that the institute could move to one of the floors and be furnished as a traditional Japanese *zendo*. Sokei-an could have one of the floors, and she and her family members could occupy other levels. (She had an elevator installed, which in the early 1940s was still unusual—this one even had a telephone, should the elevator malfunction.)

The new First Zen Institute opened its doors on East 65th Street on December 6, 1941, the day before Pearl Harbor. After Pearl Harbor, Sokei-an was considered a "security risk" since Zen Buddhism was so intimately connected with Japanese culture (and politics) in the minds of the U.S. government. After months of FBI surveillance of their new quarters, Sokei-an was arrested and interned at Fort Meade, Maryland; his existing medical problems worsened while there. (His grown son Shintaro and daughter Seiko, who had been living in the United States, were also interned in the West.) Although ill when students and influential lawyers successfully argued for his release in 1944, he and Ruth married (as Alan Watts and others observed, "they were in love"). The dark shadow of the timing of the opening of the First Zen Institute and Pearl Harbor continued to haunt Ruth and Sasaki Roshi: they married in 1944, and he died in 1945.

Ruth spent the remainder of her life (another twenty-two years) fulfilling some of Sasaki Roshi's wishes as well as her own: to work on translating classic Chinese Zen texts into English, to find a Zen teacher for the New York Institute, and to continue her Zen training with a Zen master. These tasks were to absorb her life, her time, her money, her family, and her friends. In 1949, Ruth began her life in Kyoto and resided there permanently, making trips to the United States and Europe but returning home again to Ryosen-an, until her death from a heart attack in 1967.

In addition to these endeavors, she created an environment at Ryosen-an with a library and an incomparable small *zendo*—the classic Zen meditation hall—that was to be home to many for formal Zen meditation. Here Ruth introduced westerners to Zen teachers and assisted in making arrangements so they could begin serious long-term Zen studies.

Post–World War II Japan was an exceedingly difficult place economically, especially for young scholars. The combination of the work Ruth offered and her considerable financial support (while almost always referred to as "Mrs. Sasaki," a local nickname among Daitoku-ji priests in Japanese was "*Oki na zai–san*," or "Mrs. Big Bucks") helped bring together one of the most improbable and fortuitous teams of scholars that could be imagined, and for an intense and extended period of time.

These scholars included Iriya Yoshitaka (1910–1999), Yanagida Seizan (1922–), Kanaseki Hisao (1918–1996), Philip Yampolsky

(1920–1996), Burton Watson (1925–), and Gary Snyder (1930–)—a list of individuals whose works were to become the sine qua non of a wide variety of T'ang and Sung literary works, Buddhist philosophy, translations of Chinese and Japanese literature, and poetry. All of these individuals made substantial and important contributions in person, in print, and in their spheres of influence, teaching others and having their own unique voices that were in some way influenced by this stimulating period in their lives.

These men were young and brilliant. They struggled with the cross-cultural dynamics of Japanese and American languages and society, the Chinese language and Buddhist scholarship, and a boss who was supportive but sometimes autocratic and demanding about their work. The research team, under the direction of Professor Iriya, collaborated for years until tensions with Ruth peaked and the relationships fell apart. Ruth was a roshi's wife and was incredibly disciplined, sometimes rigid, and expected the best from people. She could not always hide her frustration and disappointment when work did not go smoothly—or quickly—enough.

As the group reached its peak of productivity, Ruth started developing suspicions (which evolved into paranoia), fueled by rumors, that a member of the research team, Philip Yampolsky, was planning to steal research notes in order to publish his own versions of certain translations. A dramatic confrontation on July 13, 1961, undermined the karma of 1930: as members of her research group watched, Ruth confronted Yampolsky in the library with her suspicions, which he denied. In front of everyone, she issued a dismissal of Yampolsky. Both Burton Watson and Gary Snyder, feeling strongly that it was unfair, resigned in protest. At the heart of Ruth's suspicions was a misunderstanding, but this did not prevent the departure of Philip, Burton, and Gary. Ruth found herself continuing the translation projects alone with the Japanese scholars, some of whom did not know English well.

Ruth's heritage is in the books she saw through translation; these were published from the 1950s into the 1970s, some after her death in 1967. One of the most important is *Zen Dust* (1966); another is the *Rinzai-roku* (Chinese: *Lin-chi lu*) translation, *The Record of Lin-chi* (1975). Other English-language translations of the *Rinzai-roku* done in later years, such as the ones by Irmgard Schloegl and Burton Watson, would not exist without this original collaborative work done at Ryosen-an.

Zen Dust is an invaluable text that continues to grow in importance for research and reference. Published in 1966, it was also issued a year earlier, in 1965, in an abbreviated student version four hundred pages shorter, called *Zen Koan*. *Zen Koan* went through subsequent reprintings (the last in 1993) in paperback. The story of its creation, which I discuss in the following pages, is a fascinating one. It is seen as a fortuitous publication whose value will only continue to grow for Zen students and scholars. The Western practice of Zen is maturing from its earliest years focusing on practice to the current environment incorporating scholarship and historical Zen Buddhist texts to enhance and deepen Zen practice: *Zen Dust* provides key insights into this history.

Ruth had a fairly orthodox and conservative approach in her mission and dedication to Zen and its movement to the West. Ironically, the framework that she developed was swept up in the counterculture movement of the 1960s, when Zen Buddhism became extremely popular in many circles and in a much broader context. In part this was due to the successful writings of her son-in-law, Alan Watts.

But also it was due to Ruth—indeed, she would make trips back to the United States in the 1950s and 1960s and give talks to groups stretching from Huston Smith's gatherings at M.I.T. to Alan Watts's

Academy of Asian Studies in San Francisco. Ruth was a dynamic speaker at these events, adding luster to Zen's growing popular interest. Many of these talks were subsequently printed in pamphlet form, and three of those are reprinted in part two of this book.

By the late 1960s, Ruth was also spending her time debunking the faddish and trendy, and promoting what was core to the ideas she thought were important and which she had developed over the previous nearly forty years. Little could she have imagined that within a decade after she died, there would be Zen centers and monasteries spreading across the United States, with serious students of Zen crowding zendos such as California's Mount Baldy Zen Center and the San Francisco Zen Center. By the 1970s, a *rohatsu* in the United States might have over fifty Western students and monks in attendance: Ruth was from the era when a dozen Western students were a full house.

The popularity of the Zen movement overwhelmed Ruth in her last years while she struggled on with the details of getting translations published. Though many people who were a part of Ryosen-an or the Daitoku-ji Sodo during the 1950s and 1960s have written of their experiences meditating or doing koan study with a Zen teacher in Kyoto, Ruth is seldom mentioned, or is referred to only in passing. Perhaps writers felt that their Western readers preferred to learn about the more exotic aspects of Zen Buddhism in Japan rather than hear stories of an American woman.

For the almost two decades that Ruth presided over Ryosen-an, many westerners spent time in either the Ryosen-an Zendo or the Daitoku-ji Sodo. They lived or now live around the world, carrying with them the experiences of Ruth, their Zen teachers, fellow Zen students, and the excitement and exploration of the culture during the 1950s and 1960s.

Ruth was the only westerner, and the only woman, ever to be made a priest of a Daitoku-ji temple in its many centuries. No one else has achieved that distinction since. As I looked around the library in 1996 and saw Ruth's photograph on the altar of the Ryosen-an Zendo, I felt that she deserved to have more of her story told.

I have been fortunate to receive the incredible help and encouragement of many people who knew her, worked for her, or were influenced by her, and who provided me with marvelous insights into her life and the environment of her time. I am especially indebted to Gary Snyder and to Haru Yoshida (Ruth's personal secretary for almost two decades), who have made this book possible. Matsunami Taiun Osho, the current priest of Ryosen-an; Victor Sogen Hori, of McGill University; and Maya Hara, of Kyoto, were a critical part of the early work in preparing this book.

I describe here the events and the people that shaped important parts of Ruth's life and work. Names of Japanese people are given in Japanese order, surname first, unless they themselves used English order. In a few cases, the same individuals used both forms. There are gaps remaining, and many other stories would add to our understanding of her life. This, the first biography of Ruth Fuller Sasaki, is a beginning.

Berkeley, California   *Isabel Stirling*

PART ONE: HER LIFE

The Chicago Years, 1892–1929 1

THE CLASSIC EARLY CHILDHOOD influences and imprinting that may have shaped some of Ruth Fuller's life views and senses are mostly unknown. We have essentially no window into her life before her late teenage years. One of the few surviving anecdotes may have been a highly influential memory for Ruth: an argument between her parents when she was a young child concerning the Calvinist tenet of "infant damnation"—the controversial doctrine implying that elect infants dying in infancy are regenerated and saved, whereas those who are non-elect are damned. Ruth remembers feeling relieved that her mother sided with those who felt that infants weren't necessarily damned, leaving a path open for the exploration of the illumination of spirit and mind.

Ruth was born October 31, 1892, in Chicago, Illinois, to Clara Elizabeth and George E. Fuller. In later years she would briefly allude to her parents as "Calvinists of Canadian extraction" who had become U.S. citizens. George left when Ruth was young, and all she would say of him later was that he had acquired wealth in the Chicago grain stock market. Her only sibling was David, born in 1895. Clara had ample money, said to have been from George's success in the Chicago stock market, anecdotally in the Canadian grain futures. She sent Ruth and David to private schools, and they participated in the social activities of Chicago's privileged class.

Ruth attended Chicago's Kenwood Institute and Loring School, private schools that merged during her senior year. In 1911, as a senior, Ruth was the editor-in-chief of the high school yearbook, the *Lampadion*, which ran a small photo of Ruth showing an attractive and serious-looking young woman, with the caption, "And still they gazed and still their wonder grew, that one small head could carry all she knew."

Ruth served as president of the school's Theta Society, in addition to yearbook editor. Her junior and senior years were a whirlwind of weekly social events and group gatherings to see plays, opera, and concerts, of which Chicago, then as now, had an endless variety. These small social groups took turns entertaining each other at dinner and theater parties, such as the one Ruth and another student had hosting their classmates at a theater party to see *Disraeli*. Dame Nellie Melba in *La Boheme*, Enrico Caruso in *Pagliacci*, Sarah Bernhardt in *L'aiglon*—a stream of theater and opera in which Ruth was submerged, and which no doubt helped to shape and hone Ruth's social skills as an adult.

In her 1911 senior yearbook, Ruth wrote an essay entitled "A Night on the Rigi," describing a trip that she took with her mother and brother to Lucerne, Switzerland. Her narrative of the trip up to Mount Rigi and its famed view is concluded with the enthusiasm of a nineteen-year-old: "When everything seems to cry out 'Live! Live! The whole great world is before you!' and you do live; live with your heart overflowing with the joyousness of it all."

Ruth took piano lessons for several months in 1913 in Switzerland from Rudolf Ganz. Ganz, a pianist and composer, had been the director of the piano department at the Chicago Musical College from 1900 to 1905 before moving to Europe.

Ruth became a skilled pianist, occasionally giving recitals such as the one for the Woman's Club mentioned in a local Chicago paper, which listed her performance as including "several selections from Bach and three numbers from Mendelssohn's 'Songs without Words'..."

In addition to her piano lessons in Switzerland, Ruth said that she'd studied French and German with private tutors in Europe for a year and a half.

On April 7, 1917, at twenty-four, Ruth married Edward Warren Everett, a Chicago trial lawyer twenty years older than she. He was a senior partner with the highly successful Chicago law firm Winston, Strawn, & Shaw. They had small wedding at Chicago's Plymouth Congregational Church for relatives and a few friends. Edward gave Ruth a yellow Stutz Bearcat (a high-performance sports car that was seen as a status symbol) for a wedding present. The newlyweds went to Honolulu for their honeymoon, after which, as the *Chicago Tribune* reported, "the couple will be at home at 2122 Lincoln Park West."

The following year, on December 30, 1918, daughter Eleanor was born to Ruth and Edward; Ruth was twenty-six, Edward forty-six. This was a challenging time for Ruth both physically and emotionally. Ruth supervised a full household of people hired to help take care of Eleanor, as well as having personal assistants, cooks, gardeners, etc. She was responsible for coordinating and presiding over the many social dinners and parties that were a part of their life.

Married to a successful attorney, having an active social life in Chicago society, and being a new mother, Ruth later described this time as marking the beginning of her spiritual unrest and her interest in Buddhism. Ruth was not alone in following a trend of upper-middle-class, wealthy, privately educated, Christian women who turned to a kind of spiritual elitism, in her case the interest in a Buddhist, East Asian alternative. Ruth was able to mesh the confidence but isolation of her social environment with this pursuit of an alternative religious experience.

Ruth's daughter, Eleanor, described some of her early childhood in this family with many recollections of the food ("juxtaposition of silver, rice pudding, sauce . . .") and the parties of that time. Eleanor recalled an embarrassing occasion of a Valentine's Day party Edward and Ruth gave, where Eleanor (then six or seven) was costumed as Cupid, with nothing on but a wide, red ribbon from shoulder to hip, and then paraded among the guests holding a tiny golden bow and arrow. Eleanor always had a governess during these years.

Ruth and Eleanor both developed some medical problems: Eleanor with allergies and asthma, Ruth's resulting from childbirth complications (it was a breech birth). In 1923 and 1924, Ruth and Eleanor went for rest and healing to Nyack, New York, where there was a resort, a kind of yoga-flavored retreat in the country.

The Clarkstown Country Club was no ordinary resort. Led by a visionary named Pierre Arnold Bernard (known in the popular press as "Oom the Magnificent," it was a kind of adult spiritual education center particularly aimed at introducing Eastern philosophy, yoga, and religions. Pierre Bernard had assembled a famed library of more than seven thousand volumes on philosophy, ethics, psychology, education, metaphysics, etc., with a special collection of Sanskrit materials. The club had tennis courts, a gymnasium, even a circus with several resident elephants. Sports events were held regularly, and the club became known for the innovation of having baseball games played at night with lights on the field.

Pierre "Doc" Bernard, born in 1875 in the farming town of Leon, Iowa, had traveled to India (Kashmir and Bengal) before founding the Tantrik Order of America in 1905 and teaching at the Bacchante Academy, known for its promotion of self-hypnosis and yoga. He has been credited with bringing yoga to America. Moving to New York after the San Francisco earthquake, he began teaching yoga, exercises, and tantric techniques to "young women and tired men" in New York at his Oriental Sanctum, and in 1910 received a lot of press attention as "Oom the Omnipotent" when he was charged and arraigned by young women who felt he had taken too much psychic control over their lives. The charges were later dropped.

Beyond the sensational press, Pierre Bernard became extremely popular with upper-middle-class women, and their yearning for exotic alternatives to the conservative Christian outlook on life was given full rein through his encouragement of (tantric) yoga and Eastern thought. His clientele of New York's high society, including a Vanderbilt, thrived during the 1920s and 1930s. After having started the New York Sanskrit College in New York, he bought land in Nyack, first called the Brae Burn Country Club, then evolving into the highly successful Clarkstown Country Club. Bernard married Blanche de Vries, who was a dancer, interior decorator, and accomplished yoga practitioner (she taught yoga in New York until well into her eighties, long after Pierre Bernard passed away in 1955).

Some thought Bernard was an imposter, while others thought he was a genuine guru. As the resort flourished, with over four hundred members, Pierre became an established figure of the local Nyack, New York, community, serving as a board member for banks, and changing his style from the yoga costumes to the conservative tweeds of a senior citizen.

Later in the 1920s and early 1930s, both Ruth and Edward gave lectures at the Clarkstown Country Club, Edward on topics related to his interest in legal issues, Ruth on topics related to her study of Buddhism. Many other members also gave lectures, including people like Leopold Stokowski, conductor of the Philadelphia Symphony Orchestra. Many students of Doc Bernard went on to become influential in the yoga circles of the United States, such as Dr. Ida Rolf, who started studying yoga with Bernard in the 1920s and went on to found the popular "rolfing" movement related to yoga practice.

This concept of adult classes and lifelong learning was somewhat similar to that of Dartington in England, now Schumacher College. A book published in 1935 called *Life at the Clarkstown Country Club* describes the center as being a "place where an attempt is made to translate the business of living into an art." The Clarkstown Country Club flourished for thirty years. It shows pictures of the many buildings (over thirty), residences, and meeting areas, spread out over almost two hundred acres of prime rural land along the Palisades in South and Upper Nyack. Ruth's early interest in Sanskrit is likely a result of her exposure to Pierre Bernard's interest in Sanskrit and his lectures and classes given during their trips to the club in the 1920s.

In 1924, Ruth and Edward sold their Chicago home at Lincoln Park West and moved to the Drake Hotel while looking for a suburban home farther away from Lake Michigan where the air would be better for Eleanor's asthma (Eleanor suggested later that it was more because her mother wanted to build a house). They moved to a small house in Hinsdale in 1926 while the well-established Chicago architect Benjamin H. Marshall designed and built a house for them nearby. (Marshall also designed the Francis Peabody estate in nearby Oakbrook, Illinois, as well as several buildings in Chicago such as the Drake Hotel and the Edgewater Beach Hotel.)

In the fall of 1927, they moved into their new home, a stunning architectural marvel at 208 East 6th Street, Hinsdale, called "Swan House" because of the carved swans on the eaves.

Edward was a devout Anglophile, and a lot of the material for Swan House was brought over from England. Ruth paid attention to the details, down to the European-style lead gutters. The brick pavers were from Madison Street in Chicago, and the carved doors were of museum quality. Ruth played an active part in the design and furnishing of the house. Some of the interior features were years ahead of their time, such as the full basement with a laundry room and gas burners for drying clothes—long before automatic dryers existed. There was a carriage house, a wine cellar, and landscaped gardens for their frequent social gatherings. A neighbor said Ruth's bedroom was "out of this world." Edward's bedroom was entirely English; Ruth's was lavishly and tastefully oriental. Her room was furnished with scarlet silk draperies and a Buddha on the mantel altar. There was also a large Buddha statue outdoors by the pond, where glowing Japanese lanterns were strung up in the trees for parties.

In the late 1930s after they had moved away, the house was rented to Charles "Boss" Kettering from Detroit, who was there to "straighten out the electromotive industry." Ketering mentioned later that it was a mistake for him not to have bought the house, which sold to the publisher William F. Regnery for $50,000 as a "white elephant."

Settled into their new home, Ruth followed her curiosity about reading original Buddhist texts in Sanskrit and Pali, and went to the University of Chicago during the next two years, from 1927 to 1929, "taking all the courses and seminars offered in Sanskrit and several in Indian philosophy. . . . I also lectured and wrote on Buddhism," she said.

In later years, Ruth said that she had to do her Sanskrit and other homework late at night because Edward insisted on chatting during dinner and after, preserving family social time.

Already Ruth was demonstrating the energy and organizational abilities that characterized her later years. She did not follow the path of a formal education. When she wanted to know about something, she set about learning everything she could about the subject. This focus was evident in everything she did—whether it was building a house like Swan House, learning about yoga at the Clarkstown Country Club, or studying Sanskrit at the University of Chicago. She could have easily taken the path of a society matron, filling her life with social events. Instead, she followed her heart and developed an attitude that nothing was impossible for her to accomplish.

RUTH HAD TRAVELED to Europe several times, but she had not yet been to Asia. During the summer of 1930, Ruth, along with her husband, Edward; daughter, Eleanor; and Eleanor's governess, Miss Hoover, traveled for three months to Japan, Korea, China, and Manchuria. A narrative of this trip was written by Edward Warren Everett in a printed pamphlet called *Far East for Ninety Days: Narrative of a Trip to Japan and China in 1930.* The cover of the pamphlet says, "Read before the Law Club of Chicago and published in the Central Manufacturing District Magazine."

This trip provided the framework, context, and connections for Ruth's later involvement with Japan and China. Friends and relatives tried hard to dissuade them from making the trip to the "dangerous orient." Edward wrote of their greatly exaggerated fears, mentioning that the warnings and outcry subsided when he told them that he'd left them everything in his will should something happen to them while traveling.

They sailed out of Victoria, British Columbia, on the ship *Empress of Canada*, stopping in Hawaii for a day and arriving in Yokohama, Japan, after a two-week journey across the Pacific. They were awed by the huge, busy port of Yokohama, and were met by senior management staff of the firm Mitsui & Co., the

"J. P. Morgan's of Japan," he said. From Yokohama they traveled the twenty-five miles north to Tokyo, arriving at the only foreign hotel at that time—the Imperial Hotel, designed by fellow Chicagoan Frank Lloyd Wright, which opened in 1922. Edward's disdainful remarks about the hotel were that Frank Lloyd Wright had "sacrificed convenience, utility, and profitable operation for architectural features." They visited shrines and temples, such as the Meiji Shrine, and were invited to traditional teahouse dinners by their Mitsui company hosts.

Edward had a keen eye for the rapid westernizing occurring in the Japanese culture in 1930, observing that the jazz band had replaced the *samisen* (a three-stringed Japanese instrument similar to a banjo) for entertainment of Japanese youth. He described their visits to Nikko and Gifu, commenting on the lack of foreigners taking the time to visit famous and historic places in Japan. They rode on the nighttime fishing boats near Gifu to join the throngs out watching the cormorant fishing tradition.

They went on to Kyoto, staying at the Miyako Hotel in the hills where it was a little cooler. This hotel was to become a place where Ruth stayed frequently in later years. With special permissions granted, they visited the Imperial Palace and went to see the Nijo Castle. They visited monasteries on Mount Hiei and on Mount Koya. They stayed in guest quarters at one of the temples at Mount Koya, where they participated in the early morning rising and rituals of the monastery.

Traveling from Kyoto to Shimonoseki, they then boarded a ship for Korea, landing in Fusan (Pusan). From Korea they headed for Manchuria, first visiting Mukden (now Shenyang). Mukden was surrounded by an ancient wall, and by the Mukden Golf Club. Amused by the local rules of the golf club, Edward jotted down the instructions on the reverse side of the scorecard:

Rule 2: a ball lying within two club lengths of a tomb or boundary stone may be lifted and dropped without penalty. Graves in course of construction and open coffins shall be regarded as ground under repair. Old grave pits are not covered by this Bye Law. . . . [F]rom these rules one would think that golf courses in Manchuria are laid out in cemeteries. They are.

They stayed three weeks in Peking (Beijing) as guests at the home of an old Chicago friend, Colonel Isaac N. Newell. Edward described China as being in progressive decay and how the poverty caused temples and palaces to fall into a state of dilapidation.

During their stay in Peking, Chang Hsueh Liang's (Zhang Xueliang's) soldiers moved in and occupied the city. After some negotiation with the national government, General Yen Hsi-shan's troops moved out, and there was no trouble. Edward recounts their visits to the Forbidden City, the Summer Palace, and the Keiman Theater to hear Mei Lang Fang, the famous opera star, and mentions that the movement of soldiers prevented them from seeing the Great Wall.

They left the active foreigners' social life of Peking for Tientsin (Tianjin), seventy miles from the capital, and then went on to Shanghai by freighter, docking at Tsingtao (Qingdao) and taking a side trip into Laoshan. Edward observed that the freighter *Calchas*, which they sailed on, was presumably loaded with a million eggs in its refrigerator, consigned to New York via England to be distributed as "strictly fresh eggs."

In Shanghai they stayed at a private apartment on the Bund, and Edward and Ruth went by train to Nanking (Nanjing) where they were guests at a luncheon hosted by the legal adviser to the national government. He said that all of the department heads were present except for President Chiang Kaishek, "who was off to war trying to subdue the communists in another province."

After excursions to famous locales like Soochow (Suzhou), they started their return journey to San Francisco via Japan on a Japanese ship, the *Chichibu Maru*. They had brief stopovers in Kobe and Yokohama, and made a side trip to Kamakura.

Edward didn't mention the most significant visit they would make during their visit to Japan, which was to meet Daisetz T. Suzuki in Kyoto. They were introduced to Dr. Suzuki by an old friend of theirs from Chicago, William T. McGovern, who had many Asia and Chicago connections (he had graduated from Ryokoku University in Kyoto) and had written the book *Introduction to Mahayana Buddhism* in 1922.

Ruth later described this first visit with D. T. Suzuki. She took a trip with D. T. Suzuki and his wife, Beatrice Lane Suzuki (an American woman), a few days later to a place near Kyoto where Zen Master Kozuki Tesshu Roshi had a temple called Empuku-ji. Kozuki Roshi welcomed foreigners to practice Zen meditation (*zazen*) and study with him. In 1930, there had been only a few foreigners who were guests and students in the small dormitory and "meditation cave," which was an actual cave hollowed out of a nearby hill. Dr. and Mrs. Suzuki and the writer L. Adams Beck had been instrumental in this dormitory being established. Unfortunately, Kozuki Roshi died shortly after this visit in an automobile accident. The roshi who succeeded him closed the dormitory and no longer invited foreigners to visit.

In conversations Ruth had with Suzuki, he told her that if she really wanted to learn about Zen Buddhism, she must come to Japan for an extended stay to study with a Zen master. He gave her a copy of his *Essays in Zen Buddhism* (first series). Suzuki gave Ruth basic guidance on the correct sitting posture for meditation, as well as some breathing exercises and techniques for "handling the mind" (beginner's zazen). She continued to correspond with Suzuki and practiced the meditation techniques of beginning zazen that he had taught her. For the next year and a half, she continued her meditation practice and began planning a trip to Japan to learn more about Zen.

Life was not to be the same for the Everetts once they returned to Chicago. Edward continued his legal practice but began having health problems. Ruth, who had taken courses at the University of Chicago in Sanskrit from 1927 to 1929, joined the American Oriental Society in 1930. She hired a personal assistant, Jessie Duff, to begin organizing her growing personal collection of books on oriental subjects into a library collection.

In March 1932, Ruth sailed by ship from Seattle to Japan. Ruth knew only one other person in Japan besides the Suzukis and William McGovern. This was Ikeda, who had been secretary and guide to Ruth and Edward on their earlier trip. Ikeda met her in Yokohama, along with Dr. Suzuki. The Suzukis had originally arranged for Ruth to stay at Koto-in, where there were a few rooms in the back, and to study with the roshi at Daitoku-ji. This plan didn't work out (the Daitoku-ji roshi declined), so Dr. Suzuki took her to meet the roshi of the great Rinzai Zen monastery in Kyoto at Nanzen-ji, Nanshinken Roshi (Kono Mukai), then in his early seventies. He accepted Ruth, now forty, as a student. Ruth had rented a house (called "Shounso," Pine Cloud Villa) on the Kamo River in Kyoto where she and her family could live when they visited from Chicago, and where Kato would serve as the housekeeper.

Ruth began studying at Nanzen-ji on April 1, 1932, continuing through the end of July 1932, attending daily meditation, *sanzen* (formal interview with the roshi), and the weeklong intensive *sesshin* (formal periods of rigorously defined times for zazen and sanzen). Nanshinken Roshi gave her the use of his small private temple, Senko-an, for use between sesshins at first, because she couldn't sit in the *zendo* (meditation hall), and it wouldn't help for her to sit at home. He advised her to come at nine every morning, get the key from him, then go to Senko-an with a *bento* (boxed meal of rice and pickles, fish or sandwiches) lunch and do zazen all day until 5 or 6 P.M., and then go home to her house on the Kamo River, about four miles away.

He told her not to bring any books with her at any time, and since he had no experience with a foreigner doing zazen, he provided a special chair for her to sit in—a Morris chair, complete with a footrest, armrest, headrest, and a series of buttons on the arm. Ruth had already been sitting according to Suzuki's instructions, in a Chinese-style straight-back chair, perfecting her posture and breathing. She got tired of the Morris chair pretty quickly, and Nanshinken Roshi told her she could do zazen "*seiza*-style," kneeling on cushions in the correct meditation posture.

Ruth followed this routine six days a week, getting up and walking around the gardens when her legs got tired. For a month, she said, she got up at 5 A.M., did zazen at home until 7 A.M., then had breakfast and took a taxi to Nanzen-ji. There she would do zazen all day, fix tea and sandwiches, then walk home at 5:30 or 6 P.M. to get her exercise. She would have supper, take a bath, and do zazen until midnight, only getting about five hours of sleep a night. Nanshinken Roshi had given her a koan to work on (from the *Mumonkan*), and Suzuki initially acted as interpreter between them.

After a month, Ruth had what she called an "interesting psychological experience," and she had an interpreter write it down so she could give it to Nanshinken Roshi. He was excited by this, and told her that now she was ready to sit in the zendo. The summer sesshin was almost ready to begin, and the monks were not keen on having a woman sitting in the zendo. The senior monks agreed to let her come and sit for one night (May 3) for the evening sitting from 7 to 9:30 P.M. Because this was an important sesshin, there were forty-seven sitting in the Nanzen-ji Sodo (monastery meditation hall), which was built to hold thirty-six, so every seat was taken, and some had to sit in an overflow room.

She "sat" very well, and was invited back the next night. She told the story of having gotten seated that second night, and Roshi came in and "yowled and bellowed," and she found out later that he was saying that everyone's sanzen had been terrible and that they would have to sit all night without breaks. She said the pain was excruciating, and at the end they had to come and lift her off the *tan* (raised platform for the meditation cushions) because her legs had become completely paralyzed. The third night she also was told to go to sanzen, and Eizan, a senior monk who knew some English, came along with her as interpreter. After this, Eizan told her that the monks were inviting her to come and sit in the zendo regularly, that she was an inspiration to them.

By the time the second sesshin of the summer was held in June, they had invited her to sit with them in the zendo during the day as well, so she made Senko-an her base for breaks in the sitting. This extended full day of sitting went from 4 A.M. straight through until late evening. She was still sitting seiza, which was very difficult for her, but between occasional hot baths and walking up and down, she got through it.

It was an intense immersion for her in koan study with a Zen master, long hours of zazen meditation, and learning the monastery rituals of sutra chanting and daily life. Decades later, Ruth would refer to this extended period at Nanzen-ji as "the most completely satisfactory time I have ever had in my life."

In a speech that she gave to her club back in Chicago in 1933, called "Another Buddhist Interlude," Ruth talked about the strong and vivid memories of her first experiences in the Nanzen-ji Monastery. She wrote, "again I am back in that great dim Zendo in the pine forest of Higashiyama, back among those dark motionless figures. Around me is the same deep stillness through which again I hear the soughing of the wind in the trees, the rushing of the mountain stream and smell the acrid spicy smell of the incense. As if from far, far away, the deep sweet tone of the bell of Eikando comes floating toward me."

After returning to Chicago in the summer of 1932, Ruth continued her studies of Buddhism and gave lectures to various groups. One of these was at the Union Church in Hinsdale in March 1933, called "Talk on the contributions of Buddhism to the spiritual wealth of the world." Other lectures she gave included those at the Clarkstown Country Club in Nyack, New York, where both she and Edward were members and occasional guests. These essays, which she wrote as a basis for her talks, helped shape her published writing in later years.

Ruth corresponded with a wide variety of people. A collection of her letters to Arthur C. March in England describing her time at Nanzen-ji was published in the journal *Buddhism in England* in 1933. She also corresponded with Ogata Sohaku, a student of D. T. Suzuki's and a monk at Myoshin-ji, beginning in the 1930s. Ruth helped support Ogata so that he could take university courses at Otani University (he dedicated his thesis to her). In addition to their correspondence discussing her desire to find a Zen teacher who would come to the United States, Ruth shared some of her family struggles and conflicts in letters to Ogata, as he had met both Eleanor and Edward when they were in Kyoto. Ogata would give Ruth encouragement and remind her that Eleanor should be given support to develop her talents.

There were only a few westerners studying Zen in Kyoto before Ruth arrived in the early 1930s. Eugen Herrigel and Dwight Goddard were the best known, both publishing books in German and English that have become classic Zen Buddhist works. Two others were Georgia Forman and L. Adams Beck. Ruth became friends with all four of them, and with the exception of Beck, who died in 1931, they kept in touch over the next several decades.

Georgia, born in 1871, married a wealthy Buffalo man, Howard Forman, in 1892. Georgia traveled widely through Europe and Asia, and was an avid collector of Japanese and Chinese art. She lived for a while in Kyoto in the late 1920s. (Georgia left a large part of her print collection to the writer James Michener when she died in 1955). In 1948, in a brief letter Ruth wrote to Alan Watts, she sent "a bit of news" about Georgia, saying that Georgia was now studying yoga with one of Pierre Bernard's "oldest and best students." Ruth was amused because she had recommended yoga to Georgia in the late 1930s, and Georgia had said to Ruth, "this physical yoga is so disgusting. I am interested in spiritual things."

(Lily) Adams Beck, the daughter of Canadian admiral John Moresby, did not begin to write until 1919 (she was born around 1862), and then published thirty books, including *The Splendour of Asia: The Story and Teaching of the Buddha* and *The Story of Oriental Philosophy*. She lived the last years of her life in Japan.

Dwight Goddard, who had studied in Kyoto in the 1920s, returned to Vermont and established the ZEN Hermitage, and edited a small magazine called the *ZEN Magazine*. He is most known for the publication of his book *A Buddhist Bible* (first published in 1932), which has become a classic compilation of various Buddhist texts in English and has gone through several printings.

In March 1933, Goddard wrote to Ruth in Chicago from his home in Thetford, Vermont, suggesting that there was a Zen teacher in New York whom he thought she should meet, the Reverend Sasaki Shigetsu (Sokei-an), at 63 West 70th Street, New York. Goddard described Sokei-an as being from the autocratic and blunt "old school" of Zen masters, though also an artist and a wood carver, and Goddard thought that Ruth might enjoy meeting him. Goddard said that he earned his living carving Buddha images and repairing art treasures for Tiffany's. Ruth said later that she had also heard of Sokei-an from the *Buddhist Lodge* magazine.

Sokei-an's teacher was Sokatsu Shaku Roshi (1869–1954), who had originally been a layman specializing in the art of making Kamakura lacquer, the special deeply incised red lacquer. Sokatsu had originally studied with Kosen Imakita Roshi (1816–1892), considered somewhat of a maverick, who formed a zendo for lay-people to train without going to a monastery. When Kosen died, Sokatsu continued studying with Kosen's heir, Soyen Shaku Roshi (1859–1919). Sokatsu finished his Zen study in his early thirties and traveled to Burma, Siam, Ceylon, and India for several years dressed as an itinerant monk. Sokatsu returned from Burma to Engaku-ji, where Soyen Roshi was, and Soyen suggested that Sokatsu revive the layman's zendo, called the Ryomo Kyokai ("the Society for Abandonment of Subjectivity and Objectivity"), which Kosen Roshi had begun.

Everyone had expected that Sokatsu would succeed Soyen Roshi as the head of Engaku-ji when Soyen retired, but Sokatsu had become involved with a young woman, and after some items in the newspaper discussing this scandal, he lost the Engaku-ji elections. He never went back to temple life but continued to live with her until his death at eighty-one. Ruth said that they were a totally devoted couple, but that the experience had made him bitter about temple Zen.

In later years Sokei-an, who was Sokatsu Roshi's disciple, described how during Sokatsu's forty years of teaching, three thousand men and women had come to Zen under his direction. Nine hundred of these were initiated into Zen, thirteen of these completed their training, and four he ordained as teachers. These four were Goto Zuigan, Tatsuta Eizan, Ohasama Chikudo, and Sasaki Shigetsu. Sokatsu did not want his disciples to follow in the temple Zen tradition of monks, but rather to continue as lay teachers. Over time, there was to be a falling-out between Sokatsu and those who went back into the monk and priest culture as they began their teaching.

Goto Zuigan had come to Sokatsu as a university student in the philosophy department at Tokyo University; Sasaki Sokei-an had come to him as a student in the art department of the university. Eizan Tatsuta studied natural science at the university, and Chikudo Ohasama was a professor of ethics at a university in Tokyo.

Ruth wrote to Sokei-an in early April 1933 and told him that she was coming to New York and would like to meet him. She said sparks flew when they met. She had heard from other people that Sokei-an had made nasty remarks about American women who went to Japan when there was plenty of Zen in America. So when Ruth and Sokei-an met, Ruth said it was like "two cats spitting."

Toward the end of their first meeting, lasting less than an hour, he told Ruth that he had not yet decided exactly what kind of a Zen teacher to be, what kind of attitude to take with his students. Sometimes he thought he should be like his teacher Sokatsu Roshi, and sometimes he thought he should take an attitude more like his own father's. Ruth said he looked shocked when she said, "Why don't you just be yourself?"

Ruth said that she realized her question had made the first "dent" in him, and it was the beginning of their relationship. That evening, they were both at a dinner party at the Japan Club hosted by Ruth's friend Miya, who was friends with the Yamanaka family, and knew Sokei-an.

From that time on, when Ruth came to New York, she would meet Sokei-an and have dinner with him (or as she said, "have him for dinner"). She said he was always a very prickly kind of person. When she'd tell him that she would send a car for him, he would say he could walk. And if she didn't send a car he would say, "They have no sense of how to treat a roshi!"

Sokei-an wrote in a letter to Ruth in the summer of 1933 that he appreciated her kindness in entertaining him as a guest in her home in Chicago during the gathering of the World Fellowship of Faiths, led by Kedernath Das Gupta in Chicago. Knowing that Ruth would be going back to Japan in the autumn, he asked Ruth if she would take a message from him to his teacher in Japan.

Sokei-an wrote to Ruth, "Do we have any more opportunity to see each other before you sail? . . . Perhaps not. . . . There will be no more staring contest in our next meet[ing]. I hope you safe going to Japan. Bon Voyage and also hope you the gateless gate of MU [nothingness]." In another letter Sokei-an gave information to Ruth about how to reach his teacher's country town.

While the exact date of their first meeting is not certain, it was said to have been April 7, 1933. Sokei-an sent a letter to Dwight Goddard on April 17, 1933, in which he wrote, "About 10 days ago Mrs. Everett of Chicago came here to meet me."

In a written narrative that Ruth submitted as part of the effort to get Sokei-an released from internment in 1944, she states that she had "first made Mr. Sasaki's acquaintance in the spring of 1933," after her return from a six-month period of study at Nanzen-ji, "and shortly before my return to Japan for a second period of study extending over a year in the same monastery and under the same teacher."

Edward's health continued to decline, and he moved back into Swan House in Hinsdale, with his widowed aunt being brought in to take care of him. Ruth returned to Kyoto in the autumn of 1933, taking Eleanor with her. Ruth resumed her koan study and zazen practice at Nanzen-ji with Nanshinken Roshi, and Eleanor, now fifteen, began taking Japanese language and tea ceremony classes. They stayed in Kyoto for a year, and Ruth studied intensively at Nanzen-ji for ten months, from early autumn 1933 to the summer of 1934. After these ten months, Ruth was ordained and given the ceremonial initiation into Buddhism (*jukai*) and received the Zen Buddhist name "Kuge" from Nanshinken Roshi.

At a farewell tea party for all the monks with whom Ruth had spent her training period at Nanzen-ji, she was invited to make some remarks, and she gave each of the monks a copy of the Japanese-language version of the *Dhammapada*. She later said that Nanshinken Roshi was furious with her for having given them reading material since the rules for monks did not allow them to have written material during this period of their training.

At Nanzen-ji in the autumn of 1933, Ruth had met Miura Isshu, a senior monk who served as the monk in charge of the zendo (*jiki-jitsu*). Ruth and Miura Isshu developed a friendship, and they coauthored the classic text *Zen Dust* many years later. Miura Isshu was appointed roshi of Shokoku-ji in Kyoto, then went on to become the roshi of Koon-ji. Twenty-five years later, he would visit the First Zen Institute in New York at Ruth's invitation to give lectures, and he told the story of Ruth's experience sitting zazen through her first really intensive week at Nanzen-ji, called the Rohatsu Osesshin. He said he thought she would disappear from the zendo like the other lay students (*koji*) who were not "extremely earnest persons."

To Miura Roshi's surprise, she sat through the entire rohatsu without difficulty, and with the same sincere enthusiasm as that of the other monks—in his eyes, perhaps even more. He said it was only after watching her during this week that he came to realize the eagerness and dedication to practice zazen that had brought her all the way to Japan. After that week, they became friends, and as he said in his New York lecture, he was there twenty-five years later because of the karmic relationship binding him to Mrs. Sasaki.

While some people saw Ruth as being somewhat aloof, she had a gift for developing personal friendships with her teachers and colleagues. At Nanzen-ji, Nanshinken Roshi, who was thirty years her senior, would come to Ruth's house on the Kamo River in the summer to get away from Nanzen-ji for a few hours to relax and read in her kitchen. He would sit in the kitchen and talk with Kato, the housekeeper (Ruth said he would rather talk with Kato than her), and would eat the wonderful Western food that Ruth had prepared. They shared a joke about his love of her American food. Nanshinken Roshi would say, "when you die, I will place a beautiful arrangement on the *butsudan* [altar] in your memory. When I die, I want you to put a tomato sandwich on the altar for me."

Ruth described Nanshinken Roshi as being sincere and earnest, devoted wholeheartedly to training his monks well. He was known for his meticulously neat and clean temple, including the butsudan arrangements. Ruth said that he taught her how to have everything in clean and perfect order. Many years later when she visited the temple at Hofuku-ji and went in to look at the butsudan, she said, "only one of Nanshinken's disciples would have a butsudan that looked like this."

Ruth marveled at the simple, direct way that Nanshinken Roshi conducted the morning services, saying that his bowing was like that of a child. Nanshinken Roshi's *nyoi* (a special short wooden staff, given to him as the sign of transmission) was the same one that Hakuin had used. Nanshinken Roshi died in June 1935, when he was seventy-three. He had been the roshi at Nanzen-ji for over thirty-five years.

Ruth probably knew more Zen roshis than any other westerner during those years. Her cooking and hospitality were well-known among them, and she had fluent social skills. This gift was a little puzzling to friends like the Suzukis, and when Beatrice Suzuki would think of introducing Ruth to a roshi, such as Oyamazaki Roshi at Shokoku-ji, Ruth would say that he had already come around the back door and to Ruth's house without Beatrice Suzuki knowing it. (Ruth said she became great friends with Oyamazaki Roshi of Shokoku-ji, who died in the mid-1960s.) She referred to Nanshinken Roshi's visits by saying that he considered her house and kitchen "his private preserve."

D. T. Suzuki continued to collaborate with Ruth even though she was not a close friend. Mrs. Suzuki, formerly Beatrice Lane, was also an American, and had married D. T. Suzuki in 1911. Beatrice died in 1939. There was some friction between the two women; Ruth felt that Beatrice was "too Episcopalian," and Beatrice thought Ruth was "a little strange."

D. T. Suzuki began publishing his popular *Essays in Zen Buddhism* in 1927, three years before he and Ruth first met. His third series of the *Essays* appeared in 1934, and in his preface to this edition, he included an acknowledgment of Ruth for her assistance in reading the *Essays* in their manuscript stage.

Edward was not in robust health but was well enough to travel again to Kyoto while Ruth was studying. Ruth hired Ikeda to take care of him. In May 1934, Ruth and Edward traveled to Tokyo and had a meeting with the minister of war, General Hayashi Senjuro. Edward had been working with the Chicago Bar Association, where he was a member, to urge Congress to repeal the Japanese Exclusion Clause of the Immigration Act. This project reflected well on his being a friend to Japan, and the *Chicago Tribune* wrote about the meeting the Everetts had with General Hayashi (May 26, 1934). This brief article described Ruth as "his wife, who is a devout student of the Zen sect of Buddhism." This was the first time in years that a private American citizen was "so cordially received in the war department."

In June 1934, Ruth, Edward, and Eleanor traveled again to Manchuria. They had an audience with Emperor Pu-Yi in the new Manchurian capital. Again the *Chicago Tribune* reported on their visit (July 31, 1934), remarking that the emperor convinced Mr. Everett that the Japanese were rapidly introducing improvements. They visited Mukden, Harbin, and went on to Peking, still with Japanese troops filling the trains. They sailed back in late July on the *Asahi Maru* and returned to Chicago. They took Eleanor that fall to boarding school at Dobbs Ferry in New York.

In the winter of 1936, they rented a home in Bermuda for a few months, where Eleanor complained that, once again, she was asked to take care of her father, Edward, while Ruth "played." The *Chicago Tribune* on April 26, 1936, reported that "$5,000 Gems of Hinsdale Couple Stolen in Bermuda" and gave a description of how burglars got into the "Bermuda home" of Mr. and Mrs. Edward Warren Everett ("using a stepladder to enter an upstairs bedroom window").

Late in the summer of 1936, Ruth took Eleanor to London to study piano under an innovative teacher, George Woodhouse, who ran the George Woodhouse Pianoforte School. Eleanor, then seventeen and already having traveled to many countries with Ruth and Edward, was a sophisticated and uniquely educated young woman. Ruth took her to meet people at the Buddhist Lodge, where Ruth had been invited by founder Christmas Humphreys to give a talk about her experience studying at Nanzen-ji. (Founded in 1924, the Buddhist Lodge changed its name in 1943 to the Buddhist Society.)

Alan Watts, a regular at the Buddhist Lodge, had become interested in Zen Buddhism after reading D. T. Suzuki's writing. Watts had written a book called *The Spirit of Zen* when he was in his early twenties and was widely read and knowledgeable in Buddhism by this time.

Alan was introduced to Ruth and Eleanor, and a friendship grew among them. Alan and Eleanor began seeing each other often. A year later, Alan Watts and Eleanor became engaged, and they married in April 1938, moving to New York soon after. Their daughter Joan was born the following November, and a second daughter, Ann, was born in 1943. Although Alan and Eleanor ended their marriage eleven years later, Alan continued to visit and correspond with Ruth over the years.

Ill health had forced Edward Everett to retire in 1935 from Winston,

Strawn, & Shaw, where he had been a senior partner. Edward had begun a practice with them in August 1899 and became a partner in the firm in 1908. He had been very active in the intervening years, serving as a director of the First National Bank of Hinsdale, as a member of the school board, and as a member of the American Bar Association's committee on jurisprudence and law reform. In the summer of 1938, Edward, at age sixty-five, became mentally ill and was moved to a sanitarium in Hartford, Connecticut. Ruth moved to New York City where it would be easier to visit Edward in Hartford.

Even more significantly, this move also enabled her to begin studying Zen with Sasaki Sokei-an, which she began in June 1938. Edward lived for another year and a half with deteriorating mental health, and died in January 1940, when he was sixty-seven years old.

Ruth continued regular sanzen study with Sasaki Sokei-an Roshi, who had a small group of students at the Buddhist Society of America (officially established on May 11, 1930). One of Sokei-an's students, Mariquita Platov, said that the first time she met Ruth was when Ruth had come from Chicago to meditate and take koans with the rest of those who were attending Sokei-an's weekly sessions at his apartment on the West Side, close to the Sixth Avenue El (the old name for the elevated part of the New York subway system). Mariquita said, "she too was subjected to the rattle of passing trains, which, according to Osho, was an excellent test of the power to meditate."

Ruth brought a perspective from her intensive experience at Nanzen-ji to this group studying with Sokei-an. Ruth had noticed that "sitting" (zazen meditation) wasn't very central in their meetings. She said that after being at Nanzen-ji, she felt proper sitting was essential, and she took credit for beginning this practice among Sokei-an's students. She said that although he made people come to his lectures for a minimum of three months before he would consider them for sanzen, he was content for them to sit in chairs. She was critical of his not making any effort to have them do zazen, and he said, "well at least I have to have the roof over my head and if I put them down on cushions and make them do zazen I would have no roof over my head, nobody would come."

Years later, Ruth described Sokei-an's early style in his *teisho* (lectures) and in his sanzen with his students. The following passages are from taped conversations between Ruth and Gary Snyder made in Kyoto during the mid-1960s:

> He gave teisho twice a week in the old traditional texts and forms, translating certain portions. . . . [T]here would be six or seven of his students and perhaps twenty to thirty others in the audience. He didn't expect the students to chant sutras; he didn't ask the audience to chant. . . . He would always have sanzen first. He would ask his students to come early. . . . He would be in the shrine room, and when he was ready he would ring his little bell, then the students would go in order for sanzen. . . . After their sanzen was completed, he would come down and do the bowing. . . . When he finished his bowing and chanting in front of the altar, and burning incense, he would take his seat, and then his oldest student would go and *gassho* [bow formally] and burn incense, then the next oldest, and the next oldest, and then at the end of the line of students who had bowed and burned incense would come any of the audience who wished to do the same thing. When

that was finished, then he would sit down and begin his teisho.

Ruth also described the approach that Sokei-an used in working with his students using koans:

He was giving koans in English, and one problem that his students had with his English translations was that he would sometimes vary the English translation just a little bit. That was sometimes confusing. As for the physical situation of sanzen, he had two of these teisho-type chairs (with the round back)—he sat in one, and the student sat in the other, facing him. He did not get down on the cushion, and the student did not get down either. The student bowed outside the sanzen door, and rang the bell, and entered, and closed the door, and bowed, and stood before him, and bowed a third time, and then sat down on the seat facing him. The two chairs face-to-face. He always carried a *nyoi* [carved wood baton] in his hands, and over to the side his little bell. That was the physical situation. (tape 3, page 14)

. . .

He never modernized his koans, but stuck very, very closely, as close as he could, to the traditional koan itself. I never knew him, and I took a good many koans from him, to give any adaptations . . . but he did not, for a long time, ask for *jakugo* [capping phrases]. Even koans that should have had jakugo, he did not attempt to use *Zenrin Kushu*, because none of it was translated. When he asked for jakugo of some of his more experienced students, he would ask for something from English poetry; sometimes he also suggested *Alice in Wonderland*, of which he was very fond, and he felt that there were a number of lines that could be used as jakugo.... He suggested nursery rhymes, too. Nursery rhymes and *Alice in Wonderland*, or the others were what they had to find themselves.... But I never knew him to use anything from *Zenrin Kushu* or to ask it. Because we had no copies of it, no one knew anything about it. (tape 3, page 15)

Ruth said that no one who listened to a lecture of Sokei-an's would ever doubt that he was a completely enlightened man.

Sokei-an seemed so different to Ruth compared to her early experiences of men connected with Zen, especially D. T. Suzuki, who was the quintessential scholar, sometimes referred to as overly studious in his approach. Sokei-an was completely the opposite; in fact, the two men knew each other but were not friends. Ruth said that D. T. Suzuki and his wife looked down on Sokei-an because he wasn't from the temple Zen tradition, and Sokei-an used to speak somewhat disparagingly to Ruth about Suzuki's writing and descriptions of Zen.

Sokei-an's father began teaching him Chinese when he was four and brought him up on the Confucian classics and the old Japanese language of Shinto scriptures and hymns. A large man at six-foot-three and a heavy drinker, his father had a stroke and died when Sokei-an was fifteen. Showing an aptitude for carving, Sokei-an was apprenticed to a carpenter, where he learned to carve ornaments for buildings, such as elephant heads and dragons. Doing well at this, he endeavored to earn a living for himself. He also became interested in poetry. Carving was an art that gave him mobility, and he spent a year walking through the mountains of the Nagano prefecture, carving in different villages where temples were being restored. He developed a great love of walking.

After that year, with the support of his mother's family, he began attending the Imperial Academy of Arts in Ueno. This became the crucial period in his development. He began studying art with Takamura Koun, a leading sculptor in Japan who had studied in Paris under Rodin and who saw great promise in Sokei-an. After the first year, Takamura Koun invited Sokei-an to live with him as a house student. Sokei-an became friends then with Takamura Koun's son, also a student at the Imperial Academy, who subsequently became a great bronze caster in Japan.

Sokei-an also began meeting poets and was mentored by a well-known classical poet, whose student he was for the next couple of years. Ruth said that instead of saying he was a "disciple" of this poet, he referred to himself, with a standard Japanese expression, as "someone who carried his teacher's briefcase."

Sokei-an had a part-time job working in the post office along with several of his student friends, and they held heated discussions about all sorts of philosophical topics, one of which was about the words "objective" and "subjective." Sokei-an said one of his friends told him that if he wanted to learn more about those words, he should study Zen, and this friend referred him to Sokatsu, who had Zen students over in Ueno Park near the university.

Sokei-an graduated in 1905, having studied with Sokatsu for a couple of years. Sokei-an was called up for the Manchurian (Russo-Japanese) war, worked in a supply company (while helping to paint scenery for the dramatic events of his group), and after being demobilized, returned to Tokyo. Shortly after that, Sokatsu invited

Sokei-an to join a small group trip to America that he was planning and suggested an arrangement whereby Sokei-an could marry one of his students (Tome) and come along. They were married.

In the fall of 1906, the group arrived in California and settled in Hayward, hoping to run a successful strawberry farm. It was somewhat of a disaster, and Sokei-an quarreled with Sokatsu. Moving with Tome into San Francisco, Sokei-an started studying with Richard Partington at the California Institute of Art. Sokatsu and the others gave up on the farm, also moved into the city, and Sokei-an renewed his sanzen study with Sokatsu until 1910, when Sokatsu returned to Japan.

Sokei-an and his wife had a son, Shintaro, and in 1910 they moved to Seattle, where they had a daughter, Seiko. During the next four years Sokei-an worked for a picture-frame maker, hand-carving leaves and embellishments. With the consent of both his wife and the frame maker, Sokei-an arranged to work only six or seven months of the year, leaving the rest of the time for his own projects. One of these was a Japanese-language paper in Seattle called the *Hokubei Shinpo*. Since many of the readers of this paper were Japanese who lived on remote and isolated farms in Oregon and Washington, he made money by walking through the countryside collecting subscriptions for the paper, and exploring the northwest while he was at it.

Ruth said that one year he spent a summer in the Columbia River valley, going from one farmhouse to the next, getting lodging and food. He tramped the mountains, explored the rivers, and meditated on the koans that Sokatsu had given him. Ruth said that he worked out solutions to a hundred koans so that he would be ready for his next visit to Sokatsu, and some years later when he went back to Japan, he found that every answer was wrong.

The following summer, Sokei-an got a job for the Union Pacific Railroad in Utah, where they were laying track. He worked as the paymaster and traveled all over the Salt Lake area.

During his extensive walking periods, "tramping" as he called it, he was writing all the time. He wrote both fiction and nonfiction and sold many of his stories to the *Chuo Koron*, a prominent literary magazine in Japan, as well as the *Hokubei Shinpo* paper in Seattle. He was becoming popular as a writer.

In 1913 his mother was ailing in Tokyo, and his wife was pregnant and wanting to have her third child back in Japan. Tome returned to Japan with the children.

Sokei-an moved to New York and got jobs for several furniture companies making carvings. He moved to Greenwich Village and became friends with some of the poetry circle, including Max Bodenheim (a precursor to the Beat poets). After World War I broke out, Sokei-an tried unsuccessfully to enlist in the U. S. Army. In 1919, on a hot July day in the city, Sokei-an came upon the carcass of a dead horse, and it was a turning point for him—he went home, packed, and headed for Japan to see his teacher, Sokatsu.

He stayed in Japan for almost two years (the maximum allowed with his semipermanent visa), writing for *Chuo Koron* and studying with Sokatsu. In 1921 he returned to New York and continued with his art of carving in wood and jade for an upscale store owned by Edward Farmer, where he worked for several years while continuing to write. He told Ruth that he believed one of the reasons his writing was so popular was his curious upbringing, which included classical Chinese and Confucius, and as Ruth said, "he knew reams of Rongo" (Confucian Analects) by heart. Additionally, one of his maternal aunts was a geisha mistress, and another had a husband who was a *joruri* (ballads for puppet plays) singer doing vaudeville, so all in all he picked up much colloquial language and culture, which added to the richness and expression of his stories and writing. He stayed in New York until 1926, and during that time, the Orientalia bookstore opened. The bookshop hosted evening discussions, and so Sokei-an, around 1924 or 1925, gave some talks on Zen.

Returning to Japan, he immersed himself in his studies with Sokatsu, and in 1928 Sokatsu gave him his inka and permission to teach. He told Ruth that along with this success, there was disappointing word from *Chuo Koron*, who told him they didn't need his writing anymore. At this news he'd "thrown himself on the floor, Japanese man-fashion, [and] wept bitterly, thinking that his literary career was over."

He returned again to New York, now as a roshi but with no money and no students, and lived with various Asian families, finally connecting with Mr. Miya, who was a senior employee at the New York office of the Yamanaka firm. Miya, who had studied Zen previously, gave Sokei-an five hundred dollars to find a place to live and start teaching Zen. Sokei-an took out a lease on two rooms at 63 West 70th Street. Miya also was instrumental in getting Sokei-an to start giving lectures at the Japan Club, which were well attended by businessmen. And he continued carving at home on projects like repairing statues for museums. Ruth said that more students became interested, and along with Miya and a few others, they incorporated, first as a branch of Sokatsu's Ryomo Kyokai, a lay Zen group in Tokyo.

On December 10, 1938, Ruth took her vows and received her Buddhist name from Sokei-an, even though she had already received a Buddhist name (Kuge) from Nanshinken Roshi back in the early 1930s. The Buddhist name Sokei-an gave her was Eryu, meaning "dragon wisdom."

In 1940, Ruth became the editor of *Cat's Yawn*, a magazine that Sokei-an and his students were producing. She also took an interest in Sokei-an's well-being and began thinking about a better place for him to teach than his apartment on the Upper West Side. She was by this time the vice president of the Buddhist Society. Ruth was living at 124 East 65th Street, where she was renovating and refurbishing a brownstone building she had purchased. She planned for her mother to live on the top floor, herself to have the fourth floor, Sokei-an to have the third floor, and the second and ground floors to be for the Institute (still called the Buddhist Society of America). Sokei-an agreed. Ruth designed the interior to reflect the style of a Japanese Zen Buddhist temple. One month before they were all to move in, Ruth's mother, Clara, died at age seventy-eight, on September 18, 1941.

In later years, Ruth remarked to Richard Leavitt that her mother had been very domineering, and that she had finally freed herself from that, saying, "I broke the silver cord with a single blow." (The silver cord reference was to a play by Sidney Howard called *The Silver Cord* [1926], also made into a film in 1933. It was about a dominating and smothering mother who reduces her son to total impotence.) Leavitt said that Ruth did not elaborate on her comment.

R UTH, SOKEI-AN, and the Buddhist Society of America opened the doors of their new quarters at 124 East 65th Street on December 6, 1941, the day before Pearl Harbor was bombed by Japan. The enthusiasm and excitement of the new location were considerably dampened by this event and by the members' awareness that the FBI had them under twenty-four-hour surveillance from a stand under the Cosmopolitan Club veranda across the street. Sokei-an was interviewed by FBI staff many times, as was Ruth. The Wednesday evening lectures, sanzen for the students, and the meetings of the group continued, but by June 15, 1942, Sokei-an had given his last public talk and was interned on Ellis Island under his (birth) name, Yeita S. Sasaki.

On October 2, 1942, he was taken to the Fort Meade Internment Camp outside of Baltimore, Maryland, where he remained as an internee until August 15, 1943. All of the energy and resources of Ruth and Sokei-an's students were devoted to freeing him.

During his stay at Fort Meade, Sokei-an began woodcarving again with such tools as the authorities allowed him to have. It was some solace to him during a period when his ill health made the internment even more excruciating. His carvings were in great demand by the camp's army officers.

Sokei-an's son, Shintaro, and his daughter, Seiko, were in relocation centers in the West during this time, and he corresponded directly with them and through Ruth, trying to help get them released. In a letter Ruth wrote to Shintaro on July 10, 1942, she said, "we do not know exactly what the cause of the government's wishing to hold him is, except that I have been informed by them that they have made a translation of a certain article written by him as 'Nonsense' which appeared in the Seattle paper in 1936 and which they consider as not exactly the right tone."

At the end of his internment, there were official discussions about whether he would be allowed to remain on the East Coast or would have to live in an area of the country away from the coasts, such as Montana or Colorado. After interviews with him and some of his students who were subpoenaed to appear before a panel, he was allowed to remain in New York. Lindley Williams Hubbell, then a senior student of Sokei-an's, was the official sponsor named on the release form. Hugo Pollock, a lawyer who had been a colleague of Edward Everett's, was instrumental in gaining Sokei-an's freedom. Sokei-an was released on August 17, 1943, under a "parole" and sponsorship of Lindley Hubbell, with conditions of a weekly visit to report to the chief district parole officer of the Immigration and Naturalization Service, along with submitting a personal report semimonthly.

Sokei-an's health was unstable, and he suffered from high blood pressure. He had a coronary thrombosis right after his release, and became a complete invalid for the next seven months. His students were able to visit him, and he continued his sanzen with them, but he was unable to give any lectures. A prominent New York doctor attended him, and he slowly regained his strength. Ruth, the doctor, and the lawyer conferred about Sokei-an's future and concluded that he must marry Ruth. As Ruth recorded in taped conversations in

Kyoto with Gary Snyder many years later, the doctor had said to her, "now look here, if you want Mr. Sasaki to get well, you have got to marry him. You have got to. The divorce [from Sokei-an's estranged wife in Japan, Tome] can be arranged in this country with Pollock— we've talked it over. You have got to marry—that is the only thing that will keep him alive, because he is determined that he is going to die. And the only thing that will bring him any kind of peace of mind and possibly facilitate his recovery is for you to marry him."

Sokei-an and Ruth married within the year. There has been specu- lation of all kinds about why they married. Some suggested that it was to get Sokei-an out of the internment camp, though that aim had already been accomplished before they married. Others have written that they married so that she could have his name to con- tinue the work of the Institute. Alan Watts suggested that they were actually in love. In Watts's autobiography *In My Own Way*, he wrote, "At this time he and Ruth had just fallen in love, and we were the fascinated witnesses of their mutually fructifying relationship—she drawing out his bottomless knowledge of Buddhism; and he break- ing down her rigidities with ribald tales that made her blush and giggle" (p. 145).

Ruth said in later years that she had had many hesitations about it, even though as she said in the taped conversations with Gary Snyder, "Sokei-an was determined to marry me." Ruth told Snyder that there were several reasons, and that it was a complex thing. One reason was that Sokei-an didn't think he was going to live very long, and there was nobody else to whom to leave the Institute. If they married, she would have his name, and that would "more or less" put the Institute in her hands. Sokei-an wanted her to continue to pursue the study she wanted to do in Japan if he died, and again, he felt she could do it better if she had his name. She said that she had refused for a long time, not because she objected to a marriage, but because she felt that because he was a roshi, and because his Japanese wife was still alive, the obstacles to marriage seemed insurmountable. Ruth said that the question of Sokei-an getting a Japanese divorce from Tome seemed impossible for the simple reason that his teacher, Sokatsu, had arranged the wedding in the first place. So he would have to ask Sokatsu for permission to obtain the divorce, and that would be an insult since Sokatsu had arranged the marriage. Ruth said that Sokei-an had written to his wife in Japan many times and asked her to divorce him, and she repeatedly refused.

Nevertheless, Sokei-an went to Little Rock, Arkansas, in the spring of 1944, where he could stay for the required period of time to obtain a divorce from Tome. Still weak, he was accompanied by Hugo Pollock and Ruth. Since the war was still going on, Sokei-an was required to have a "reputable citizen" serve as his sponsor. Pollock found a minister of the Congregational church in Hot Springs to be his sponsor. Ruth took an apartment in the same hotel. After eight weeks the divorce became final, and Ruth and Sokei-an were free to obtain a marriage license.

Sokei-an and Ruth had planned to marry and take the train back to Chicago the same day. But on July 10, when they went to get the marriage license, they learned that Little Rock still observed the southern miscegenation law forbidding marriage between races. They had to make a mad dash across county lines to Hot Springs, Arkansas, where they found a judge willing to marry them. Because the war was still on, there was gasoline rationing, and Ruth said they had trouble getting a taxi to drive them twenty miles to the judge. There they obtained a legal divorce and a legal marriage, and barely caught their train to Chicago. The stress of the events took their toll, and as their train neared Chicago, Sokei-an collapsed in the observation car while they were standing in line for breakfast. They sent a telegram at the next station to a doctor Ruth knew in Chicago, and an ambulance and wheelchair met them when they arrived.

After visiting Eleanor and Alan (who was then at Northwestern University in Chicago), they went on (via ambulance and wheelchair to the station) by train to their home in New York. After Sokei-an's release, the Buddhist Society of America changed its name to the First Zen Institute of America. The new name had been a dream of Sokei-an's, and he said, "If you will do this, I will die the happiest man in the world." Sokei-an continued to have trouble with high blood pressure and intense headaches in the next several months. In the spring of 1945, he became weaker instead of stronger, and he died on May 17, at sixty-three, from kidney thrombosis. His ashes were buried at Woodlawn Cemetery in Upper Manhattan.

Ruth was fifty-two years old when Sokei-an died. She continued working with other students at the First Zen Institute to keep alive the projects that Sokei-an had started. During the next few years, they republished the lectures of Sokei-an (first published by the Buddhist Society of America, the earlier name of the First Zen Institute) that had been in the thirteen issues of *Cat's Yawn*. This book, also called *Cat's Yawn*, was a facsimile printing of the magazine issues along with a foreword, appendix, glossary, and index. It was published in 1947 under the imprint of the First Zen Institute of America, and was the first of many book projects for both author and publisher.

Foremost in the minds of Ruth and the other members of the First Zen Institute was their desire to find another Zen master for their group. Ruth, as vice president of the Institute, Mary Farkas as secretary, and George Fowler as president began writing letters to roshis in Japan who had connections with Sokei-an and who might be sympathetic to the Institute's need for a new teacher.

In June 1949, both Ruth and Mary Farkas corresponded with Goto Zuigan Roshi, then *kancho* (head) of the headquarters temple of Daitoku-ji. Goto Roshi was a dharma-brother of Sokei-an, having shared the same teacher. Ruth enlisted the help of her old friend Ogata Sohaku, a monk she had known in her Nanzen-ji days and kept in touch with, to carry the letters to Goto Roshi on her behalf.

In their letters they pleaded with Goto Roshi, arguing their need as persuasively as they could. They felt that having the head of Daitoku-ji come to New York would enhance their credibility and prestige among scholars and others who had begun to be impressed with the First Zen Institute and its growth under Sokei-an. They were told by Ogata Sohaku that Goto Roshi considered himself too old for such an undertaking, and they responded that Nyogen Senzaki (another dharma-brother who had shared the same teacher with Sokei-an and Goto Zuigan) was then actively teaching in Los Angeles at the age of seventy-six, and that D. T. Suzuki, at eighty, was just preparing to come again to the United States for several years of teaching.

Their second line of argument to Goto Roshi was that he should come and should bring along a younger roshi who might be more suitable. None of these letters brought the desired result, so the next step was to get permission from Goto Roshi for Ruth to go to Japan so that she could discuss these urgent matters with him personally. In a letter to Goto Roshi, Mary Farkas said that it had been Sokei-an's wish that Ruth go to Japan and discuss the future need of the Institute for a teacher with both Goto Roshi and Awano Roshi (at Manman-ji), the two people Sokei-an considered most knowledgeable about finding a successor.

After several months, Ruth finally received the necessary military permission to travel to Japan in October 1949. Shortly before she left New York, she hired a new personal assistant, Haru Yoshida, who was to provide the essential backup and support for Ruth in Japan for the next sixteen years. Haru's first letter to Ruth in Japan in October 1949 was the beginning of frequent and continuing correspondence between them for the next sixteen years. Haru was asked to take charge of the library at the First Zen Institute, and she organized relationships with publishers and book dealers to provide books for the Institute as well as for Ruth in Japan.

In November 1949, Ruth stopped in Tokyo on her way to Kyoto and paid her respects at the little layperson's zendo first established by Sokatsu Roshi, Sokei-an's teacher, in Tokyo's Nippori district, not far from the Imperial University.

Once in Kyoto, she immediately started to work with Goto Roshi on translation projects, and Goto Roshi accepted her as a student for continuing her koan study. She began to fit into the daily routines at Daitoku-ji, and wrote in a letter to Haru Yoshida, "tell Walter [Nowick, a member of the Institute preparing to come to Japan] my sitting is getting to be superb."

Being in Kyoto and embarking on these projects gave Ruth renewed energy. She was in excellent health and walked at least an hour a day. She said it helped her to think things out when she walked, and that she had much to think about in addition to her koan. Ruth was beginning to realize that she would need years in Japan rather than months, so she began looking for a house to live in.

She asked Goto Roshi for assistance in finding a house, and Goto Roshi consulted with his disciple Oda Sesso Roshi, who had become the new roshi of the Daitoku-ji Sodo. Oda Roshi offered a house on some land in the Daitoku-ji complex. This house had been built for a former Daitoku-ji Sodo roshi, Denenshitsu Roshi, some thirty years earlier when he had retired. Denenshitsu Roshi only lived in the house for a couple of years. Since then, the Daitoku-ji Sodo had rented the house before the war (Daitoku-ji was closed during the war) to the principal of a high school in Osaka. At the end of the war the house was rented to the head priest of a nearby Shinto shrine, Shiramine Jingu. The Shinto priest was agreeable to moving out, as he had lost interest in Zen and was devoting himself to the study of Christianity.

Oda Roshi offered the house to Ruth rent-free, partly because he wished to indicate his appreciation of the work Ruth was engaged in for Zen and partly because the house had fallen into such serious disrepair that the sodo could not afford to put it in order. Ruth accepted and spent about 1,000,000 yen (about $2,800) making the house livable. She also asked if she might have an unused patch of ground at the back of the house for a place to raise chickens and have a small vegetable garden. Several months later, after a six-month visit back in New York during February–August 1950, her request was granted, but she was asked to pay 1,000 yen (about $2.80) per month to the Daitoku-ji Sodo for the use of it.

While getting ready for the trip back to New York, Ruth had traveled to a few temples, hoping to find a roshi to come to the First Zen Institute. One of these temples was at Ibuka. She took a translator along to assist her. About forty monks gathered in the reception room in the evening after their daily sanzen with the roshi. After introductions by Kajiura Itsugai Roshi, Ruth was asked by the monks to tell them about those who studied Zen in America and how the temple was founded in New York. When she told them of her search, they asked her what the qualifications were for a roshi to go to New York. She said later that they looked pretty discouraged when she finished listing the qualifications. One of the monks asked her if she thought she'd ever find someone like that, and she admitted she might not. When asked what was the most important attribute, she told them "that he have what is known as daigo, that is, complete enlightenment from a Zen standpoint."

Kajiura Roshi had tentatively selected a candidate for Ruth, Awano Osho. When she returned to see Goto Roshi, being diplomatic about her lack of interest in the candidate from Ibuka, she asked his advice about what to do next. Goto Roshi replied that there was an interesting man at Heirin-ji she should visit.

Kyoto Beginnings, 1949–1955 4

GOTO ROSHI gave Ruth a letter to read to the members of the First Zen Institute for her visit to New York in February 1950. He described Ruth's earnest efforts to find a new teacher, and of her having interviewed many roshis in various parts of Japan. Goto Roshi said that he, too, had made many efforts to locate a teacher, but that so far they had not found someone with the appropriate qualifications. He apologized for not himself being able to come and visit them, but he advised them to be patient. He said that their zazen practice would benefit from Ruth's direction since she was "quite an experienced student in Zazen."

Meanwhile the East 65th Street brownstone hummed with activity. Eleanor had moved into Ruth's apartment on the fourth floor with daughters Ann and Joan after having separated from her husband, Alan Watts, the previous year. The First Zen Institute was having regular meetings. Walter Nowick, twenty-four, an advanced student who had been with the Institute since 1948, was starting to hold sesshin for the members, even though they had no teacher. Walter was a pianist studying at Juilliard, and his father was from a Russian immigrant family who had started successful potato farming on Long Island. His piano teacher had introduced him to the First Zen Institute, and Walter was preparing himself for a trip to Japan to study Zen by learning Chinese and Japanese, and by reading Buddhist texts that were available.

Ruth had started her work of introducing potential American Zen students to Japanese roshis with her letter of introduction for Walter Nowick to Goto Roshi, and through Goto Roshi, to Oda Sesso Roshi. Shortly after she arrived back in New York in February 1950, Goto Roshi sent her a letter thanking her for the several presents she had sent him and telling her that he would talk with Oda Sesso Roshi about having Walter come to Kyoto as a formal student.

By the end of March 1950, plans were firming up for Walter Nowick to sail to Japan on the SS *General Gordon* on June 1 for a six-month stay at Daitoku-ji. Ruth began giving talks at the weekly meetings of the Institute, describing in detail the places she had stayed and the people she had visited in her four months in Kyoto during the winter. Woven in with her remarks were stories of people who had become connected to her and the First Zen Institute. She prepared stories of the roshis and their historical context. One of her most interesting was that of Goto Zuigan Roshi himself.

Goto Roshi was the oldest disciple of Sokatsu, who was also Sokei-an's teacher. As head abbot of the Daitoku-ji temples, Goto Roshi was surrounded by formality. As a balance, he found a temple a short distance away on the outskirts of Kyoto, and would come in to Daitoku-ji only when it was necessary. His retreat was the temple Daishu-in on the grounds of Ryoan-ji (Temple of Dragon of Peace), a temple famous for its rock garden popularly ascribed, at least in part, to Soami in the fifteenth century. On the autumn day Ruth went out to visit him, his seventieth birthday, she took a streetcar and an "interurban tram" from Shokoku-ji.

It had been sixteen years since Ruth had last seen Goto Roshi in

1933–1934, when he was living at Tokai-an in Myoshin-ji. Ruth said she had not remembered his appearance after such a long time, but that she thought he didn't look quite his age. She also commented that he was all shaven, and that Zen priests didn't go in much for shaving except on the days stipulated by monastery regulations, about once in five days. She said they preferred the unshaven look, as it made them appear a little more venerable, a little older.

His small temple had a guest room, a room for the image and the tablets of the families who are connected with the temple, a small room off that, a tearoom of four and a half mats (about eighty square feet) in which he made his study and spent most of his time, a kitchen, and some dressing rooms behind that. Ruth said he thoroughly enjoyed living in this temple.

Goto Roshi's life intertwined with Sokei-an's life as they joined their teacher, Sokatsu, in coming to America in 1906. This trip of Sokatsu and his disciples is depicted in the book *Cat's Yawn* (1947, p. 19). Goto Roshi served as a translator for Sokatsu and the group as they struggled to make ends meet in the San Francisco Bay area. Goto Roshi was also the one who had picked out the "no-good" farm in Hayward, a disaster of trying to make a living growing strawberries on worn-out land. At the end of four years, Sokatsu decided to return to Japan. Sokatsu had also opened a small zendo in San Francisco. When he went back to Japan in 1910, Sokatsu left Sokei-an with the instructions that he was to stay and study English and learn about American culture. Goto Roshi accompanied the rest of the small group back to Japan, where Sokatsu built a temple in the outskirts of Tokyo. Goto served as his personal assistant for six more years, as secretary, cook, etc. At the end of that time Goto had completed his Zen study and received his *inka* (seal of dharma transmission).

Goto Roshi then returned to his old temple at Myoshin-ji and

went to Korea on behalf of Myoshin-ji headquarters to do mission-
ary work. Ruth said he spent fifteen years in Seoul. He started by
living in a couple of rooms, and by the time he left, he'd built a magnificent temple.

Goto Roshi first became the abbot of the Myoshin-ji Temples
(Myoshin-ji was the largest of the Rinzai Zen headquarter temples),
then became the abbot of the Daitoku-ji Temples. Ruth said that
although Daitoku-ji had only 260 subtemples, it was the most powerful temple in Japan. The abbot, at that time Goto Roshi, held the
most important position within Rinzai Zen. Ruth was particularly
enthusiastic about Goto Roshi's story, because she felt that members of the Institute should know about Sokei-an's lineage and
interconnections.

Ruth also liked to recount the life of Oda Sesso Roshi (1901–
1966), the disciple of Goto Roshi who had become roshi of the
Daitoku-ji Sodo. Oda Roshi became the roshi whom several First
Zen Institute members would meet and study under in Japan. Oda
Roshi was Goto Roshi's only heir. Ruth said he was a man of about
forty-five (actually he was forty-nine years old) and so handsome
that when the question came up of his being a possible candidate for
the First Zen Institute position, Ruth had said, "No, no, no, there
would be nothing but girl trouble from beginning to end . . . looks
just like a Hollywood boy." She said Oda Roshi called her "aunt," or
"*oba-san*," since Sokei-an was his "uncle" (Goto's dharma-brother).
Oda Roshi studied with Goto Roshi at Myoshin-ji and was also with
Goto Roshi when he went to Korea.

In July 1950, Walter Nowick wrote his first letter to Ruth from
Daitoku-ji. By the middle of that summer, Ruth was busy planning
her return to Kyoto for early fall. She wrote to Goto Roshi that she
would take care of family business and household matters during the

summer, and would move her invalid brother, David, to Honolulu with a nurse for an indefinite stay. David had had a difficult life. It was said that he was a homosexual who had a knack for getting beaten up. This resulted in injuries that were to plague him and indirectly lead to his early death in 1954.

Ruth also wrote that she would like to bring her new assistant, Haru Yoshida, back to Kyoto for several months. Haru was known in those years as "Penny," and as Haru explained, after the war there was some resistance to young women with Japanese names. After Haru got out of the relocation camp at Tule Lake, she got a job in an art gallery in Manhattan. Her boss told her that people wouldn't like hearing a Japanese name, that she should call herself "Miss Penny." So, for a few years, she did.

Haru met Ruth because a silkscreen artist who had a space next to the art gallery Haru worked at invited her to go along to the First Zen Institute meetings that he attended. He also told Haru that Ruth needed a part-time secretary, so she went over to 65th Street, and Ruth put her to work taking dictation. After a few weeks, Ruth asked Haru if she would work for her full-time, explaining that the "part-time" had just been a test, that she really needed someone full-time.

Ruth wrote several letters from New York to Goto Roshi that summer emphasizing the urgency of finding a Zen teacher for Sokei-an's former students in New York. Everything else in the world at that time seemed to be peripheral to these matters. "The problem of how to get the true line of Zen teaching transplanted into America in the shortest possible time is with me night and day," she wrote. "I feel its speedy accomplishment is imperative or Zen may be lost to humanity."

In her urging, she said that she had done everything she could to get the organization ready, but that she could not be the teacher or create a teacher out of the empty void. "Japanese Zen must supply that man, and I think all Japanese Zen has no more important work at this moment than to bend all its energies to find the man who should come. I am fully convinced that this will be the last opportunity." She didn't explain why she felt it was a "last opportunity," but it appears to have been her method of persuasion.

Shortly before Ruth's departure to Japan in August 1950, Eleanor, who had gotten a divorce from Alan Watts, married Carlton Gamer on August 4. Eleanor and Carlton had met in Chicago while Alan was connected with Northwestern University.

Ruth returned to Kyoto and her little house in Daitoku-ji on August 31, 1950, accompanied by her new assistant, Haru Yoshida. When they arrived, Ruth found that Kato, her housekeeper from twenty years earlier, had cleaned the little house and installed what remained of furniture Ruth had left behind in her house on the Kamo River from her days studying at Nanzen-ji in the 1930s.

Kanaseki Hisao began assisting Ruth with many small tasks: letters, appointments, translating assistance, etc. (Kanaseki's birth name was Takemura Hisao, but after marrying, he changed his name to Kanaseki, which is what most people remember him by. This Japanese custom was followed sometimes in families with several sons: when one of those sons married into a family with only daughters, the husband would assume his wife's family name.) Over the next several months, Kanaseki Hisao and Haru Yoshida kept Ruth's projects and the household going as Ruth became settled. Haru began teaching English classes at Doshisha University in addition to assisting Ruth.

At the end of April 1951, Haru returned home to New York and described in a letter to Ruth her first meeting back at the First Zen Institute. "In the evening I sat with Fielder [Schillinberg], Walter [Nowick], Miss Severin, Jesse, Gerry and Ida-Mae. Fielder is still in charge of the bells and Walter has introduced the practice of bowing before sitting and upon getting up, and he serves them tea at their places, so there is no talking all evening. The sitting starts at 7:45 P.M. with three sessions of 25 minutes each with five minute breaks. Then tea is served, followed by two more sessions. About Fielder being in charge, they say he has been wonderful and they all seem to go for him."

One day Ruth mentioned to Goto Roshi that her house should have a name, as most Japanese houses did. When she went to see him next, he told her to call it "Ryosen-an," and that there had once been an old temple by that name on those grounds. He wrote out the characters for the name, and Ruth had them carved on a wooden board and hung over the front door. She didn't know then about the long and important part that Ryosen-an had played in Daitoku-ji history.

Daitoku-ji, translated as the Temple of Great Virtue, was founded in the early 1300s by Daito Kokushi. One of the headquarter temples of Rinzai Zen in Kyoto, it initially had several hundred subtemples spread throughout Japan. It was rebuilt after being destroyed by fire in 1453 and by war in 1468. It had many subtemples in the main compound, where there are currently about twenty-five subtemples. Originally these temples were organized into four sublineages, and Ryosen-an was at that time the head of one of the sublineages, controlling many temples in that sublineage in the northern part of the country around Tokyo.

Ruth described the history of this subtemple called Ryosen-an in one of her "Dear Everyone" letters, July 1, 1956, issued with *Zen Notes* III, nos. 8 and 9 (August–September 1956):

The first Ryosen-an stood just to the north of the Dai-toku-ji Honzan (main administrative building) and was under the patronage of the powerful Taga family. Between 1615 and 1623 new temple buildings, the gift of a pious daughter of Ieyasu, founder of the Tokugawa Shogunate, were constructed under the direction of the 162nd Kancho, Nisshin Zenji. In 1636, only fifteen years later, due to the reconstruction and enlarging of the Honzan, the new Ryosen-an was taken down and rebuilt on its present site. This is of woodwork fitted together almost without nails, and the inner and outer walls consisting mainly of sliding panels that a child can remove—plaster is used very sparingly—the entire build-ing can be taken apart with ease.

Then in 1870, with the end of the Shogunate and the beginning of the Meiji Restoration, Ryosen-an lost its patronage, as was the case with hundreds of other temples, and many of the temples were destroyed or fell into disrepair. Ruth described the intervening years, and how gradually the Ryosen-an land, tended by the care-taker responsible for the Daitoku-ji Honzan, became the site of a house for retired roshi Denenshitsu, who wanted to live in a house near the sodo. This in turn became the house that Goto Roshi and the Daitoku-ji Sodo ended up renting to Ruth.

During the Meiji Restoration, at the end of the Tokugawa period, Shinto became more important than Buddhism because the new emperor was also the chief priest of Shinto. The Meiji Restoration coincided with the opening of Japan to the outside after 250 years when it had been a closed country. Two prevailing attitudes, that all things Western were wonderful and that all things traditional were wonderful, coincided in a lack of support for Buddhism, which was now depicted as neither Japanese (coming from China fourteen centuries earlier) nor Western. Buddhist temples were closed, property and possessions confiscated, and priests turned out. Ryosen-an was destroyed, and its property was reduced to its present size. When Ruth arrived, there was only the small cabin left on the land.

Her house was small. After the winter, Ruth knew that she needed more space, such as a *kura*, or storehouse, for storing winter things in the summer and summer things in the winter. She also wanted a place to leave things when she made trips back to New York. She consulted Oda Roshi about building a kura on part of the vegetable patch, and he didn't object. So a kura was built with a connecting passage to the house, at a cost of several hundred thousand yen (between one and two thousand dollars). When the rooftree was raised, the chief secretary of the *honzan* (headquarters) at that time conducted a little ceremony. The building of the kura was the start of complicated political exchanges among Ruth, the priest of Hosshun-in (the subtemple next door), and Daitoku-ji headquarters.

Ruth was immersed in her projects in Kyoto, one of which was her work with Goto Roshi on the study and correction of Sokeian's English translation of *Rinzai-roku*. Haru Yoshida was kept busy in New York shipping project supplies (file cards, paper, work supplies) and books for Ruth. Because of the difficulty in the postwar years of getting clothing, scarce food items like coffee and sugar, vitamins, clothes, and cosmetics, Haru shipped a running stream of packages to Ruth to keep her stocked with things she needed and requested.

Packages were also flowing from Kyoto to New York. Ruth sent *zabuton* (large square cushions) and zazen (round) cushions made in Kyoto to members of the First Zen Institute, and she facilitated requests for *tansu* (storage chests) and other Japanese furniture items to be made and shipped. Ruth also had a very special touch with gifts for new members of the First Zen Institute. Among the most treasured items were small celadon incense burners, called *koro*, copies made from the original incense burner on Goto Roshi's altar in Seoul, which Goto had brought back from Korea. Ruth had a well known Japanese potter named Zuiho make them, and they were very carefully packed in boxes made of *hinoki* (*Chamaecyparis obtusa*, Japanese white cedar—this wood has become so rare that now Port Orford cedar, a closely related and almost identical wood, is used instead) and tied with special woven ribbon. New members of the Institute, when they "entered the *sangha*," were given this incense burner along with a box of incense. Ruth also sent authentic sutra books for chanting, especially useful to Mary Farkas and First Zen Institute students who had begun studying Chinese.

Ruth had started publishing essays in Buddhist magazines and periodicals. In June 1951, she wrote an article published in *Bukkyogaku-Kenkyu* (Studies in Buddhism) no. 5, titled "Why Zen Buddhism Appeals to American People." The only essay written in English in this issue, it was the text of a talk she had given on October 31, 1950 (her fifty-eighth birthday), to students at Ryokoku University in Kyoto. She said in this talk that one of Ryokoku's graduates, William Montgomery McGovern (1897–1964), was responsible for introducing her to D. T. Suzuki, and thus for her first study of Zen at Nanzen-ji.

When Professor Kimura of Ryokoku had invited her to speak, he had asked her to address the question of why, with several Japanese Buddhist sects in existence, Americans should want to study only Zen. Ruth gave a succinct picture of the interest, both popular and serious. She said, "to those Americans who have once tasted the tasteless tea of Zen, the more highly flavored beverages of other Buddhist sects seem less appealing."

Ruth had been sending regular letters about her activities to First Zen Institute members, and by July 1951 these letters were becoming more like essays. Her "Dear Everyone" letters were three-hole punched and filed in notebooks in the Institute library. By 1954 they had become formalized and were included in issues of *Zen Notes*, the First Zen Institute newsletter, which began with Volume 1 in 1954, under the editorship of Mary Farkas, and is still being published by the Institute. She signed her letters "Eryu," the Buddhist name given to her by Sokei-an Roshi.

One of her earliest "letters" was a ten-page description of one of D. T. Suzuki's visits to her. She had asked him about his perspective on American interest in Buddhism, and he had talked for quite a while about it. He was especially enthusiastic at that time about how psychoanalysis and the psychoanalytic experience might potentially be combined with Zen guidance to reach ultimate Zen understanding. Suzuki was then preparing for another extended stay in the United States to teach at Claremont College in California (on Buddhist thought of the Kamakura period), and to give a series of lectures in New York at Columbia University. He had returned from a visit to New York not long before, and he had visited the First Zen Institute.

Ruth asked Suzuki about all of the members of the Institute, since he had met several of them on his visit. She reported in her letter that he had not been optimistic about the future of the First Zen Institute. He told her that he did not think the New York center would succeed. Ruth asked him how, then, Zen would be transplanted to America, and he told her, "you must move all your people to Japan. That is quite expensive an undertaking and many cannot leave America. Nevertheless, you must manage somehow to do this. Otherwise your efforts are useless."

He explained his opinion by commenting that America had no tradition and no background (science and Christianity evidently not offering tradition). He felt that Americans should come and live in Japan—many people for many years—and then gradually return to America, bringing with them the Zen traditions, reestablishing and adapting them to American life.

Ruth finished her "Dear Everyone" letter with an account of a visit later that day to a neighboring temple called Ryoko-in, the temple of the Kobori family. Her description shows her growing interaction with others at Daitoku-ji. Kobori Sohaku had been a student of D. T. Suzuki's at Otani University, and Beatrice Suzuki had taught him English. He recounted to Ruth the lively supper discussion they had had with Suzuki. Ruth mentioned that Kobori had been "a great help to me in reading footnotes and I thereby help his English." In fact, she relied heavily on his counsel, encouragement, and help many times in the coming years.

By early fall of 1951, two people associated with the First Zen Institute were in Kyoto for Zen study, Walter Nowick and Albert Craig. Albert Craig (later professor of Japanese history at Harvard University) was accepted for study at Kyoto University, and Ruth had plans for him to help her with some of her projects. Others were starting to think about how to save money to get to Japan, and some were taking Japanese-language conversation lessons.

January 1952 opened with an essay by Ruth published in the new magazine called the *Young East*. The first issue included Ruth's essay, "An American Appreciation," a lengthy review of the life and work of D. T. Suzuki. In it, Ruth mentioned Suzuki's return to the United States to continue his teaching and to work on his projected translation of the *Gandavyuha*. She wrote, "He has been one of the master-builders of the bridge over which Buddhist thought is slowly traveling from the East to the West. His influence in this movement is beyond being measured or assessed."

Devoting all of her time to her projects that winter, Ruth caused other Institute members to worry about her since she had not written. By March 1952, she had completed her translation from German of Heinrich Dumoulin's *The Development of Chinese Zen After the Sixth Patriarch in the Light of Mumonkan*. She sent drafts of the manuscript to Rahder and Mary Farkas for their comments, and in 1953 the book was published as the second title under the imprint of the First Zen Institute of America, following the earlier publication of *Cat's Yawn*. Her introduction to the translation shows the thoroughness and intensive efforts that she put into scholarship and research, including extensive footnotes and appendices. She had Albert Craig help her with the first rough translation. From that beginning, she continued working on it, believing that it would be "valuable for the students of the First Zen Institute of America in New York, who long had been clamoring for some material in English on the history of Zen after the Sixth Patriarch." Others who assisted her on this book project included Philipp Karl Eidmann of Ryokoku University, and Ogata Sohaku, then abbot of Chotoku-in at Shokoku-ji. Goto Zuigan Roshi was acknowledged as well for his support and encouragement.

This translation included additional material that Ruth prepared as appendices: a four-section glossary (Japanese, Chinese, Chinese character, and Sanskrit) and elegant fold-out charts of Rinzai Zen lineages. It was published in Kyoto in November 1953. Her attention to detail shines in small ways, including the design of the dustjacket, created from handmade, persimmon juice–coated Japanese paper known as *shibugami*, "popular in Japan in feudal times, but rare today." This same persimmon juice was used to treat the straw hats worn by monks for *takuhatsu* (weekly Zen monk begging practice).

Gary Snyder, who had just graduated from Reed College and was living in San Francisco, became an associate member of the First Zen Institute in 1952 after having corresponded with them, and a note was sent to Ruth that he had joined as a member and had been sent the gift incense burner (koro) and a box of incense. (Gary's is still in use in his home, as no doubt are many others' as well.)

Haru Yoshida wrote to Ruth in November that Nyogen Senzaki had come for a visit from Los Angeles to the Institute—he arrived with long-stemmed red roses and a poem in English and Japanese "in memory of Sokei-an." He read three short stories, asked for questions, and after eating some tea and cake he was gone "like a breeze." Haru said that Senzaki was staying in New York at Rushkin's and giving a lecture every Saturday night in addition to sutra chanting every morning. In late October he held a commemoration service in honor of his teacher, Shaku Soyen, which Haru Yoshida and others from the Institute attended. Around sixty showed up for the service, and the tribute he gave to his teacher showed deep devotion. Haru was asked to accompany Nyogen Senzaki on a pilgrimage to Sokei-an's grave in Woodlawn Cemetery.

The 1950s and early 1960s in Kyoto are considered the most important years of Ruth's life and work. She needed a lot of help to make her vision and plans a reality. She had been accustomed since the early days of her marriage to Edward Everett in Chicago to having a large household staff (housekeeper, cook, gardener, driver, and personal assistant for her projects and library), and in her life at Daitoku-ji, she began assembling the many people who would be able to help with household and landscape work as well as those she was hiring to assist on the research and translation projects. She had a reputation for being fair and generous with those who worked for her.

In March 1952, Ruth hired another personal assistant, Washino Akiko, in Kyoto. Washino had studied flower arranging with a Japanese relative of Haru Yoshida's. Ruth also hired other help with the cooking, house-cleaning, and gardening. Washino became an indispensable part of Ruth's operation, and the ideal housekeeper and companion for the rest of Ruth's life.

Washino was tuned in to all the social nuances important in the temple community, such as the gift-giving obligations. She learned English, and handled Ruth's personal calendar and travel arrangements as well as supervising the household. She accompanied Ruth on all of her travels. Ruth was finding that living in Japan was different from visiting even for several months, and Washino was a positive force behind the scenes, with complete loyalty to Ruth.

On October 6, 1953, Lindley Williams Hubbell arrived in Kyoto at Ruth's invitation to help catalog books for her library and to do other work associated with her writing projects. Lindley, a Yale Younger Poet from Hartford, Connecticut, had known Ruth for several years through their connection with Sokei-an. Lindley was a senior member of the First Zen Institute, having been a student of Sokei-an's since the early 1930s, longer than either Ruth or Mary Farkas. Lindley had published books of poetry, beginning in 1927 with *Dark Pavilion*.

Lindley had worked in the Map Division of the New York Public Library since 1925. While he'd had no training in cartography, he provided reference services in the Map Room with its rare maps and atlases. Since the reading room was not heavily used, Lindley had time to devote to his poetry and to assisting his friends and colleagues with questions about poetry and literature (he was an expert on Shakespeare). Walter Ristow, chief of the Map Division from 1937 to 1946, described Lindley's daily stream of visitors, including visits by Louise Bogan, then the poetry editor of the *New Yorker* magazine. Lindley was also friends with Gertrude Stein and Alice B. Toklas.

Shortly after Lindley arrived in Kyoto, Ruth invited Lindley and Kanaseki Hisao to dinner one evening. After discussing their love of Shakespeare, Lindley was invited by Kanaseki to meet Ueno Naozo, then the president of Doshisha University. President Ueno invited Lindley to give a lecture in English on Shakespeare at Doshisha, at the end of which Lindley was offered a professorship. He gave lectures there while working with Ruth. Ruth was very grateful for Lindley's presence and help in Kyoto. Lindley became a citizen of Japan in 1960, and was given the Japanese name Hayashi Shuseki ("Autumn Stone in the Woods").

Ruth helped Lindley find a place to live near Kinkaku-ji, also known as the "Golden Pavilion." After a few years, Lindley stopped working at Ryosen-an as his teaching at Doshisha and his poetry circles evolved, but he remained one of Ruth's closest friends. In addition to his expertise in Shakespeare, he became a devoted student of Noh (musical dramas developed in the fourteenth century), attending hundreds of performances of the classical plays. A wonderful tribute to Lindley by his friends, colleagues, and students, was published when he died in 1994, called *Autumn Stone in the Woods: A Tribute to Lindley Williams Hubbell* (1997). Lindley never returned to the United States. It was said that he had a photograph of the Showa Emperor (Hirohito) on his wall, and that when he died, he left a big piece of his estate to the neighborhood Shinto shrine in Kyoto.

Ruth's publishing success with *The Development of Chinese Zen* did not result in a better financial picture for her. This was the beginning of her worries about how to balance the budget for her enterprises in Kyoto as well as back in New York.

Ruth was learning a little more about temple politics when she found out that the house she was getting rent-free was in arrears for taxes. The Daitoku-ji Sodo gave her the bill for the back taxes, about 50,000 yen (about $140). It was explained to her that if the sodo once paid taxes, they would have to always do so, whereas if Ruth paid them, then no one would have to after she left. She suspected the neighbors had reported to the tax office that she was living there, for the house was not registered in the name of the sodo. As time went on she learned more details about these complicated property arrangements of where she was living, and about the historical complexity between her neighboring subtemple of Hoshun-in and the Daitoku-ji headquarters.

Meanwhile, presentation copies of *The Development of Chinese Zen* had gone to many of Ruth's friends and associates, and favorable reviews were being written. Ruth learned that a review of the book was about to be published in the *Harvard Journal of Asiatic Studies*, which delighted her even if it wasn't going to be favorable. She said, "I wonder what they'll say about the *Ho Koji*. That is really going to be a book. I am hard at it now. The English translation is all but finished and much done on the footnotes. I only need time . . . a couple more sessions with Iriya Sensei and I shall get at the footnotes and general cleaning up."

Ruth was lucky to have found Professor Iriya Yoshitaka to help her. She told others that it was wonderful to have such a good scholar with whom to work, and one who was sympathetic to her and to her projects as well as having such a deep knowledge of the texts and materials.

Other reviews also appeared, including a very positive one in the *Monumenta Nipponica* in May 1954. Ruth was now working on other translation projects. In a letter to D. T. Suzuki in January 1954, she said that she was working on the *Mumonkan* and also on Maspero's *Early T'ang Colloquial Grammar*.

Most of Ruth's correspondence with D. T. Suzuki was not preserved, but her mention of her translation projects was in response to a letter he'd sent requesting her to ask some questions of Goto Roshi at Daitoku-ji, and then to send Goto Roshi's answers back to him.

Suzuki hoped to use the answers of Goto Roshi in the classes he was starting to teach at Columbia University that year. He told her that he was lecturing on the role of the *Hekiganroku* (the *Blue Cliff Record*, a core koan collection of one hundred koan cases originally from China, used in the development of Zen thought). The questions were quite technical, about what cases were the most important in the eyes of Goto Roshi. Ruth's response to Suzuki was that, regretfully, Goto Roshi was seriously ill with pneumonia and visitors were forbidden, so that Suzuki's questions would have to wait for another time. There was also an indication that Suzuki's request was a bold one.

Publishing was also getting under way in New York at the First Zen Institute, and Mary Farkas, as editor, issued the first *Zen Notes* in January 1954. Mary wanted to publish monthly rather than quarterly, with about four pages for each issue—more than a pamphlet, less than a periodical. It was a newsletter for members, but it also had a nonmember subscriber list. The first issue carried a two-page essay by Ruth on New Year customs in Japan. *Zen Notes* provided a good record of the comings and goings of its members to Kyoto and other places of interest. In the second issue, the departure of

Walter Nowick for his third trip back to Kyoto for Zen study was announced. Each issue had an article by Ruth, about a sesshin in Kyoto or another topic of her choice. These articles, in addition to her "Dear Everyone" letters, became an ongoing journal of Ruth's activities in Kyoto, visitors to Daitoku-ji, and her visits to other temples and places in Japan. Since she did not keep personal journals, these more public equivalents provide an excellent framework for her life and activities in the 1950s and 1960s.

In the May 1954 issue of *Zen Notes*, Mary Farkas included English translations of some *Zenrin* poems done by Ruth and Lindley Hubbell.

The end of an era came with the death of Sokatsu Roshi, Sokei-an's teacher, on July 6, 1954. Ruth wrote a memorial tribute to Sokatsu Roshi for the October 1954 issue of *Zen Notes*. Others have written of Sokatsu's early years and coming to America in 1906, but none had written of his later years. Sokatsu had not kept up with what had happened to Sokei-an in his later years in New York, so Ruth had had opportunities to visit him and fill him in on details during the late 1940s and early 1950s.

She said he was delighted to learn of his "grandchildren" in America (Sokei-an's students). On one occasion Ruth took Walter Nowick to meet Sokatsu Roshi, an "exhibit" of one of Sokatsu's "grandchildren." On that visit she described Sokatsu sitting on his zabuton cushion in his room surrounded by relics of his great days: paintings, bronzes, sculptures, pottery—sitting erect and immovable despite his severe arthritic condition.

Ruth's translation projects and connections with Zen scholars, students, and teachers in Kyoto and New York were gaining momentum. In addition to Western scholars such as Leon Hurvitz and Burton Watson, some of her old friends from Nanzen-ji days, Ogata Sohaku and Miura Isshu, were also working on projects. A sense of that activity was reflected in a letter Ruth wrote to Mary Farkas describing Ogata's translation progress on the *Keitoku dento-roku* (Record of the Transmission of the Lamp), of which she'd sent Mary the draft of chapter 1. Ruth said, "I am going this afternoon to Hiezan with Walter [Nowick] for three days, but when I get back I'll send you Chapter II. It continues the story of the Indian patriarchs. In the meanwhile Hurvitz is engaged in translating for me a very brilliant article by a young Japanese scholar interested in Zen on the historical view of this patriarchal lineage."

One of Ruth's ideas was to prepare biographical stories of living Zen masters for the members of the Institute and for publication in *Zen Notes*. She would visit the roshis and tell them to start thinking about their biographies. She said, for example, that Goto Roshi would be glad to write his, as he liked to write. He would be especially interested, she said, once he learned that Asahina Roshi had given his biography for *Zen Notes*. Asahina Roshi had visited the First Zen Institute while on a trip to New York in June 1954 and had given lectures to the members.

Ruth said she had Eizan Roshi's biography in part from a lecture he gave on his sixtieth birthday, and that Kanaseki Hisao had translated it already. She had asked Miura Roshi to provide the story of his experiences in the zendo, bringing in the progressive steps in koan study. She wanted to call it "The Making of a Roshi." Even though he was quite shy, Ruth said he had agreed.

Ogata and Miura Roshi were key contacts for Ruth in her efforts to provide Japanese connections for students from the First Zen Institute who wanted to go to Japan. Ogata, who received financial support from Ruth, had made several trips to Europe and the United States, and knew English well. As the priest of the subtemple

Chotoku-in at Shokoku-ji, Ogata and his wife were able to host a few westerners as they came to Kyoto to study Zen.

Ruth tried to prepare hopeful students for disappointments when they would be confronted with the realities of living in these temples. Americans had some idealistic notions of what monks, temples, and monastery life would be like. Walter Nowick, who stayed at Miura Roshi's temple for a brief time, had the impression of monks being arbitrary and unfair. Ruth would sympathize, telling some people that she was convinced that there was a deterioration at work. When she told Miura Roshi her observations, he said, "Oh, never mind, the time will come when another Hakuin will come along."

Zen Notes published some interesting essays by its members. In November 1954 (Volume I, No. 11), an essay was published called "Anyone with Yama-Bushi Tendencies: A Message from a California Member of Special Interest to Those Seeking Jobs Which Leave Time for Study and Zazen." Written by Gary Snyder, then twenty-three, it described his experiences fire-watching in the Pacific Northwest. Gary was a graduate student in what was then called the Department of Oriental Languages at the University of California, Berkeley. His interest in Zen brought him to Ruth's attention, along with a conversation she had with a scholar friend of hers, Donald Shively (born and raised in Japan and at the time teaching at Berkeley) who visited her in Kyoto. Ruth said Shively had told her that Gary Snyder was one of the students that professors dream of having in their classes, and he knew of Gary's interest in Zen.

Ruth sent regular notes about visits to other temples and monasteries for the *Zen Notes* readers, such as the trip she, Walter Nowick, and Kanaseki had made to Mount Hiei to visit Enryaku-ji for a few days. And she described Walter's experiences at Mudo-ji (Temple of Immovability), partway down the mountain where the monks' meditation practice included going on long walks circumambulating Mount Hiei.

Ruth tried to disenchant students from idealistic notions they might have of temple life, while at the same time sending glowing and romantic descriptions of zendo experiences. Even though she would say that zendos were not like those in the "old days" (e.g., Nanzen-ji in the early 1930s), "under any circumstances sitting in a zendo is wonderful . . . the big quiet room, the dim light, the faint smell of coarse incense, the cold fresh air, the sounds of the night coming from a distance—passing voices, the throb of the Nichiren drum, the notes of a flute, the Chinese noodle man's whistle, all melt into you and you into them. . . . sometime I hope you may all know the experience."

A publications department was set up at the First Zen Institute in addition to the growing library. Haru Yoshida, Ruth's assistant, handled the incoming and outgoing publication requests. In the mid-1950s, the Institute was getting many orders for copies of *The Development of Chinese Zen* from Europe and the United States. Haru also became an expert at locating copies of works on Zen, Buddhism, and Chinese and Japanese studies that scholars at the First Zen Institute or other places were trying to locate. She carefully selected copies of new books for the Institute library as well as for Ruth's library in Kyoto. While it was a part-time job for Haru, correspondence with Ruth showed how time-consuming it was, corresponding with book dealers and publishers as well as individuals in England, Europe, Japan, and the United States.

Senior members from the Institute were all interested in going to Kyoto to visit, some to make extended stays, hoping be able to study and take sanzen with a teacher. Late in 1954, Ruth began arranging for a house in Kyoto for Vanessa Coward and her husband,

Henry Platov, two of Sokei-an's senior students, to come for a year and study with Oda Roshi.

To complicate the autumn of that year, Ruth's only brother and remaining family member died after his long illness in Honolulu. Ruth went to Hawaii to take care of his affairs, and then flew his ashes to rest next to their mother's at the Bronswood Cemetery in Oak Brook, Illinois.

Rebuilding Ryosen-an, 1955–1960 5

T HE FIRST ZEN INSTITUTE in New York celebrated its twenty-fifth anniversary in February 1955. Institute members received the very welcome news from Ruth that she would be bringing Miura Isshu Roshi to the United States to visit them. There was great excitement as they started to plan his New York itinerary. The "Monday-nighters," as they called themselves, were the core group of the Institute. After the announcement of Miura Roshi's impending visit, the Monday night sittings jumped to eight people. By late March, preparations were complete for the arrival of Ruth, Washino, and Miura Roshi.

Zen Notes issues for April, May, and June 1955 all reflected the importance of this visit by Miura Roshi, who represented the possibility of the Institute's getting a real Zen teacher from Japan after the decade since Sokei-an died. A biographical sketch (complete with footnotes) of Miura Roshi was published in the April (1955) issue, highlighting the connection Ruth had with him from her Nanzen-ji days in 1933 where he had been a senior monk.

While Miura Roshi was in New York, the First Zen Institute planned for him to preside over a formal ceremony for members who wished to formalize their becoming Buddhists and entering the *sangha* (community). *Zen Notes* (June) included portions of Sokei-an's ceremony for this along with the calligraphy and text of a talk by Miura Roshi called "The Four Vows" from a lecture he had given in April.

Goto Zuigan Roshi, Ruth's sanzen teacher in Kyoto and Sokei-an's dharma-brother and eldest heir of Shaku Soyatsu of Engaku-ji, had sent along a present for the First Zen Institute in celebration of this anniversary. It was a painting of Daio Kokushi, teacher of the founder of Daitoku-ji, painted by Zengyu Kunmoku. Goto Roshi wrote an inscription and a poem at the top of the painting. The poem was about Kido Osho (Chinese: Xutang, [Hsu t'ang]), a famous Chinese Zen priest who lived in eastern China, where Daio Kokushi went to study Zen in 1265. The poem that Xutang gave to Daio Kokushi at their parting is the verse that Goto Roshi inscribed on the painting.

Goto Roshi explained the verse in detail for Ruth so that she could better translate it. He asked her to convey his greetings and to work on fulfilling the prophecy of Xutang, which reflected the movement of Zen from China to Japan, and then from Japan to American and Europe (children of the eastern seas). It said, "It is the expressed hope of Goto Roshi that the torch of Zen, handed to those in the still more easterly lands of America and Europe, may continue to burn brightly, until it forms one continuous encircling light, dispelling the darkness of ignorance and bringing awakening to men in all lands" (*Zen Notes*, August 1955).

The following issue of *Zen Notes* carried the first half of an essay by Goto Roshi on the highlights of Zen Buddhist history. The second half appeared in the following issue. The first of Ruth's "letters" from Kyoto, later to be called "Dear Everyone" letters and included as inserts in issues of *Zen Notes*, appeared in the September issue. It was an account of the trip that Ruth, Washino, and Miura Roshi took after leaving the Institute in mid-June. They traveled west to

Colorado and New Mexico for a two-week vacation to rest and visit Ruth's daughter, Eleanor, her husband, Carlton Gamer, and their son, Michael, who made their home in Colorado Springs, where Carlton had a faculty position on the Music Department of Colorado College. They visited the Museum of Navajo Ceremonial Art, and villages and old Spanish churches in Santa Fe and Taos. After leaving Colorado Springs, they went on to San Francisco, where they had several visitors, including Gary Snyder, who was starting to plan his first trip to Kyoto for Zen study that fall (delayed some by passport problems). The letter concluded with a mention of their visit to the Soto Zen Mission in Hawaii on their way back to Japan.

These "Dear Everyone" letters provide a fascinating and detailed glimpse of the flow of people through Kyoto, and of Ruth's hospitality. A good example is her account of the visit of the scholar and writer Joseph Campbell, which she published in the August 1955 issue of *Zen Notes*. Campbell had been in India for six months prior to his arrival in Kyoto. Ruth described taking him to see Oda Roshi in the Daitoku-ji Sodo, and how Oda Roshi had provided a tour of all the buildings. Another afternoon, along with Lindley Hubbell, they went to visit Ryoan-ji and Goto Roshi. On one of Joseph Campbell's last days there, they went with Walter Nowick for a picnic on Mount Hiei and visited Dengyo Daishi's temple (Dengyo Daishi, or Saicho, was the founder of Japanese *tendai*, another Buddhist sect), where Walter was giving English lessons to one of the priests.

Another visitor Ruth described became a part of Ruth's activities for the next few years, Donatienne Lebovich (now Sapriel), an artist living in Kyoto with her two children while her husband conducted business in Japan and Korea. Donatienne had attended meditation at Ogata's temple when she first came to Kyoto, and had met Ruth through D. T. Suzuki. She took sanzen with Oda

Roshi for several years, and helped provide artwork for some of Ruth's publications.

Ruth was legendary for her dinners and parties and her introduction of Western foods at these events. In October, Ruth's entire "Dear Everyone" letter was devoted to a description of Goto Roshi's seventy-seventh birthday, an auspicious one (double numbers), and the celebration by his students on the occasion. She had a small private party for him that included Walter Nowick, Kanaseki Hisao, and Washino. "I had made a great big angel-food cake, iced it with fresh orange icing and decorated it with fifty candles, all the cake would hold—Roshi's first birthday cake with candles. We had coffee and cake and birthday presents sitting with the warm sunshine pouring in the open shoji, and looking over the lovely lake on the bank of which Daishu-in is built. Then we leisurely ambled down the mountainside" (*Zen Notes*, October 22, 1955).

Occasionally Ruth would apologize for her letters being "too garrulous," but it is precisely because of these lengthy anecdotes that so much of her life and those events connected with her have been preserved.

Goto Roshi retired from his position of abbot of Daitoku-ji, and Oda Sesso Roshi, then head of the Daitoku-ji Sodo (and Goto Roshi's heir), barely fifty-five years old, was elected *kancho* (head abbot). Being elected to this position was the highest honor possible for a priest in Rinzai Zen. When he became kancho as well as roshi of the monastery of Daitoku-ji, Goto Roshi asked him to open Daitoku-ji to foreigners.

Oda Roshi played a fundamental role in the next several years for Ruth and the Zen students connected with her and the First Zen Institute. Foreigners could come and sit in the monastery, and if they were still there after a year, they might be admitted for sanzen and study with Oda Roshi. Many westerners became his students, including Gary Snyder, Janwillem van de Wetering from the Netherlands (who subsequently wrote some popular fictionalized books about his experiences), Irmgard Schloegl from England, and Philip Yampolsky.

Gary Snyder once said that Oda Roshi "was the subtlest and most perceptive man I've ever met. . . . His teisho were inaudible, his voice was so soft. Yet as one of the head monks at Daitoku-ji Sodo said much later, 'Those lectures of Oda Roshi we couldn't hear I am beginning to hear today.'"

Mary Farkas, the main person coordinating the activities of the First Zen Institute in New York, began planning her first trip to Japan and Ryosen-an, and Ruth wrote of the warm welcome she was planning for Mary's three-month stay in Kyoto. "We hope she [Mary] is going to like Japanese food for we eat a good deal of it at Ryosen-an. However Mitsue and Washino have become quite capable in American cooking, too. Their layer cakes and pies and cookies and muffins, to say nothing of casseroles of chicken and curries and stews, have become the wonder of our visitors. We have even taken to making schnecken (with the help of bread mixes) and hot rolls."

Meanwhile Walter Nowick had moved into the *inryo* (priest's private rooms) at Rinko-in, a Shokoku-ji temple. The First Zen Institute had assumed a "long lease" on it after Vanessa Coward had stayed in it and renovated the kitchen and bath during the previous year. This would put Walter closer to Miura Roshi, so that Walter could keep Miura Roshi company and help him learn English. In November, Walter gave a piano recital together with a young Japanese violinist. Miura Roshi was there that evening, as were Nakagawa Soen Roshi, who had come to Kyoto with Nyogen Senzaki. Ruth said, "The two roshis, both of whom love western Classical music, attended the recital and we had a little ice cream party afterwards."

The year 1955 closed during the final weeks of Mary Farkas's three-month visit to Kyoto. Details of all the places and people that Mary and Ruth visited (including Walter Nowick or Kanaseki on some of the visits) were written up for *Zen Notes*. These included local visits like the formal tea for them at Ryoko-in, a subtemple of Daitoku-ji, by the Kobori brothers, both Zen priests and descendants of Kobori Enshu, famous garden maker of the sixteenth century. Other visits included the Inari Shrine at Fushimi, where they walked the entire circuit of eight kilometers up the mountain; Nara city to visit Todai-ji and the Great Buddha; and the Great Shrine of Ise, where they were offered consecrated sake to drink.

Ruth and Mary had dinner with Miura Roshi, R. H. Blyth (the haiku scholar), and Father Heinrich Dumoulin at a famous old tempura restaurant in Kyoto called Hanacho, and on the following day they visited Eizan Roshi, third heir of Sokatsu Roshi and younger dharma-brother of Sokei-an, in Ichikawa (Chiba prefecture). Eizan Roshi was the head of Ningen Zen, a large Zen layperson's group with branches throughout Japan. In the evening, Miura Roshi joined them for a performance of kabuki.

The following day they had lunch with an old friend of Sokei-an's from his New York days, Eichi Araki, governor of the Bank of Japan. They went to Engaku-ji, D. T. Suzuki's hermitage then occupied by his disciple Furuta Shokin, and on February 10, they visited Asahina Roshi, went to Kamakura, and paid their respects at the tomb of Kosen Osho, Shaku Soyen's Zen teacher. Furuta then took them to Tokei-ji, Shaku Soyen's personal temple just across the railroad tracks, where they burned incense at the tombs of Shaku Soyen, Ida Russell of San Francisco (an

American disciple of Shaku Soyen), and Beatrice Lane Suzuki, after which they climbed the three hundred steps behind the temple to see the permanent home of Suzuki's large library, Matsuoka Bunko.

After this last whirlwind week of activities, Miura Roshi joined Mary Farkas and Walter Nowick for their journey back to New York. The members of the First Zen Institute were delighted to have Miura Roshi back to visit them, and Walter Nowick served as a translator for him. Senior members, including Walter Nowick, Mary Farkas, Fielder Schillinberg, Haru Yoshida, and Kimo Martin, arranged dinners and visits for him. On the occasion of the twenty-sixth anniversary of the First Zen Institute, February 15, 1956, Miura Roshi sat with the members for the second time in the master's place. He presented to the First Zen Institute a bronze (*kansho*) sanzen bell that had been presented to him by his teacher, Seigo Hogaku, one of Shaku Soyen's heirs. The wooden stand that held the bell was made to Miura Roshi's specifications by Kyoto craftsmen whose family had made these stands for Daitoku-ji for eight generations.

The students of the Institute, now numbering about fifteen regularly attending, eagerly hoped that Miura Roshi would establish permanent connections with them after this two-month visit. He was still responsible for his temple in Japan, Koon-ji, and its eighteen subtemples.

Although the group at the First Zen Institute was still fairly small, the politics within it were not always smooth. With the possibility of Miura Roshi's future return to New York, the group went through some organizational shifts. Fowler was then the chair of the First Zen Institute Council, Sam Reiser served as vice-chair, and Mary Farkas was secretary.

Mary had in mind that Secki Shapiro would take over for her as secretary. Mary was assuming more leadership of the Institute as Ruth's attention focused increasingly on her activities in Kyoto. Ruth kept up an active correspondence with the officers and members of the Institute, and letters from Ruth were read aloud at the council meetings. Agenda items for the Institute's council included discussions on how the organization might be able to support Miura Roshi should he return to New York, and whether or not the top floor of the building (currently Ruth's apartment, used occasionally by Eleanor and Carlton Gamer) could be converted for use by the Institute. Until now, expenses incurred during Miura Roshi's visit were paid by Ruth and were supplemented by small personal donations from First Zen Institute members directly to Miura Roshi.

Ruth's "Dear Everyone" letters from Kyoto continued to arrive with the issues of *Zen Notes*. Usually around a dozen paragraphs, they were summaries of Ruth's activities in Kyoto, her thoughts about the seasons and landscapes, and notes about Zen temples and their historical significance. Monthly circulation of *Zen Notes* with Ruth's "Letters" inserted was about 125 copies. In the May 3, 1956, letter (issued with *Zen Notes* III, no. 6), Ruth wrote of the splendid profusion of spring-flowering plants and trees, the flaming scarlet azalea in the Ryosen-an garden, and the sudden spurts of growth in the bamboo. In this same issue, she also wrote about the end of Lindley Hubbell's work at Ryosen-an as he went on to teach at Doshisha University; the arrival of Yanagida Seizan (then Yokoi Seizan) to join the research efforts; and the arrival of Gary Snyder, who had finally received his passport clearance.

The construction of a library at Ryosen-an was begun in July 1956. Hoshun-in, the temple from which Ruth was leasing the Ryosen-an land, and the Daitoku-ji Sodo (headquarters) both approved her building of the library. It was located in the northeast corner of the rented land (many years later when Ruth was having difficulties at Ryosen-an, she mused over the coincidence of having chosen the northeast corner, which she had heard was considered "unlucky" in Japanese culture). It had a large central room for work and study, with a fireplace and a butsudan (altar). It had a small kitchen, dressing room, bathroom, and an adjoining room for book stacks. It was built with a tile roof and walls of white plaster with sliding glass doors opening to the main room. The cost of the construction in 1956 was about $8,000.

Because the unoccupied land to the east of the house was used for community vegetable gardens, children's playing, and exercising, Ruth decided to build a wall to surround the property for more privacy and quiet. She was permitted to build a traditional plaster temple wall around the front area, with a temple-style gate and solid wooden doors that could be closed to keep the public out. After the wall was in place, the gardens were developed with an old pine, camellias, rocks, and moss.

As the library went up, Ruth realized that what she had originally thought of as a quiet residence and study for herself would have to become the Kyoto headquarters of the First Zen Institute. She began the arrangements to form a Japanese religious corporation under the name Nichibei Daiichi Zen Kyokai (The First Zen Institute of America in Japan). Ruth later signed a lease for the land for a twenty-year period beginning January 1, 1957, and all of the buildings on the land—main house, kura (storehouse), study, library, and zendo (to be built later)—would be registered as possessions of the corporation.

Ruth thought that the twenty-year time frame would be ample to accomplish the goals of the translation projects she had in mind. By this time she had a small group of scholars to work on these translation projects, and she felt that even if she died before the end of a twenty-year lease, they would be able to continue work on the projects. The lease provided for indefinite renewal should they wish to remain longer than twenty years, and when the time came, the corporation could be dissolved, the lease terminated, and the buildings presented to the Daitoku-ji Honzan. In a memorandum, she said that if she should die, Walter Nowick or someone else could be appointed to take over.

Although devoting intense energy and time to her work at Ryosen-an, Ruth maintained close connections with her family. In the summer of 1956, Joan Watts, Ruth's granddaughter (Eleanor's daughter), came to Kyoto to spend a year with her at Ryosen-an. Joan began studying Japanese, painting, and tea ceremony. Ruth would take Joan along on trips to visit temples and historical sites, and would describe some of these outings for *Zen Notes*. On one occasion, Ruth took Joan to visit the monastery at Hosshin-ji and Harada Roshi, then eighty-six. She described Harada Roshi's combination of Soto and Rinzai teaching methods for his students since he had taken sanzen from two Zen masters. She said that he used Joshu's "MU" as a first koan ("usually for several years") in the Rinzai method, rather than the Soto "this very body is Buddha."

Ruth took Joan on outings to visit artists and craftsmen. She describes visiting paper maker Abe, from a family of paper makers going back three hundred years, and a visit to the kiln of a famous Izumo potter. Ruth had a keen eye and delight in the traditional Japanese craftsmanship and art.

Just as Ruth's "Dear Everyone" letters reflected on the history and building at Ryosen-an, later letters were about individuals arriving and living in the community surrounding her. Ruth wrote about

Walter Nowick, who was in Kyoto both to study Zen and to earn a living. He taught English at Doshisha University initially, but as his talents as a pianist became known, he got more involved in music and was offered a teaching position at Kyoto Women's University. Walter and others who came in the early 1950s had the tremendous advantage of being able to study with a Zen teacher who knew English, Goto Zuigan Roshi. Even with this advantage, these students still worked hard on Japanese language study in addition to their other activities.

Finding a place to live for long-term visiting students was always a challenge. When Vanessa Coward arrived from the First Zen Institute, arrangements were made with Ruth's old colleague Ogata Sohaku for Vanessa to live in the *inryo* (detached living quarters) at Rinko-in, one of the subtemples of Shokoku-ji, and as Ruth said, "another of the Rinzai Zen headquarters in Kyoto with which we have always had the happiest of relations." Ruth described Vanessa's extensive remodeling of the inryo, adding a Western-style kitchen, bath, and dressing room. Vanessa remained there for a year, taking sanzen with Goto Roshi. On returning to New York, she suggested that the inryo be used by other students of the Institute if need be. After Vanessa had left, Miura Roshi lived there while he was in Kyoto, and Walter Nowick and Gary Snyder also stayed there.

Vanessa Coward decided to return to Kyoto, and since the inryo that she had previously occupied was taken, Ogata found her a place to stay at Chotoku-in, his temple in Shokoku-ji. Vanessa remodeled this residence as well, furnishing it with Western-style appliances. Ruth wrote of the convenience of Walter and Vanessa both being in the same temple compound. Walter would call for Vanessa at five-thirty every morning, and sitting on the back of his scooter they would head up to Daishu-in for their sanzen with

Goto Roshi. Goto Roshi's personal monk attendant returned to the Daitoku-ji Sodo, and Walter assumed some of his duties with Goto Roshi.

Every morning, Walter, as attendant, and Vanessa, as assistant attendant, would sweep the verandas and scrub all surfaces, with Roshi directing them both. Ruth said that on some mornings Walter's duties included sweeping the garden as well, and she said, "the tea master Rikyu was not more arbitrary with his disciples in the matter of what leaves should be raked up or let lie than is Goto Roshi. All this is a part of Zen study and practice."

On May 21, 1956, Gary Snyder arrived at Ryosen-an. He had initially been rejected for a passport because of his left-wing associations in college, and because he had shipped out on a freighter from New York in 1948 with the Marine Cooks and Stewards Union, which was considered Communist-dominated. Ruth "didn't blink an eye," as Gary said, advising him to keep on working to get the passport. She later told him that she fully expected anyone who "thinks and works and studies" might be drawn to the left, as he was, with good cause. As Gary explained, when the chips were down, Ruth could be surprising.

Gary was becoming established as a poet and presence in the San Francisco literary scene, and in 1955 and early 1956, prior to leaving for Japan, he had become very involved with Allen Ginsberg, Jack Kerouac, Kenneth Rexroth, Lawrence Ferlinghetti, Michael Mc-Clure, Jack Spicer, and a circle of writers and cultural figures who were bringing new and dramatic energy to the San Francisco literary scene. Gary had been part of the famous poetry reading at the Six Gallery in San Francisco in 1955, which is now referred to as a pivotal point in mid-century popular culture and the start of the Beat Generation. In addition to his growing recognition as a poet, Gary had made some well-received translations of the famous Chinese Zen poet Han Shan (*Cold Mountain*).

Goto Roshi was too old and frail by 1956 to take on new students, and Gary's spoken Japanese was not considered adequate yet to embark on koan study with a non–English-speaking roshi. Gary entered language school for a year long intensive course in spoken Japanese, and Ruth helped him make arrangements to live at Rinko-in. Gary became the personal assistant for Miura Roshi, who was staying at Rinko-in. He would rise at five in the morning for zazen practice and sutra chanting with Miura Roshi, prepare Roshi's breakfast, clean the inryo, then go to Japanese language classes. In the afternoon he would work with Miura Roshi on English language lessons, followed by shopping and preparing supper for Miura Roshi and himself.

Gary's arrival also sparked a lifelong friendship with Philip Yampolsky. Philip, who had already begun working for Ruth part-time while writing his dissertation, became a guide for Gary in Kyoto life and culture. Gary fondly remembers the coffee shops, bookstores, map stores, and Korean workingmen's *doburoku* (home-brewed saké) bars that Philip would take him to. Gary and Philip also sat together at the Daitoku-ji Sodo as they began their studies with Oda Sesso Roshi, and what started as mentoring by Philip grew into close friendship between the two. Gary said that Philip regularly spoke the Kyoto dialect that he'd learned during his first year in Japan while on his Fulbright scholarship, living in housing around 5th Street in Gojo. It contained an extreme slang that shocked and entertained those who heard him speak. Even in sanzen with Oda Roshi, Philip told Gary that Roshi had asked him, "please try to speak standard Japanese. The slang in the Kyoto dialect makes you seem so low class."

The reverse was also of some amusement to those who recall Goto Roshi sometimes talking "salty workers' American slang," which Goto Roshi had picked up as a young man in the East Bay of California.

At the end of 1956, Ruth held a large Christmas Eve party for those connected with Ryosen-an, including her granddaughter, Joan. Ruth wrote in great detail of the party, describing the roasting of the turkey—she had been raising turkeys in the backyard—and the desserts of pumpkin and mince pies with homemade vanilla ice cream. She wrote, "Everyone said that Ryosen-an had lived up to its reputation of having the finest food in Japan." After the dinner they opened presents, Kanaseki serving as master of ceremonies (he was getting ready to leave for New York in January 1957). Vanessa Coward hosted a New Year's Eve party for everyone in her rooms at Ogata's temple, Chotoku-in.

There was a growing interest in Zen Buddhism in the United States, and Ruth was getting more letters at Ryosen-an inquiring about how to go about studying Zen in Japan. On February 4, 1957, *Time* magazine published in its "Religion" section a small essay on Zen. It mentioned Alan Watts on the West Coast, the First Zen Institute on the East Coast, and said that "in an aromatic garden in Kyoto, the first Zen study center in Japan for Westerners was formally opened this month. Last week its builder, Ruth Fuller Everett Sasaki, Chicago-born widow of a Zen teacher, announced that enough new U.S. students were expected so that a meditation hall would have to be built to accommodate them."

The *Time* essay discussed the contributions of D. T. Suzuki, then teaching at Columbia University. The article closed with the comment that the future of Zen in the United States depended on having English-speaking Zen teachers. It mentioned Walter Nowick as a likely candidate.

Ruth was caught in the dilemma of a growing interest from westerners along with the confusion these people had about what it meant to "learn about Zen." She was especially disturbed by those who, without any knowledge of the Japanese language, would write that they were coming to Kyoto for three or four weeks to find out as much as they could about Zen. She said that it would be like a Japanese person not knowing English going to England for a few weeks' visit to find out as much as possible about Episcopalians—only more so.

In March 1957, posted on the Ryosen-an main gate was a sign stating, "Observing public notice of incorporation of the Kyoto Branch [of the First Zen Institute of America] signed by Miura Roshi, Ruth Fuller Sasaki, Vanessa Coward, and Gary Snyder."

The first service of Ryosen-an was held in the new library building in March 1957. Miura Roshi presided, and Ruth, Donatienne Lebovich, Gary Snyder, Philip Yampolsky, Vanessa Coward, Manzoji Yoko, Walter Nowick, and Yanagida Seizan were in attendance.

Ruth realized that the library, once it was furnished and operating as a library and study room, could not serve well as a zendo. It was too cumbersome to move the furniture out of the way for use as a zendo. So she announced that Ryosen-an would build a separate zendo, marking a widening of purpose for the activities of Ryosen-an. She said, "It [the library] cannot acquire for evenings only the undisturbed and calm atmosphere so necessary for good sitting. And since we want very much to make Ryosen-an a true center in which foreigners, whether they remain for a short or a long time[,] can carry on their Zen study and practice, we feel we must provide this basic requirement, a suitable place for zazen."

She planned for the zendo to be a small-scale model of a traditional monastery zendo that would seat sixteen people.

Kyoto was a major tourist destination, and hotels and inns were expensive. Finding places for foreigners who wanted to visit Ryosen-an was a problem, and Ruth urged people to plan ahead. Ruth always had plenty of advice about what visitors could do and see in a few weeks in Kyoto in addition to experiencing some of the routines of Ryosen-an. She would offer the quiet of the zendo as a perfect counterpart to busy sightseeing activities. "And you will hear the sharp clack of the clappers and the ching of the bell, you will smell the incense, and you will share in the deep silence that envelops that most wonderful of rooms, a zendo." She went on to say, "When you return home and your friends ask you what you have learned about Zen in your three or four weeks' stay in Kyoto, perhaps you will have to say, 'Not much.' Not much you can speak about, perhaps, but much you will never forget."

A few weeks' stay was enough for a small taste, but she recommended that students from the First Zen Institute plan on at least three or four months if they really wanted to experience more of what went on in a monastery. She described in detail the obstacles, while at the same time making the experience seem very compelling. Cold water, mosquitoes, harsh conditions in summer and winter—all paled next to the descriptions of the depth and peace of the zendo experience.

By the end of April, the construction on the new zendo was beginning. A big ceremony that takes place when the framework of a building is set up was held on April 26, 1957. While new growth for Ryosen-an was under way, the First Zen Institute in New York received a blow to its dream that Miura Roshi would accept their offer to become their new Zen teacher. He sent his resignation to them in late spring 1957. In June, Ruth wrote a letter to members of the Institute's council, discussing the sad turn of events, saying that Miura Roshi knew his heart was not at the First Zen Institute, but instead back at his temple, Koon-ji. It became even more complicated when Miura Roshi reversed his resignation (some said it was in part to circumvent Ruth's direction) and continued to serve as teacher to the members of the Institute through March 1960.

The story of his relationship with them was not yet over. For the next several years, Miura Roshi continued teaching. He eventually ended his formal relationship with the First Zen Institute but taught a few of the students on his own in New York, using his apartment as a sanzen and meditation room.

As Ruth thought about the direction of Ryosen-an once the zendo was built, she anticipated being able to focus more attention on her primary work of the translations. In a letter to Haru Yoshida in February 1957, she wrote, "When the zendo is completed and the wall around the entire place finished, there will be nothing of any consequence more to do here. . . . I want a peaceful stretch of time in which to write and translate. I am just now beginning to feel that I have the translation work well in my hand, and feel a kind of competency in doing it. My period of study and preparation is gradually coming to an end. The period of production must begin, late as it is, and short as it is sure to be." Ruth was sixty-six years old.

She had visions of quiet days when she could work on her translations without interruption. But the reality was that Ryosen-an was becoming an even more active place for visitors and social events. Ruth's granddaughter, Joan, became engaged to a young man at the U.S. Army post in Kobe, and Ruth began planning for a large wedding to be held in Kyoto in August. Ruth's attention to the wedding plans included much correspondence with Haru Yoshida in making arrangements for wedding gowns and many other details of things to acquire from New York. The wedding was to be an elaborate affair held at the old St. Francis Xavier Catholic Church in Kyoto, followed by a huge reception and family gathering.

Once the wedding was over, Ruth began working earnestly in the Ryosen-an library on the project for *Zen Dust*. Gary Snyder had returned to San Francisco for the winter, and Ruth expected him back in the spring of 1958 (he came in 1959). Keeping her company in the library were Yanagida Seizan and Manzoji Yoko, the secretary (whose father was a scholar). Ruth's goal was to complete the manuscript for *Zen Dust* during the winter.

Ruth had stopped taking sanzen with Goto Roshi at Daishu-in, and wrote that her koan study was "gradually reaching its conclusion." Her early morning walks to Daishu-in at Ryoan-ji had become such a part of her daily routine that she continued these dawn walks through the summer. When she would return from her walk, Tanimoto, her gardener, would bring her "his daily summer offering, a morning-glory plant with one fresh bloom on it." He also brought her news of the daily activities of the neighbors.

Ruth was extremely appreciative of her good fortune in finding Iriya Yoshitaka, who taught in the Department of Chinese at Kyoto University, and later became head of the Department of Chinese at Nagoya University. By 1957, she had been learning from Professor Iriya for almost four years, working with him on Saturday or Sunday afternoons on Zen texts and related material. Iriya was considered the foremost authority in the field of the colloquial language of the T'ang and Sung dynasties, in which many of the Zen texts had been written.

The book *Zen Dust* was to be the translation of Miura Roshi's eight talks at the First Zen Institute in New York in the winter of 1955 on the history and system of koan study in use in the Rinzai monasteries in Japan. The title "Zen Dust" was chosen by Miura Roshi. Ruth had made the original English translations of these lectures but wanted to finish more of her own koan study before adding translations of the *Zenrin kushu* (a collection of verses used to state one's understanding of a koan after the study of a koan has been completed). Working with Miura Roshi, some two hundred of the phrases and verses of the English translation of *Zenrin kushu* were being worked on for the final draft of *Zen Dust*. In the Ryosen-an Library, several people worked together on the research for this and other publication projects.

Ruth elaborated on the activities of "literary Ryosen-an" for the November 1957 *Zen Notes*, outlining her projected translation projects. She described *Zen Dust* as being nearly completed, and "The Conversations of Layman P'ang" as being the next translation in line. Her idea was that all of the translations would be published with Chinese-character text and Japanese romanization on the left-hand page, and the English translation on the facing right-hand page.

Another project awaiting her attention was *The Record of Rinzai*, which Sokei-an had translated. She said, "here again the Chinese text has already been studied, and the Japanese roman-letter reading completed. In addition, all the special terms have been indexed, a total of some 3,000 cards."

Next in line after *The Record of Rinzai* was to be an English translation of the *Mumonkan* (Chinese: *Wumenguan* [*Wumen kuan*]). She said that the Chinese text and Japanese roman-letter reading of this were already completed, and most of the koans translated—"these as I studied them myself"—but "Mumon Osho's prose and poetical commentaries are still to be done in English."

Ruth, who had just celebrated her sixty-fifth birthday, went on to describe what other projects she was lining up, "if I am still living after this," which included tackling the *Rokuso dankyo* (Chinese: *Liuzu tanjing* [*Liutsu t'anching*]; The Sixth Patriarch's *Platform Sutra*), which she'd studied with Sokei-an at one time. In between these major translations, she was yearning to complete a dictionary of Zen Buddhist terms. She said that she devoted her spare minutes between appointments, or "while waiting for dinner to be served or her study to be cleaned," to this dictionary so needed by those who had to "make bricks almost without straw." She said that what she could not get from translating the Japanese explanations in Japanese dictionaries she would have to get someone to translate for her from the Chinese dictionaries, then ask Iriya about it, and finally go to Goto Roshi for the traditional Rinzai Zen explanation. "Roundabout and tedious," she wrote.

The actual process of creating the dictionary was something she felt would benefit her and the others connected with the Institute. She would note on library file cards all the interesting names and terms from every bit of material they were translating at Ryosen-an. She was adding terms from already published translations of Zen, Buddhist, and Taoist texts by "authoritative translators." All of these index cards would contain Chinese characters, Chinese and Japanese roman-letter readings, and Sanskrit readings where those existed. There were four sets of cards, one for each, and separate files so they could have a four-language, cross-reference dictionary file. On the master card, filed by the Chinese characters, she would note the text from which each term was taken and the name of the translator, so that "eventually we shall be able to build up a dictionary based more or less on historical principles."

By the fall of 1957, Ruth had assembled the core of her research team. They mostly worked at other jobs, and helped on the Ryosen-an research and translation work during their spare time. Each member of the research team deserves a biographical book of his or her own—some had already achieved prominence in their areas of specialty; some were yet to grow into their fame and importance. It was a remarkable gathering of individuals, and the stories and reminiscences of that time show the rich texture of Ruth's resourcefulness in facilitating the complexities of these massive publication efforts. At times, as Iriya mentioned a few years ago in reminiscing about Ruth, "she was an autocrat," and he even told her that on occasion when she would ask for his opinion or advice.

Iriya Yoshitaka, then forty-seven years old (1910–1999), was the senior member and director of the research team. He taught at Kyoto University and later became professor and head of the Department of Chinese Literature at Nagoya University. Joining him were Kanaseki Hisao, thirty-five (1918–1996); Yokoi (later Yanagida) Seizan, thirty-four (1922–), who taught at the Research Institute for Humanistic Studies at Kyoto University; Burton Watson, thirty-one (1925–), teaching at Kyoto University; Philip Yampolsky, thirty-six (1920–1996); and Gary Snyder, twenty-six (1930–). Manzoji Yoko assisted the team as secretary.

In many ways, Iriya was the mentor of this group, particularly of the three Americans, Burton, Philip, and Gary. Iriya led the weekly seminars and discussions, focusing on the *Rinzai-roku* translations, and inspiring the others with his careful attention to the nuance and subtle meanings of the T'ang dynasty colloquial language that was used in the old texts. His meticulous attention to these details provided inspiration to the others, demonstrating how a scholar worked. Iriya maintained his friendships with these men for the next several decades, combining his passionate curiosity and scholarship with his love of hiking and the outdoors.

In a letter to Haru Yoshida in June 1957, Ruth wrote, "Phil Yampolsky will return [to the United States] about the middle of August. He will stay two months with his parents, then return to Kyoto to work for me five days a week for an indefinite period, four or five years, if I live that long . . . he is the most wonderful help in my work I could possibly have. I have given him a long trial and I find him simply invaluable . . . he loves working here better than any place in the world." Philip Yampolsky was the grandson of the great anthropologist Franz Boas, who started the Anthropology Department at Columbia University. Philip had come to Japan on a Fulbright from Columbia University to work on his dissertation project on Hui Neng, the Sixth Patriarch of early Ch'an.

Burton Watson, now known as one of the world's best translators of Chinese and Japanese, had completed his Columbia University Ph.D. in 1956, writing his dissertation on Ssu-ma Ch'ien, the historian, and his work. For the next four years, the research team worked intensely. The major research projects were not published until after the demise of the original research group, but many smaller publications were written and published during the next few years.

Many years later, Philip Yampolsky wrote about the remarkable individuals on the research team in a chapter for the book *Gary Snyder: Dimensions of a Life*, commemorating Snyder's sixtieth birthday. He spoke highly of Iriya Yoshitaka and of Kanaseki Hisao, "an English professor of great good humor, wit, and competence, who helped Mrs. Sasaki in assorted ways."

Philip wrote of a younger scholar, Yanagida Seizan, "an expert on Chinese Zen, who had an unparalleled knowledge of its texts as well as Buddhist texts in general." Yanagida, retired now from the Research Institute for Humanistic Studies at Kyoto University, is, in Philip Yampolsky's words, "recognized as the foremost scholar of Zen Buddhism in both China and Japan." Yanagida wrote and published numerous books, and became the director of the International Research Institute for Zen Buddhism. He also became a leader in a citywide environmental/quality-of-life movement to block high-rise-building development in Kyoto.

Burton Watson worked part-time for the research team. He is renowned for his translations of both Chinese and Japanese works of literature, history, and poetry into English. In an essay written for a Festschrift after Iriya died in 1998, Burton described attending the sessions in which Ruth and Iriya worked together. He said that before the library was built, they used to have the working sessions in her living room, and that he learned a lot from Iriya's expertise and scholarship in T'ang-period texts. In this and subsequent translation projects at Ryosen-an, especially when they worked on the *Rinzai-roku,* Burton said that with Iriya Yoshitaka, Yanagida Seizan, Philip Yampolsky, and others, it was equal to a university seminar environment and provided them with valuable experience in the understanding of Zen works in Chinese and Japanese.

Iriya also loved hiking and often went out on long day and weekend hikes in the Kitayama, the mountain region north of Kyoto. Sometimes one of his sons would accompany him, and Gary also hiked with him. Iriya described to Gary the hiking route he'd taken once on a walk all the way from Kyoto to the Japan Sea, going north through the mountains. Gary took good notes of the route, and later he and Joanne Kyger replicated the beautiful, rugged hike. Gary recalled going over passes on three ridges, part of the time on ancient worn footpaths with the *li* (distance) markers for stretches through the forests.

At times there was a great deal of tension, however, between Ruth and her research staff. She was the boss, and she paid the salaries (considerable, especially at that time, when Japan was still recovering from the war). She brought to the group Sokei-an's translation of the *Rinzai-roku*, while the research staff were doing research that arrived at quite different translations from that of Sokei-an. As both Burton Watson and Iriya described, Ruth would bring out a few pages of translation, the research staff would make numerous changes, and she would type up the clean copy ignoring their suggestions. The tension seemed to have been aggravated by the fact that Ruth did not have a scholar's command of either Japanese or Chinese. The dynamics that existed among the members of the team and Ruth were problematic, but nonetheless resulted in some important contributions, significant publications, and lifelong friendships. This collaboration may also have spurred on the individual work of each of the research experts in their own particular endeavors, and the *Lin-chi Lu* translations received more of their individual attention in later years.

Ruth, now sixty-six years old, made history when she was ordained a priest with the Buddhist name Jokei ("Jo" from founding Roshi Daio Kokushi's temple name Nanpo Jomyo and "kei" from Sokei-an's name) by Oda Sesso Roshi, and installed as the abbot of the restored Ryosen-an. A ceremony was held on May 17, 1958, to name Sasaki Sokei-an Founder of the Restored Ryosen-an, and to ordain Ruth Fuller Sasaki as priestess, and appointed as abbot, or *jushoku*. Nineteen fifty-eight was a fruitful year for Ruth, and she was involved in the many events leading up to the grand ceremony for Ryosen-an as well as the work with her research team on the translations.

Late in February, Ruth wrote a letter to Gary Snyder, who was back in the United States for the winter. She said, "all the boys are working hard in the library. Watson comes as often as he can. We are now sitting seven nights the first week in every month, and four nights the other three. During the Osesshin week several Japanese students come; otherwise there is Phil [Yampolsky]—he is sitting as quiet as a lamb though he is suffering terrible pain in his legs. Between sitting periods he runs around the Zendo as if he were training for an Olympic Marathon."

She continued, "When are you coming back to us? We look for you the first part of September. I wish you were going to be here this summer to look over the MS of *Zen Dust* for me and proofread it as it comes from the printers."

In writing to Haru Yoshida about the new honor of being the jushoku of Ryosen-an, Ruth said that nothing had really changed, "except that I shall now have freedom of action." She said, "I had to go contrary to many of my strongly held ideas to accomplish this. I did not want to make this a *matsuji* [subtemple] and I certainly did not want to become the first foreigner, let alone a foreign woman, to become the priest of a Rinzai Zen temple. If I had been told in the beginning what the irrevocable rules of Daitoku-ji were, first among them that no buildings except temple buildings or buildings for temple purposes could be built on Daitoku-ji land, I should probably never have stayed here beyond the first six months. . . . Memoranda attached to the basic papers relieve me and any future foreign jushoku from the usual duties of a priest, such as reciting sutras, holding office at the Honzan, etc."

Ruth wrote a letter to Kobori Sohaku, who had been helping

her with the negotiations at Daitoku-ji, in which she said, "in our conference with Fukutomi Roshi and Nagata [an attorney] I clearly stated that, if I became the jushoku of Ryosen-an, I could not assume the usual duties of jushoku because I was a foreigner, a woman, untrained in temple procedures, and because I needed the years left to me to carry on the work of spreading Zen to the west. You accepted me as jushoku with these limitations."

Ruth could see the many advantages of this honor, and in a fourteen-page memorandum to the First Zen Institute, she wrote, "As far as the American Institute is concerned, I am also happy. I think, from the conversations I have with various thoughtful guests from foreign countries, that there is more and more a feeling of dissatisfaction with Zen as it is being presented non-traditionally, for the simple reason that there seems nothing firm to take hold of. With the Kyoto arm of our Institute solidly established within Daitoku-ji itself, everything that we write, teach, or do will bear the stamp of traditional Zen. The Daitoku-ji connection makes it obvious at once that what we are teaching is just that without our having to say anything."

She went on to describe the coming ceremony: "On May 17th ... the buildings of the Restored Ryosen-an will be dedicated, the statue of Manjusri will be placed in its shrine in the zendo, and I shall be presented with a *koromo* [robe] from the Honzan in recognition of the work I have done and my appointment as priest of Ryosen-an. At the Honzan, later the same day, I shall be presented with a *kesa* [shoulder robe] by the Kancho, acknowledging my *tokudo* [ordination of priest], and an elaborate ceremony will be held in commemoration of the 13th anniversary of Sokei-an's death. Present at the ceremony will be the Kanchos and Roshis of all the Rinzai Zen Honzans and Sodos in Kyoto, all the Daitoku-ji priests in Kyoto, and some Ryosen-an Ha priests from Tokyo, in addition to the Kyoto members of the Institute and a few immediate friends—about eighty persons in all.

"Daitoku-ji is very happy about the way matters have turned out and every kind of cooperation is being given to me and every kindness possible being shown. Of course, they are going to get considerable glory for themselves from it because they will be the first Rinzai Zen Honzan to have such an organization for foreigners' study of Zen under their jurisdiction and within their walls."

The pamphlet Ruth had written, *Zen: A Religion*, was published in time for the printer to produce one hundred copies for the ceremony, one for each guest. Subsequently, two thousand copies of this pamphlet were printed.

Events at Daitoku-ji surrounding the ceremony were newsworthy in Japan, and word spread to the United States. Ruth was photographed by *Kyoto Shinbun* for *Time* magazine, where an article appeared noting the historical significance of this event. The formal ceremonies of the day, the great honor to Ruth, and the nuances and details of the behind-the-scenes activities make this one of the most interesting days of Ruth's life.

Ruth decided to record the details in a letter for the First Zen Institute members, knowing that it was a historical moment in the transmission of Zen to the West. She described the day's special ceremony in six pages of single-spaced type in the July 1958 issue of *Zen Notes*. It was such a mystery that Sokei-an turned out to have been a priest of Daitoku-ji and was, unknown until a short time before, a member of the Ryosen-an line of priests within Daitoku-ji. Oda Sesso Roshi gave her the vows as she took tokudo to become a Daitoku-ji priest. As part of this ceremony, Ruth was taken to the *hondo*, the main hall of Daitoku-ji, and allowed to enter the special place where stood the statue of Daio Kokushi, founder of the line of Daitoku-ji teaching that Kokushi brought from China when he returned to Japan in 1269 as the dharma-heir of Kido Osho of Kinzan. She bowed, burned incense, and marveled at the experience of standing face-to-face with this life-size figure deep within the main shrine of the hondo.

Ruth's descriptions of the day covered the extensive preparation of guest lists, gifts to be given, food to be served, clothes to wear, each detail of the ceremony such as who would stand where, and which sutras would be chanted. Ruth said that her constant mentor over a period of weeks for the day's complexities was her friend and colleague Kobori Sohaku, another priest at Daitoku-ji, who had learned English from Beatrice Lane Suzuki when he was younger.

The guests were all to receive purple silk *furoshiki* (square scarves for wrapping packages), with the seal of the First Zen Institute of America in Japan in white at one corner, as mementos for the dedication of the zendo.

For the ceremony that would be the memorial service for Sokeian, the presents were to be *rakusus*, the small bib with the ivory ring always worn by Zen priests (except when they wore the kesa). The guest lists included the kanchos and roshis of all the Rinzai headquarter temples in Kyoto, all the priests within Daitoku-ji, the leading priests of the Ryosen-an line from out of town, the members of the First Zen Institute of America in Japan, and other close associates. Ninety people were on the invitation list, and just sending invitations was not enough. Ruth had to personally visit each of the kanchos and roshis to invite them, and the wrapping on their gifts had to be marked with special calligraphy. Kobori spent many days on the calligraphy.

The day's events were divided into two parts. The first part was to be at Ryosen-an, beginning at 9 A.M., when the figure of Manjusri, the Bodhisattva of Intrinsic Wisdom, was installed in every zendo, along with a memorial service for Yoho Zenji, the original founder of Ryosen-an. Ruth was presented with a special black robe from Daitoku-ji.

The second part was to be held in the main hall of Daitoku-ji, where a tablet to Sokei-an, inscribed with his new title "Founder of the Restored Ryosen-an," would be installed on the main altar next to other tablets of the most important priests of past generations. Ruth was formally presented with a kesa, and a sutra-chanting service was held in Sokei-an's memory. The last of these events was to be a formal and very elaborate dinner.

One of the few treasures of the old Ryosen-an was a portrait of the original founder painted in 1500, inscribed in his own hand and hung above the temporary altar. Since Ruth's entire house was to be open to guests, much care was taken in arranging the *tokonomas* (alcoves)—all of them with flower arrangements of roses from Kobori's garden. Preparations on the day itself began at 5 A.M., and Ruth described the entry of the guests into the zendo and onto the *tan* (bench) in their appropriate order. The formal proclamation was followed by lighting the incense and reading an *eko* (memorial sutra reading for a dead person/priest) to Manjusri and an *eko* for the founder. At 10 A.M., they all went over in appropriate sequence to the main hall, where an *eko* was read for Sokei-an, and Ruth bowed to the altar of the founder of Daitoku-ji. As Ruth described it:

> One must see such a scene with one's own eyes to realize its full beauty. Against old gold painted screens and black and white painted sliding panels, all National Treasures, the priests sit in their purple robes and gold brocaded

rakusus. In front of them stand the red lacquer trays; high on the walls behind hang famous paintings from Sung and Ming China. To the side stretch the age-darkened timbers of the deep veranda, and beyond, the white sand, rocks, and trees of one of Kyoto's most famous gardens.

Through the popularity and influence of D. T. Suzuki, Alan Watts, and others, there were starting to be more publications about Zen in English. In the summer of 1958, the magazine *Chicago Review* published an entire issue on Zen, including an essay by Ruth along with essays by D. T. Suzuki, Alan Watts, Gary Snyder, and others. Gary Snyder, in a letter to Ruth written from Marin-an, the zendo in Marin County he'd created, said, "the summer issue of *Chicago Review* is the best selling issue they've ever had."

In the fall of 1958, after things had settled down somewhat, Ruth and Washino planned a journey back to the United States with stops in Copenhagen, Zurich, Geneva, Paris, and London for a six-month visit to take care of publication business and to see family and friends. Shortly before leaving Kyoto in the early autumn, Ruth seemed content with the direction that Ryosen-an was going. In a letter to Gary Snyder she wrote, "We still miss you and hope you will be back among our group. A very nice man of twenty-seven is here from Holland [Janwillem van de Wetering]. He is living as a lay visitor in the sodo for the next year, studying Japanese with Mrs. Fujitani and practicing zazen every night in the zendo. Walter [Nowick] is tiptop. Goto Roshi is frail but in good spirits. Everyone is fine and working hard."

Janwillem van de Wetering later went on to write of his experiences during this time in widely popular fiction. He wrote of his first meeting with Ruth when he was sent over to Ryosen-an by Morinaga Roshi (then a head monk called Fu). He mentioned her deep, throaty, somewhat hoarse voice as she offered him a Camel cigarette from her pack and served him Lipton tea, graham crackers, and chocolate chip cookies. He began sitting in the zendo and talked of Ruth's generosity in serving meals to Institute members. He had been living on the monastery's daily fare of boiled cabbage, rice, and barley, and he said her generosity probably saved his life. He became acquainted with all kinds of American food served at these meals, which included chops with gravy and mashed potatoes, steaks, vanilla ice cream over canned cherries, and open-faced beef sandwiches with fries.

During this time, Jack Kerouac's book *Dharma Bums* was published, and Ruth's Victorian upper-middle-class upbringing, as well as her strong opinions about how Zen should be presented, were expressed in a letter (November 13, 1958) written from her hotel in New York to Gary Snyder, who was out in the San Francisco Bay Area. "His Buddhism is the most garbled and mistaken I have read in many a day.... I expect you to consider these words of a 'square' old woman, but when you have lived as long as I you will see that present day 'Dharma bums' are just the same type of boys that appear in every generation, each time with a new name and a new line, but intrinsically just the same 'bums.'"

She commented on Kerouac's thin disguising of Gary in the book. She said, "I think everyone grants Kerouac's sensitivity of reaction and his ability to vividly write those reactions. I found the first mountain climbing episode quite exciting. But as a novelist he shows no talent whatsoever and no imagination."

She went on in the letter to confirm Gary's return to Ryosen-an, saying, "You know I am very, very fond of you, and while I have no desire or intention to make you other than you are, I want you to become what you really are. I am looking forward very much to having you around."

Gary Snyder had connected his friend Claude Dalenberg with Ruth, and Claude went to Ryosen-an in 1959 for a year and a half. In Ruth's letter to Gary in February 1959, shortly before she would finish her six-month trip to the United States, she said, "I will be glad to talk with your friend Claude Dalenberg when I get to San Francisco on March 16 [1959]. . . . I shall have to see Mr. Dalenberg and then think the matter over. The fact that he has appeared in *Dharma Bums* doesn't endear him to me. . . . Naturally I have no desire to make the least move to prevent anyone whatsoever [from] coming to Japan to study Zen, but since even the using of my name is equivalent over there to a recommendation from me, I have to be very careful. And I don't want the Institute there to become a nursery for boys whose mothers couldn't bring them up properly at home."

Ruth read widely in the areas of fiction and popular culture, and had strong opinions that she was not shy about sharing, and which were often impressive in their breadth. Gary Snyder said that on an occasion shortly after he arrived, he accompanied Ruth on a business trip to Tokyo, and on the return train trip, she talked impressively about her ideas and opinions of the writings of Henry Miller.

The work of the big translation projects continued, along with the Saturday afternoon research team meetings. Ruth had to organize the Saturday study group for *The Record of Rinzai* directed by Iriya Yoshitaka, composed of Philip Yampolsky, Burton Watson, Gary Snyder, Walter Nowick, and herself, to discuss the Chinese text of the *Rinzai* using Sokei-an's English translation as a guide.

Frustration was growing among the research team about the size and ambitious nature of the undertakings, and the fact that it took so many years with nothing published to show for such intense efforts. Meanwhile, several smaller efforts were starting to get published.

Institute members all helped in some way to get these small books and pamphlets published. They were elegantly printed and a big success. Between 1959 and 1963, four were printed under the imprint of the First Zen Institute of America in Japan:

> *Zen: A Religion*, 1958 and 1963, 32 pp.
> *Zen: A Method for Religious Awakening*, 1959, 28 pp.
> *Rinzai Zen Study for Foreigners in Japan*, 1960, 104 pp.
> *The First Zen Institute of America in Japan*, 1959, 42 pp.

The first three were attractively printed, bound, and contained in a boxed set—and are also reprinted in part two of this book. In the foreword to *Zen: A Method for Religious Awakening*, Ruth explained that this publication was from the text of a lecture at M.I.T. that she had been invited to give by Huston Smith. Smith had visited Ryosen-an in 1958 and had gotten to know Ruth and the work of the Institute.

The third of these, *Rinzai Zen Study for Foreigners in Japan*, was written in response to the numerous requests for additional copies of Ruth's "Letters from Kyoto" that were included in issues of *Zen Notes*. Seven of her "Letters" were devoted to topics on how foreigners might begin Zen practice in Japan, and Ruth decided to reissue these "Letters" along with additional material, all in a more convenient form. Donatienne Lebovich provided drawings relevant to instructions for zazen practice, and Ruth included an essential reading list of books on both Hinayana and Mahayana Buddhism as background ("an absolute necessity," as Ruth said) for students interested in studying Zen.

The last pamphlet, *The First Zen Institute of America in Japan*, describes the purpose of the work at Ryosen-an, and the facilities of the library and the zendo for sixteen people. The Ryosen-an Library was open to members of the Institute every day except Monday from 9 A.M. to 5 P.M. Holdings in the library included major Japanese collections of Chinese and Japanese Buddhist scriptures; Japanese translations of Chinese scriptures; old and new Chinese and Japanese texts on Buddhism, history, and literature; reference works; and a large Western language section of works in French, German, and English on religion, philosophy, psychology, and Buddhism. Major European, American, and Japanese scholarly journals of Far Eastern studies were subscribed to, and there was access for students and scholars to "English translations, still in manuscript, of old and modern Zen works."

Ruth outlined the expectations for visitors and students at the Institute, explaining that "transient visitors" might be permitted to sit once or twice in the zendo during the evening meditation, but that serious students must commit to a minimum of two months, "provided they have completed most of their sightseeing and shopping previously, so that when they begin their zazen practice they may have adequate time and undivided attention to devote to it" (p. 13).

Membership was listed in categories: associate member ($5/1,800 yen per year) for "Persons interested in Zen, regardless of their place of residence"; governing member ($3 per month) for foreigners resident in Japan, Japanese persons interested in furthering the work of the Kyoto Institute, and foreign students living in Japan and engaged in Rinzai Zen study under a Zen teacher; supporting member ($100 per year) for individuals, corporations, associations, or partnerships; and visiting student member ($6 per month) for foreigners temporarily resident in Japan and regularly attending meditation sessions at the Institute. Holding office at the Institute was restricted to governing members. A listing of the advisors, officers, and members of the research team finishes the text.

This pamphlet concluded with sixteen pages of black-and-white photographs of Ryosen-an in 1959, including interior and exterior pictures of the library and zendo, which provide excellent documentation for comparison with how Ryosen-an looks today.

Ruth was pleased with the compliments she received on the publication of these pamphlets. She said that their success made quite an impression on some of the research team who had said that the pamphlets were no good and that no one would buy them or pay any attention to them.

Two additional pamphlets were published, one in 1960 called *Ryosen-an Zendo Practice*, a compilation of the rules and customs observed at the Ryosen-an Zendo, and another in 1961 called *The Wooden Fish: Basic Sutras and Gathas of Rinzai Zen*. The imprint says that the translations are by Gary Snyder and Gutetsu Kanetsuki, but Ruth said, "*The Wooden Fish* is now out. . . . It is Gary's work from beginning to end."

The Wooden Fish describes the sodo-year schedule for Daitoku-ji as an example of a Rinzai Zen monastery in Japan. An introduction of sutra chanting is followed by the actual sutras along with their English translations, which were from Sasaki Sokei-an (Heart of Great Wisdom Sutra); D. T. Suzuki (Dharani of Removing Disasters), Ruth F. Sasaki (The Four Vows), and the various ekos read at Ryosen-an and Zuiun-ken. Sutras and gathas for mealtime chanting are followed by a collection of other sutras and gathas, and included at the end is an appendix of English, Sanskrit, and Japanese terminology. *The Wooden Fish* sold for $1.00 and became highly sought after.

Orders were sent to the First Zen Institute, and bookstores such as City Lights in San Francisco sold them. It has become a scarce and valuable publication over the years.

In the spring, Ruth was back in Kyoto after her six-month trip to Europe and the United States. Gary Snyder returned after a year away. Paul Wienpahl, a professor at the University of California, Santa Barbara, spent the summer studying and sitting at the Ryosen-an Zendo and later wrote a book about his experience at Daitoku-ji that summer.

Trouble was growing with Walter Nowick. In December, Walter verbally resigned from the Institute, where he had been serving as vice president. His formal resignation letter was sent on January 17, 1960. Walter was then living at Rinko-in, the subtemple at Shokoku-ji, and said that he needed to devote all his time and energy to Zen study and practice under Goto Roshi.

Goto Roshi also resigned from his advisory position on the board. His stated reason was that he needed to relieve himself of all responsibilities except for his teaching. Ruth stopped her sanzen study with Goto Roshi at this time. Ruth felt that it was Walter's problem, and that after his departure things were quieter around the zendo. One of the misunderstandings among Walter, Goto Roshi, and Ruth apparently concerned the financial support provided to Goto Roshi by Ruth. Another difficulty was that Ruth sometimes avoided following advice from Goto Roshi. It was suggested by Philip Yampolsky that Ruth's insistence on building Zuiun-ken as a dormitory for the Western Zen students connected with Ryosen-an and Daitoku-ji was the final straw for Goto Roshi. Yampolsky wrote that he, Gary Snyder, and Walter were summoned by Goto Roshi, who explained his reasons for resigning and ending the relationship with Ruth and Ryosen-an.

Not long after, Ruth went to visit Goto Roshi, and they resumed their good relations. Goto Roshi indicated that he would like Ruth to come back for sanzen with him. It would be more years before Ruth and Walter began mending their relationship.

Ruth was reaching a troubled time with the First Zen Institute in New York as well. She felt that the content of *Zen Notes* had deteriorated to the point that she wanted to discontinue sending her "Letters" for inclusion.

Research and Translation, 1960–1967 6

A^S THE DIRECTOR of the First Zen Institute of America in Japan, Ruth naturally became a social director, concerned with the successes and relationships of the students. Ruth got to know the families of some of the students, and sometimes parents would correspond with her. With the growing publicity of the First Zen Institute in Japan, Ruth began to receive voluminous correspondence from people who were curious or who wanted to arrange visits, and she received visits from westerners in Japan who had read about the Institute. Over the next several years, she had secretarial assistance in answering queries from Furuta Kazuhiro, Dana Fraser, and Richard Leavitt.

Ruth had strong opinions about her visitors and those who sent her letters. She did not waste time on people who were not serious about Zen. The decade of the sixties intensified the challenges of the work Ruth had undertaken. On one hand, she had the burning desire to complete the publications and translations. On the other hand, she found herself running a growing institute for Zen students planning long-term residence to study.

The accompanying social community of westerners from the United States and Europe, along with the Japanese scholars and workers who were part of the Institute, made a lively social scene, and as might be expected, one that had its fair share of difficulties and challenges. This was a period of cultural change in Japan as well as in the United States, and Ruth was from the "old school" of etiquette and social norms, not quite prepared for the growing momentum of the counterculture movement of the sixties.

Many of the popular books on Zen coming out during this time thanked Ruth and/or quoted from her writings. One book Ruth praised was *Anthology of Zen* (1961), by William Briggs, which included short essays by Ruth, Sasaki Sokei-an, Soyen Shaku, Goto Zuigan, Senzaki Nyogen, and Mary Farkas. Many other authors also gave tribute to Ruth in their publications, including Huston Smith, Paul Wienpahl, Nancy Wilson Ross, and Joseph Campbell.

Gary Snyder, one of the principal long-term members of the Institute, had met the poet Joanne Kyger when he was in San Francisco in 1958 and had invited her to come to Japan. Ruth had some unwritten social customs for those connected with the Institute that she adhered to, and despite the growing cultural acceptance in the United States of unmarried couples living together, Ruth insisted that Gary and Joanne get married if they were going to live together in Kyoto.

Joanne and Gary married on February 28, 1960, as soon as Joanne arrived in Japan. After the civil ceremony in Kobe, they had a wedding ceremony at Daitoku-ji, and Ruth had a reception for them at Ryosen-an. Later Ruth wrote up the event for her "Letter" for *Zen Notes*, explaining that her detailed account of the wedding ceremony held at Daitoku-ji would serve future "American Zennists" who would probably be interested in having similar Buddhist weddings.

Joanne published a book about her time in Kyoto in the early sixties, *The Japan and India Journals, 1960–1964* (1981), and the entries show a perspective on Ruth and the Ryosen-an life different from that of the men in Ruth's employ or connected with the Institute.

Joanne said in conversations that the whole feeling in Ruth's residence and the rest of Ryosen-an was of "fine craftsmanship, comfort, and visual pleasure." Joanne described the Ryosen-an Zendo as small and beautifully proportioned, a pleasure for meditation.

Ruth took great care with the zendo, and for her the attendance and the respect with which the students participated in the zendo were very important. She tried to instill the formality of traditional zendo ritual, and to adapt only a little for foreigners. A priest or monk was always in charge of the zendo sittings. Some were stricter than others. Ruth tried to get students to understand why sitting correctly was an essential part of zazen practice. She would say that lots of people thought they were sitting properly when they were comfortable. "Here we aim to teach people to sit correctly, and everyone who does not do so is corrected until he learns how to sit properly and then comfortably in the correct position. This is a practice hall, not a place for comfort."

The first *rohatsu* (intensive sesshin) was held at the Ryosen-an Zendo on December 1–8, 1960, and included fifteen people: five Japanese, with Gutetsu serving as jikijitsu; Yamada Sobin, priest of Shinju-an, serving as jisha; one English; one Swiss; three American women; and five American men. The schedule included zazen twice daily from 5:30 to 7:30 A.M. and 6:30 to 9:30 P.M., and, on the seventh day, also 6:30 P.M. to midnight.

Joanne Kyger echoed the remarks of many other westerners in Kyoto who were associated with Ryosen-an about the satisfaction of meals that Ruth provided to them. Joanne said that for those who had "culture shock palate," occasional meals at Ruth's with beef, potatoes, and mushrooms, preceded by a gin martini, were a wonderfully nurturing generosity on Ruth's part. Al Klyce, a student from California who had been associated with Ryosen-an for a brief time, said that even though he felt that Ruth did not totally approve of him since he wasn't a Zen scholar or a long-term student, when it came time for him to leave Kyoto and return to the United States, she graciously invited him over for a nice farewell dinner.

Joanne also spoke highly of Ruth's personal assistant, Washino. Joanne took flower-arranging lessons with Washino for over a year and described her as "calm, sweet, humorous, patient." Washino was an ever-present and essential part of Ruth's daily life, a loyal combination of administrative assistant, translator, cultural advisor, companion, and household manager. Washino was the go-between for Ruth and the other temples at Daitoku-ji, informally visiting and keeping the social nuances of the Daitoku-ji life and Ryosen-an flowing smoothly.

Ruth's social visits and outings were often to people connected with the Institute in some way. On one occasion, Ruth, Washino, Donatienne Lebovich, and Vanessa Coward took a trip to the Tokyo Museum to look at paintings, some of which Ruth was interested in making arrangements to photograph as part of the illustrations she wanted to include in *Zen Dust*. One night while they were on this trip, Ruth said that Philip Kapleau; his new wife, deLancey; and Bernard Philips, who was living at Kamakura for the year, came to dinner. She said that all three were practicing Zen under Yasutani Roshi, heir of Harada Roshi of Hosshin-ji, who instructed only lay students. In the afternoon they had climbed the 174 steps to D. T. Suzuki's at the top of Pine Hill, just across from Engaku-ji. She said, "at ninety-one he is in excellent health and bubbling over with good spirits."

Housing for some long-term Ryosen-an students was available at the remodeled and refurbished dormitory called Zuiun-ken, "House of the Auspicious Cloud," a building disassembled from the second floor of Empuku-ji and reassembled at Daitoku-ji in the traditional modular way of Japanese temple buildings. This building had originally been given to Empuku-ji by the Arisugawa family.

Claude Dalenberg resided in it, as did Irmgard Schloegl (now the Venerable Myokyo-ni of the Zen Centre of London), who had just arrived from the Buddhist Society of London to spend several years in Kyoto. It had room for six or seven students, and was within the Daitoku-ji complex, only a two-minute walk from Ryosen-an. The renovation of Zuiun-ken, funded by members of the First Zen Institute, even included installations of Western bathrooms. There was ample room for both male and female student residents.

By the end of the year, Judith and Bill Laws, from the First Zen Institute in New York, and their young son had also moved in to Zuiun-ken while they looked for a place to live in Kyoto. Ruth's daughter, Eleanor, and her husband, Carlton, and son, Michael, stayed there in 1962, as did Ken Walden and Jacques May in 1963.

Being a dormitory, Zuiun-ken had the inevitable difficulties of different personalities trying to get along in a semistructured environment. There was a resident monk, a housekeeper/cook, and short- and long-term residents. Regulations were simple: getting up in the morning for early zazen, attendance at early sutra chanting, cleaning one's own room, and eating breakfast. They were free to do whatever they liked until 5:30 P.M., when dinner was served, and they were expected to be at the Ryosen-an Zendo for zazen from 7 to 9 P.M. There was complete freedom from Saturday after breakfast until Monday morning.

There were political problems over letting Ryosen-an use Zuiun-ken in the first place. These controversies did not completely disappear, and Ruth played as integral a part in Daitoku-ji behind the scenes as the other priests, who perhaps wanted Zuiun-ken for their own purposes. Ryosen-an had the use of Zuiun-ken until 1964, when the lack of students interested in staying there made the expense of renting it infeasible. Ruth also referred students who needed a place to live to her longtime friend Ogata Sohaku, priest of the subtemple Chotoku-in at Shokoku-ji. Renovated quarters with Western conveniences at Chotoku-in were rented, but there was no room for more than one or two residents.

The Institute had regular director's meetings. A meeting held on June 5, 1960, was attended by:

Mr. Oda Sesso Kancho	Mr. Gary Snyder
Mrs. Ruth Fuller Sasaki	Mr. Saichiro Kitamoto
Rev. Isei Fukutomi	Mrs. Donatienne Lebovich
Rev. Kobori Sohaku	Mr. Toyokichi Shimotsuma
Mr. Philip Yampolsky	Mr. Fred Summer

Minutes of the meeting stated a membership of forty-two: ten governing members, thirty associate members, one visiting, and one nonpaying temporary. Since Walter Nowick had resigned, it was reported that Kobori Sohaku had been serving as jikijitsu, and that a "small but steady" group had been sitting. Other activities included a mention of the Friday evening meetings in which "the Director reads from her MSS of Sokei-an," and the Monday afternoon meetings in which Kobori read from the *Mumonkan*.

In the spring, George Kennedy, head of the Chinese Department at Yale University, was in Kyoto on sabbatical. He dropped by

Ryosen-an and volunteered to help. Ruth had the idea for a little class in Chinese grammar studies, and so Philip, Gary, Kobori, and Ruth began a class with him using the *Keitoku dento roku* (Chinese: *Chiangte Ch'uanteng lu* [*Jingde chuan deng lu*]; *Transmission of the Lamp*) as a study text. Ruth was delighted that this would give them material both for the *Zen Dust* appendices and for future issues of *Zen Notes*.

The hundredth anniversary of the opening of trade relations between Japan and the United States took place in 1960. At a formal event held in Tokyo in November, Ruth was awarded a special citation for promoting "religious, educational, economic, industrial, political, diplomatic, social and cultural relations." These citations were awarded to 298 Americans, of whom only seventy were still living. Ruth and Ryosen-an also received a Bollingen Foundation grant ($5,000 each year for 1961–1963) to assist with the translation and publication projects.

In September 1960, Philip Yampolsky gave a paper at an international conference of Orientalists held in Tokyo called "Some Problems in the Translation of Chinese Zen Material." In particular, he described the difficulties encountered by the research team in working on the translation of the *Rinzai-roku*. His paper was published in two issues of *Zen Notes*. He divided the problems into three major categories: the problem of Zen meaning, the problem of the Chinese in which the text was written, and the problem of rendering the text into adequate and appropriate English. It was a brilliant analysis of these scholarly challenges.

The Saturday work of the research team on the *Rinzai-roku* continued. By July 1961, the tensions of the research team came to a boil with misunderstandings between Ruth and Philip Yampolsky. Philip was "dismissed" on July 13, and Burton Watson and Gary Snyder resigned in protest of the dismissal. The misunderstandings revolved around Ruth's perceptions and some rumors that Philip was secretly planning his own translation of the *Rinzai-roku.*

Ruth's perception edged into the realm of paranoia, and she was said to have stormed into the library where work was going on, demanding that Philip produce the papers and accusing him of going behind her back to undermine their work.

As Gary recollects, Philip went to a filing cabinet, retrieved the papers, and handed them to her. She left, somewhat deflated, but still believing that Philip was planning something underhanded.

Her extreme behavior with Philip worried Burton Watson and Gary Snyder, and they tendered their resignations (thinking that this would reverse itself if she apologized and reinstated Yampolsky).

A day or two later, Ruth had a meeting with her lawyers in her office, while the research team worked in the library. One of the lawyers went back and forth between the two locations in an effort to smooth things out. Because Ruth was not able to make a serious apology to Philip, the others felt that none of the terms they were offering would suffice to heal the breach.

Gary took the lead in trying to resolve the situation, asking the others if things could be patched up, and all three agreed that they probably couldn't be. Gary decided to speed up the process, walked directly to the other room where the lawyers and Ruth were meeting, and informed them that they were all wasting their time, that the three of them were formally resigning.

Gary learned that, although it was rough at the time, Ruth never seemed to hold it against him, and that they had a good relationship subsequently. Gary went to work teaching English conversation part-time, and Watson and Yampolsky left.

Yanagida and Iriya continued to work with Ruth, but in a much more scaled-down way. They continued to be frustrated by Ruth's "perfectionism," as Yampolsky had described it, saying that if she'd had more academic training, she would have had the confidence to work more quickly through the process. This breakup of the research team was indicative of the frustration they had with Ruth's style. It was likely that her financial support was a motivating factor in keeping things together for as long as it did.

Some have called this event the pivotal point in the entire life of the Institute, and it is certainly an example of the difficulties of Ruth's relationships with those who worked with her. In the beginning, she was thrilled to have Philip Yampolsky at Ryosen-an, and she raved about him and his work often. She set such high expectations that when there were disagreements, she ended up feeling great disappointment and betrayal.

Washino had also told Ruth that rumors were circulating that she should retire as director, letting Walter assume the position of priest of Ryosen-an, and that Philip be made the head of the library. But Ruth was not ready to retire, even though she was close to seventy.

It was an explosive end to an intense working relationship. But other than being deeply distressed over the events, Ruth did not acknowledge the significance of the breakup of the research team. By the end of the year, only the original three Japanese scholars remained to assist her with the ongoing work of *Zen Dust*.

Ruth had turned sixty-nine, and she realized that the translation projects, the zendo, and the Zuiun-ken dormitory were all in crisis. Still, she pushed on toward the goal of getting *Zen Dust* published. She was growing discouraged at the task of completing the research of the three who had left.

Ruth described the process of working on the manuscript. It involved checking each phrase, through Kanaseki asking for Yanagida's input, and then rechecking and working with Professor Iriya to double-check the meanings. The scholarly translation difficulties were compounded by Ruth's limited Japanese and Yanagida's limited English. Kanaseki was heroically patient during this process, and Ruth gave him a lot of credit for any progress that was made. Ruth acknowledged the frustration that everyone felt, including her own, saying: "It makes one wild, especially at my age, and wanting so much to finish *Zen Dust* and have a vacation at home. But there is nothing to do but plug away. I expect other scholars—for if I complete this I shall certainly qualify for a scholar—have had like problems."

The First Zen Institute in New York, meanwhile, was hoping to have Miura Roshi continue there as their Zen teacher. An apartment was being created for him in the Institute's new space on East 30th Street, after moving from the Farkases' building on Waverly Place. Neither Miura Roshi nor the Institute members were sure of the permanency of his connection to them.

On a trip back to his home temple of Koon-ji in the fall, Miura Roshi stopped at Ryosen-an to visit Ruth. They had a long talk about the First Zen Institute, and he seemed happy with his new quarters and hoped that the Institute would reorganize itself into a system with which he could be more comfortable. One of Miura Roshi's difficulties was that he seemed caught between Ruth's and Mary Farkas's differing visions of what a Zen teacher at the First Zen Institute should be.

One of Miura Roshi's conditions for continuing was that there always be a man in charge at the Institute. He was uncomfortable with there being more female than male students. Partly this was due to his background and cultural differences between Japan and New York. His entire experience had been in monastery temples, and he was not used to women being part of the hierarchy. He would refer to it as "Farkas Zen," feeling like he was being "managed" and was more of a guest than a roshi to them.

At the same time, Mary Farkas was working hard to keep the Institute going. There were misunderstandings about whether the First Zen Institute was still in a "pioneer Zen" phase or had developed into a more mature organization. As things turned out, Miura Roshi separated from the Institute before long, sending a letter of resignation in November 1963.

After traveling to Japan for a big ceremony at his temple, Koon-ji, Miura Roshi returned to New York and moved into an apartment on East 72nd Street. A few of the former First Zen Institute students continued to study with him (ones that he selected), and he remained in this role as an independent teacher in New York, beginning with a Nirvana Day ceremony at his apartment in February 1964, and continuing until 1976, when he died. His independence surprised, dismayed, and intrigued both Ruth and Mary Farkas, who couldn't understand just why he was staying in New York without being connected to them.

By mid-July 1962, Ruth wrote that the notes for the first half of *Zen Dust* would be finished "this week," and by the middle of September, "all will be on their way to the printer." However, in mid-November, she said, "it is almost done, but there are so many, many little things that must be checked and rechecked and rechecked again. You will see what I mean when you see the final text."

In the end, the book *Zen Koan* (over four hundred pages shorter than *Zen Dust*, considered to be the "student version") was published first, in 1965, printed in Japan first, then in New York by Harcourt.

Zen Dust, which had several printing glitches, finally followed in 1966, to critical acclaim. It was printed first in Japan; the U.S. edition by Harcourt did not get published until 1967.

Ruth's zeal and dedication to her work took a toll on her health and energy. In the spring of 1962, she had need for serious dental work, and made a quick trip to New York so that she could get a new bridge made by her longtime dentist. This gave her a chance to see up close what was happening with the First Zen Institute, and to talk in depth with Miura Roshi about the deteriorating situation.

Her health problems persisted. In January 1963, she fell outside a Kyoto restaurant and broke her left arm, which meant having a heavy cast for a few months. Gradually she was able to return again to her work. Fortunately Ken Walden was providing secretarial help during this time. By February 1963, she wrote that *Zen Dust* was almost finished except for the index. She was amazed at how big the book had become, over 450 pages. Every page had elements of Sanskrit, Chinese translation (transliteration in roman letters), and Japanese reading of the Chinese, also in roman letters, and they constituted over a thousand pages of proofs to read and correct. The text was going through its third proofs, and the index would not be created until that task was finished.

Ruth was starting to think about the process of printing and publication in Japan, the United States, and Europe. She said she was thinking of printing only 1,000 copies, with 300 of those for Miura Roshi and herself to present as gifts. She was going to have paper molds made so that it could be easily reprinted when more became necessary.

Ruth was mending some of her relationships with those who had left and resigned, and in the summer of 1963, she wrote that Walter had sent his regards to her through Gary Snyder. Gary and his wife,

Joanne, had renewed relations with Ruth, and she felt that they were now on excellent terms. She was happy they were coming for dinner in late June, bringing with them Allen Ginsberg, who had been with them on their trip to India. Ruth said that she, too, might go to India at the beginning of the following year to attend an international meeting in New Delhi of Far Eastern scholars and give a paper, as well as travel to the Buddhist holy places (by September she had changed her mind about going).

In an example of Ruth's capacity to stay current and actively interested in things beyond her daily work, Gary Snyder recounted that during this dinner with Allen at Ruth's, she spent the entire evening discussing Allen's book *Howl*, which Gary had given her a copy of not long before. For Gary Snyder, who had left behind a new era of poetry and public performance in the company of Allen Ginsberg to go to Kyoto and work with Ruth, it was an odd kind of fulfillment to see the two halves of his life brought together at this dinner.

Ruth was in good spirits, and she wrote on June 27 that Ryosen-an had some really nice students, nine or ten total, and that "the library is simply heaven from one week to the other." She said, "If only I were fifty instead of seventy and knew as much as I know now! Anyway, personal relations on all levels are wonderful."

In addition to the work of finishing up the "last tag ends" of *Zen Dust*, they had begun work in March on the *Rinzai-roku* again, and had called in Leon Hurvitz to help, with the research team working on it one day a week (by late June, he was working three full days a week). She said that Hurvitz would be able to work on it through July, and that he was trying to get a four- to six-month extension from the University of Washington so that he could stay until it was finished (it turned out that he wasn't able to extend his time beyond July). She said, "We're all happy to have him because we can work with him and because he is brilliant, but most of all because he can look at the material with a western scholar's eye."

Ruth and Washino left for a trip to New York in early January 1964. Ruth relied heavily on the assistance of Richard Leavitt and Furuta Kazuhiro at Ryosen-an with handling the correspondence and the visitors, and on Haru Yoshida in New York to help with preparations and itineraries for the trip, which was to be a combination of meetings in New York and a vacation to visit her daughter Eleanor's family in Colorado.

By September 1964, Ruth was already contemplating a permanent return to the United States, but she wrote that it would probably not take place for several years. A combination of her health problems, "climate and age" as she put it, and severe rheumatism brought her to this conclusion. She invited her friends, Zen priests Fukutomi Roshi and Kobori, over for dinner on September 20, and told them that she was giving up the lease on Zuiun-ken as of March 31, 1965 (she was required to give six months' notice), and that she was closing the zendo schedule of zazen and work with students as of January 1, 1965.

She said that they had had only three new students since the spring of 1964; of these, only one wanted to attend a monastery, and she had sent him to Tokyo to live with Fukutomi Roshi's heir at Kotoku-ji. During this period, Irmgard Schloegl was studying with Oda Sesso Roshi and doing zazen at the Daitoku-ji Sodo; Ken Walden was sitting at the sodo also and living at Gary Snyder's house while Gary was away; and Richard Leavitt was sitting in the zendo and also teaching two evenings a week. Ruth said that Kobori was sad over her decision, but that Fukutomi Isei thought it was a wise one.

Ruth's plans were to focus the energy and years remaining to her on the *Rinzai-roku* and the *Hokoji goroku* (Chinese: *P'ang Chushin Yulu*

[*Pang Jushi Yulu*]; *The Recorded Sayings of Layman P'ang)*, trying to get those manuscripts ready for publication. This became a turning point for Ryosen-an: the First Zen Institute would become exclusively a research institute for translation and linguistic work, and Ruth said she would not accept any more new students.

Printing problems dogged the final stages of *Zen Dust* and *Zen Koan*, and Ruth delayed a trip to New York from January 1965 to later in the winter, trying to get things straightened out with the Japanese printing company. She had the page proofs by now, but just trying to buy the paper for printing was difficult. There were complicated arrangements between the printing in Japan and the publishing of the two books in New York by Harcourt. Ruth delayed her trip to New York twice because of problems with the *Zen Dust* printing in Tokyo. It turned out that the paper itself was unsuitable, so the printing run had to be stopped and completely restarted. She said that the new paper was going to cost between $600 and $800, and reflecting on the extremely expensive paper used earlier in the printing for *The Development of Chinese Zen*, she hoped that the new hard-coated paper would stand up to the printing on the second try.

She was starting to think about a printer for the *Rinzai-roku*, and was interested in talking with a printer in Belgium that had done work she liked. She thought that the Belgium printers would be able to print the *Hokoji goroku*, which she was hoping to finish on a trip to Colorado Springs to house-sit for Eleanor and Carlton while they were away. She said that the length of time it took her to put the *Rinzai* manuscript in its final form would determine how much longer she would live in Japan, thinking two years would do it, after which she would plan to move back to the States in 1967.

During 1965 and 1966, many of her close associates and friends

passed away. Former members of the Institute, such as Walter Nowick, were also drifting out of her life completely. The day after
Ruth returned to Kyoto from New York, Goto Roshi died. After all
the ceremonies were over, Walter decided to return to the United
States to his farm in Maine, and he met with Ruth before he left.
Walter had lived in the United States during the past few years, traveling back and forth to Japan while Goto Roshi was still alive.

In June 1965, Ruth wrote that she had put "the last period to
the Index for *Zen Dust*." The next day she received two copies from
the printer of the Japanese edition of *Zen Koan*, and they rushed the
unbound sheets to New York for the Harcourt publication of 1,300
copies scheduled for October. Ruth had hoped that the Japanese edition would be printed by Weatherhill, but in the end she decided to
print the 200 copies of the Japanese edition under the imprint of
the First Zen Institute of America in Japan, keeping the copyright
of the Japanese as well as the American editions in her own name.
They planned on printing 1,500 copies of *Zen Koan* in addition to the
1,000 copies of *Zen Dust*.

Zen Koan had unexpectedly large sales, and Ruth ordered a thousand sets of extra plates so that they could issue more copies of both
Zen Koan and *Zen Dust* on short notice without waiting the extra four
months for clean collotype plates. Ruth was also starting a detailed
itinerary for a trip to Europe to talk with printers in Brussels, The
Hague, and Leiden. She had been leaning toward St. Catherine's (a
Catholic printer), but after having dinner with Paul Demiéville of
Paris, she hoped to talk with Brill in Leiden because they had bought
a new set of Chinese type and were prepared to print scholarly books
on Chinese subjects.

In early January 1966, Kanaseki surprised Ruth by a sudden invitation to his wedding. She was already starting to miss the incredible

help he had been to her; since September 1965, he had been on a Fulbright scholarship to the United States. He was going to teach at Columbia and also take Donald Keene's courses in Japanese literature, which would begin in February 1967. Kanaseki had been a crucial link in her work with Iriya on the *Rinzai* translation, and she was trying hard to figure out how to get Kanaseki to help before he left and after he returned in the summer of 1967.

In April 1966, Ruth and Washino headed for Europe to visit friends and talk with printers about the *Rinzai*. So many foreigners had stopped at Ryosen-an in the past few years that Ruth had many people to visit. Their first stop in Amsterdam included a dinner at the palace with the brother of the king of Denmark, who had visited Ryosen-an in 1965. In Paris, Ruth came down with pneumonia, so she had to skip the London portion while she recovered. They sailed from Le Havre on May 6 for New York.

D. T. Suzuki passed away on July 12, 1966, and Oda Sesso Roshi died on September 16, 1966. A couple of days later, Ruth collapsed in her bath at Ryosen-an. It turned out not to be a stroke but the cumulative result of deep fatigue from her work and her travels. Richard Leavitt, who was working at Ryosen-an as Ruth's secretary at that time, sent a letter to Ruth's assistant in New York, Haru Yoshida, indicating that had it been more severe, it might well have become a stroke. He said that it was the "result of a long and deep fatigue, induced by her recent trip, the lack of any chance to rest during it, and the multitude of problems to be faced here."

Ruth reaffirmed late in 1966 that she would stay in Japan only a few more years. She informed Daitoku-ji that she would be leaving for good in the spring of 1969 and suggested that they consider what to do with Ryosen-an. Oda Sesso Roshi, who was not in the best of health, had retired as the abbot of Daitoku-ji before he passed away in September, and no one yet knew who would be elected.

Ruth was finally able to get up and walk around after her sudden attack six weeks earlier, but it wasn't until late October that she could start typing again. She was pleased when Harcourt wrote her in October saying that they had already sold 500 copies of *Zen Dust*.

In August 1966, Ruth had made advance reservations for herself and Washino to stay at the Kokusai Hotel in Kyoto at night to avoid the damp chill of winter, returning to Ryosen-an during the day to work. Despite her statements that they would take no more students, Ruth said in December that they had accepted three new students, Americans. Dana Fraser, one of the older Ryosen-an students who was then staying at Ryosen-an during the nights, helped them with zazen during the 7 to 9 P.M. sittings in the zendo.

A new kancho for Daitoku-ji was picked, and Ruth explained that he was a roshi from Kyushu, very good, but very frail with tuberculosis, who would only come up to Daitoku-ji for the ceremonies. Ruth was quite pleased that her good friend Fukutomi Isei was elected chief secretary. She said that she and Fukutomi Isei saw "eye to eye" on almost everything. (In May 1967, she said that Fukutomi Isei told her that he would like to be the resident priest at Ryosen-an so that he could clear up relations with Hoshun-in, from whom Ryosen-an rented its land, and get them to return art objects belonging to Ryosen-an that Hoshun-in had had for well over a century.)

In a newsy letter of March 6, 1967, to Irmgard Schloegl, then in London, Ruth described the election politics at Daitoku-ji, with the Fukutomi–Kobori–Shinju-an "crowd" becoming more influential. She wrote, "other splendid plans are afoot about which I cannot say anything as yet. But if these boys accomplish half [of what] they set out to do, there will be an entirely new spirit and life in Daitoku-ji. I had the lot of them over for dinner last Sunday."

In May 1967, Ruth made plans to leave Kyoto for the summer. She said that when she told her coworkers, they seemed pleased: "The English professor wants a long vacation; Iriya wants to work in Nagoya where he has an extra job in a big library there; Furuta has plenty to do here and prefers to do it uninterrupted."

By June, Harcourt had sold all of its copies of *Zen Dust*, and was hoping to get more sent. Another 900 sets of plates were ready for printing (and 30 already complete) and only needed some minor proofing. Harcourt placed an order for 930. Surprisingly, Ruth had still not heard from her coauthor, Miura Roshi, about whether he had received his copies.

On July 25, 1967, Ruth and Washino traveled to Colorado Springs. Ruth had bronchitis and general exhaustion. The Gamers were heading to Europe on vacation, and Ruth and Washino enjoyed some rest (along with the Gamers' two beagles and a dachshund, who showered them with attention). She continued her travels after Colorado Springs, heading to New York on September 12, then on to Europe, before traveling back to Kyoto in mid-October.

At the age of seventy-four, on October 24, 1967, a week before her seventy-fifth birthday, Ruth died suddenly of a heart attack at Ryosen-an. The subsequent funeral ceremony and cremation was a huge event that involved all of those connected with the First Zen Institute in Kyoto and some from New York, her family, and all connected to her through Daitoku-ji. Eleanor's description of the events, as well as comments by Richard Leavitt, reveals the profound cultural differences in memorial services and burial practices in Japan and the United States. Indeed, it was also the end of an era of Japanese cultural practices, since the methods of cremation have changed over the subsequent decades.

Ruth's body was packed in dry ice and covered with banks of flowers, her face still visible, and there were vigils every night until the cremation. Individuals sat for four-hour shifts in the Ryosen-an Library where the coffin was. On Saturday, October 28, the service began in front of the temporary altar, elaborately constructed of fresh green bamboo, surrounding the coffin. A recent photo of Ruth with a black bow attached rested on the coffin, which was draped with her official priest's robes.

It was pouring rain, but dozens of priests and guests sat just outside the open glass-panel sliding doors under awnings, while eulogies were given and incense burned. At the end of the ceremony, all the flower heads were cut off, and people tossed them into the opened coffin. The hearse arrived, and then a smaller group including the three officiating priests, the First Zen Institute board members, Eleanor, Gary Snyder, Richard Leavitt, and a few others followed the hearse to the crematorium up the hill behind Kinkaku-ji.

After the cremation, lasting a little over an hour, a smaller group gathered around the long metal stretchers near the two white porcelain urns. Half of Ruth's ashes were to go to the Woodlawn Cemetery in New York where Sokei-an's ashes were buried, and half were to be buried at Ryosen-an. The American guests did not know that the custom was to pick out the bones with chopsticks, so when they were each handed a pair of chopsticks with a running commentary by the undertaker about the various items that weren't ash, there was shock and disorientation. After the appropriate division of items and ashes into the two urns, the urns were wrapped and packed in boxes to be placed in the tokonoma of Ruth's study at Ryosen-an after sutra chanting and incense burning.

A more public service was conducted a couple of weeks later at the Woodlawn Cemetery in New York when Ruth's ashes arrived there.

In an obituary published in the *Mainichi Daily News*, Iriya was quoted as saying of his sixteen years working with Ruth, "She never compromised in the quest of truth. Our work is now confronted with insurmountable difficulties with the passing of Priest Jokei."

Beyond her obituaries, which include ones written by both Mary Farkas and Irmgard Schloegl, many individuals who knew Ruth have reflected on her contributions, strong presence, and the complexity of her personality and character. Richard Leavitt perhaps summarized best the various comments of those who knew her well. He said, "She was very fair in all her dealings. . . . She was not parsimonious or mean-spirited. She was manipulative for her purposes, of course; but she was never sneaky, malicious, duplicitous, or ungrateful. She was unwavering in her devotion to the memory of Sokei-an and to carrying on the work he had entrusted to her. She was always clear, open and above-board in what she said and did. She helped many people."

There were still ongoing translation projects that continued after Ruth died, resulting in two important books in the following decade. *The Recorded Sayings of Layman P'ang* (*P'ang Chushih Yulu*) came out in 1971, published in Tokyo by Weatherhill. In 1975, *The Recorded Sayings of Ch'an Master Lin-chi Hui-chao of Chen Prefecture* (*Lin-chi lu*) was published in Kyoto by the Institute for Zen Studies.

Fukutomi Isei, then chief secretary of Daitoku-ji, wrote the inscription for Ruth's tomb at Woodlawn (here roughly translated into English):

Tomb of Sokei-an Shigetsu
And Zen Priestess Jokei

Ode on Zen Priestess Jokei composed on her departure
Receiving Sokei's way to spread the true school
   [Sixth Patriarch]
She has sat heroically at the Dragon Spring [Ryosen-an]
For five and seventy turns of the ring of jade
Leaving behind not a speck of dust
In her complete whiteness.
Observe the meaning of the dead leaves [her ashes]
Returning to their original place!
One leaf flying to the West, another
To the East!

>   —Respectfully composed by
>   Isei of Ryosen-an, Daitoku-ji

>   (from Eleanor Gamer's letter
>   dated November 23, 1968)

When Miura Roshi visited the Woodlawn gravesite with Haru
Yoshida, he remarked that Fukutomi Roshi had used Ruth Fuller
Sasaki's real Buddhist name, "Jokei," rather than "Eryu." He said
that the inscription was a capsule of her biography condensed from
Fukutomi Roshi's eulogy.

RYOSEN-AN IS ONCE AGAIN a place for zazen. It is open to foreigners as well as locals who might be interested, for regular periods of sitting in the mornings. There has been a revival of interest in the translation and publication of material that has lain dormant in the library of Ryosen-an for the decades since Ruth died.

Matsunami Taiun Osho, the current priest in charge of Ryosen-an, maintains an open and regular schedule for the zendo. Ryosen-an is still the only place in Daitoku-ji that has a place for foreign visitors who want to experience Zen meditation in the midst of the great Rinzai Zen Temple complex. Even when there are no visitors, Matsunami Osho presides over the small, perfectly sized Ryosen-an Zendo with his resonant sutra chanting. For many years, Ryosen-an was quiet and closed. Now it has become a relaxed and open place for long-term Kyoto residents as well as for short-term visitors.

Photographs of Ruth sit on the butsudan of the zendo as well as in other places at Ryosen-an, wearing her robes and gazing outward. The Western conveniences that she introduced and imported are still operating: the stove and hot water system in the kitchen, the kitchen altar, and other pieces of furnishings and artwork. The library is fairly quiet, but in the past few years a growing interest in some of the unfinished work has drawn scholars to pore over Ruth's notes. Tom Kirchner, from the International Research Institute for the Study of Zen Buddhism at Hanazono University, has been working on a manuscript on the *Rinzai-roku*. Victor Sogen Hori, professor at McGill University and longtime friend of fellow Zen priest Matsunami Osho, has used the resources of Ruth's work in the library for his recently published book, *Zen Sand*, a masterful continuation and completion of the history and use of the jakugo for koan study that Ruth and the research team had begun.

Matsunami Osho traveled widely in the United States and Europe in the early 1970s and has been a colleague and teacher at the Trappist Abbey in Lafayette, Oregon, in Zen meditation practice. He also visited the Zen monasteries connected with Joshu Sasaki Roshi (no relation to Ruth) in New Mexico and California. He regularly travels to Europe to give instruction in Zen meditation practice, including summers in Switzerland and Germany. Fukutomi Settei Roshi, a temple lineage heir of Fukutomi Isei, with whom Ruth was close friends, became the kancho of Daitoku-ji, and after retirement, he has stayed at Ryosen-an on his visits to Kyoto. He met Ruth when he was a younger priest and has fond memories of her and of his teacher's high esteem for her.

I have stayed in the library at Ryosen-an on my visits, unrolling my futon and settling my pillow in the library where the ghosts of Ruth, the research team, and the visitors float under the same ceiling lamps that lit the evenings for them several decades earlier. Descendants of Ruth's cats purr in the armchair as I make tea and browse through the somewhat dusty books and card catalogs.

I assist with the early morning chores, weeding the grass seedlings out of the moss gardens, fighting the mosquitoes, settling in to analyze the files and folders left behind. I inventory Ruth's collection of personal books, not fitting for the library shelves, but an interesting mix of cookbooks, fiction, and nonfiction, many of them signed by the authors to their friend Ruth—packed away in boxes with no purpose except a reluctance to get rid of them.

I muse over the notes Ruth wrote in the margins of some of the books on the library shelves, and her strong opinions of various books that were published in the 1950s and 1960s that did not find their way into book reviews, opinions that those who knew her have commented on.

Ruth and books: she loved them and struggled with them. They have made her a household name among Zen students in subsequent years, for *Zen Koan* at the very least, even though there is little awareness of who she was or what part she played in the development of Zen in the West.

She knew she was part of a historical movement, and that her role in it was unique and remarkable. Based on what I've read of Ruth's many writings and correspondence, I believe that Ruth didn't have a clear sense of how she *didn't* fit into the categories of those who traditionally have carried Zen forward—she was not a teacher with a lineage, although she definitely had a lineage of Zen teachers that shaped her, and she strongly resisted the role of a Zen nun in a more traditional and subservient hierarchy. She preferred instead to have the honor of being an abbot tempered by the conditions of an American woman with other concerns and obligations on her mind and in her heart. She never shaved her head as do most Zen nuns, and she always wore earrings, which seemed an anomaly to many who met her.

Some thought she was too attached to her American cultural customs to enter fully into the Japanese Zen experience of leading Ryosen-an. Others have felt, in looking back at the fifties and sixties, that she had a strong sense of herself and what she was bringing to the enterprise, that she melded a respect for the traditional Japanese Zen culture with an understanding of herself as an American individualist, bringing the best strengths of her own style and character to the work at hand. Either perspective reflects well on her lifetime of observing, reflecting, and acting in ways that influenced scores of people who came into contact with her or with publications she had a hand in creating.

Irmgard Schloegl remarked after Ruth died that she was a "fundamentally warm-hearted person with her feet planted on the earth." Traces of Ruth's impact on Zen authors of the time are reflected in D. T. Suzuki's preface to the third series of *Essays in Zen Buddhism (1933)*, and in Alan Watts's dedication to her in a wonderful short book he wrote in 1948, called *Zen*. American Zen Center teisho and newsletters in the past decades (such as the Mount Baldy Zen Center) have used as their subject matter material from the books published as a result of Ruth and her research team's translation work.

The threads of Ruth Fuller Sasaki are woven through the subsequent years of Japanese, American, and European Zen centers and zendos, in anecdotes and in published works. The resulting fabric is a tribute to the energy, character, and contributions of this remarkable woman.

PART TWO: HER WORK

ZEN:
A RELIGION

by Ruth Fuller Sasaki

NEW YORK, THE FIRST ZEN INSTITUTE
OF AMERICA, INC., 1958

I SHOULD LIKE TO SPEAK a little about Zen as a religion. For, above everything else, Zen is a religion. Since Zen began to be known in the West, various aspects of it have been emphasized and various elements in its teachings stressed—Zen is a kind of nature mysticism; Zen is a kind of existentialism; Zen is a kind of mental therapy; Zen is a discipline in which blows and conundrums are used as teaching devices; Zen advocates a humble, retired mode of life, the main activity of which is the practice of meditation; Zen aims at the attainment of *satori*[1] and with satori comes total knowledge and understanding; Zen is everyday life; Zen is complete freedom; the man who has attained the aim of Zen, that is, satori, is beyond law, beyond the regulations laid down for human society.

While these statements cannot be said to be totally incorrect, each taken by itself gives but a fragmentary and distorted view of what Zen really is, and all miss what, to my mind, is the fundamental aim and meaning of Zen.

Fundamentally Zen is a religion. Whatever other qualities or aspects it may have, all derive from or are by-products of the particular kind of religion Zen is. But a religion Zen certainly is, and of first importance in knowing something about Zen is to know it as a religion.

I shall not try to define the term "religion." Discussions on that subject still go on and, like most discussions, arrive at no final answer satisfactory to everyone concerned. If, however, you demand of a religion that it have a God external to the universe and man; if you demand that it have a uniquely revealed scripture in which there must be an individual soul that exists throughout all eternity and eventually comes to reside either in eternal bliss in a heaven, or in eternal damnation in a hell; if you believe in sin that can be washed away by the sacrifice of another, or salvation that can be attained through a savior, then for you Zen will not be a religion and Zen will not be for you.

And here I should like to define what I am speaking about when I use the word "Zen." The word Zen has been used to connote many things. At the expense of being called ultra-traditional and authoritarian, I prefer to apply it, for the moment at least, to that sect of Buddhism developed in China, of which Bodhidharma is traditionally considered to be the founder, and to the teachings of this sect.

Though, as its name indicates, the Zen Sect emphasizes meditation and is sometimes even called the Meditation Sect, the fundamental core of Zen, as of all Buddhism, Hinayana[2] or Mahayana,[3] is what is usually termed "enlightenment." There are several words used to denote this experience of enlightenment. Sokei-an[4] preferred the English word "awakening." In Japanese it is known as *satori*, a word now gradually coming into English usage. Rinzai[5] called it "true understanding" or "true comprehension."[6] Another word, dating from Bodhidharma's time, is *kensho*,[7] "seeing into one's own true nature."

When Shakamuni Buddha attained his Highest Perfect Awakening he manifested the fundamental principle of the religion which he was later to develop. And when, after some inner struggle, symbolized by his conversation with the god Brahma, he determined to reveal his experience to all men and thus show them how they might attain release from sorrow and suffering, he demonstrated the natural corollary of enlightenment and took the first step toward making his experience the pivot of a world religion.

For the Hinayana or, more precisely, the Theravada schools, the main aim is the attainment of individual enlightenment. For this reason men and women leave their homes to become monks and nuns, believing that in the monastic life they will find the best opportunity to accomplish this aim. The role of the lay believer in Hinayana Buddhism is largely that of sustaining the clergy who are actively seeking this enlightenment, and by thus doing to lay up for himself merit which, in some future life, will permit him to retire from the world and seek Nirvana for himself.

For the Mahayana schools, one's own enlightenment and the assisting of others to attain their enlightenment are two aspects of the one fundamental principle. Self-awakening must be attained first, but just self-awakening is not sufficient. The luminousness of the experience of awakening must be shed abroad for all men to share in. Awakening itself cannot be given to anyone by another, but the awakened man can and must assist others on their path toward the goal, otherwise he has not understood the full import of his experience. This is the role of the Bodhisattva, stressed in the Mahayana schools. To me, Shakamuni Buddha is the perfect example of the complete Buddhist teaching—the Buddha, the Perfectly Awakened One, whose aim was not to attain enlightenment for himself, but to solve the problem of human suffering, and whose life after his enlightenment was for forty-nine years devoted to showing others how they might solve this problem for themselves. It is interesting to note that one of the favorite subjects in Zen *sumi* or black ink paintings is Shakamuni coming down from the mountain, the mountain-top representing his awakening and his coming down from the mountain-top his return to the everyday world.

For most of the Mahayanist schools one further characteristic must be mentioned. That is, that any man, whether he become a monk or remain a layman, may attain this awakening. The layman's role is not merely that of sustaining the clergy and laying up merit through good deeds. That he must do, but even in the midst of his everyday life, if he exert himself to that end, he also can attain enlightenment.

That this summary characterization of the two divisions of Buddhism is inadequate, I am quite well aware. But if you will keep it in mind, you will have a useful, though brief, guide for distinguishing them.

Zen, perhaps even more than other Mahayana sects, stresses the importance of awakening for the layman and makes available to him all the teaching and discipline it affords the monk. One of the names most honored in Zen is that of the Indian layman Vimalakirti of Vaisali, known in Japan as Yuimakitsu or Yuima.[8] Yuima takes his place on an equal footing with all the great figures of monastic Zen. Both in China and Japan during the course of the centuries, many great laymen have appeared in Zen history. Among them, for instance, Fu Daishi[9] of the 6th century, known as the inventor of the revolving bookcase. Another well-known person is the layman Ho[10] of the T'ang dynasty, a disciple of the early Chinese Zen masters Baso[11] and Sekito.[12] The fact that Zen considers the layman as well as the priest a candidate for satori and offers its teaching and discipline to both without discrimination is one of the several reasons why, in my opinion, among Buddhist sects Zen is particularly suited for American and European people.

Most of you have heard of or read the famous verse descriptive of Zen attributed to Bodhidharma which begins with the line: "A separate transmission outside the scriptures; not established on words or phrases."[13] By many people in the past, and in the present as well, these lines have been taken to mean that Zen has no doctrine and no relationship to the scriptures. The Sixth Patriarch,[14] who is said to have been an illiterate seller of kindling wood, is held up as the most illustrious example of this premise. The study of the lives of the great men of Zen demolishes this thesis, however. I have yet, in my own studies, to find one who, either before or after his attainment, has not zealously studied one or more of the traditional Buddhist sutras, or scriptures, and who in his writings or talks did not quote from them freely. All had a thorough grounding in basic Buddhist doctrines as they were taught in their times. Bodhidharma is said to have handed the *Lankavatara-sutra*[15] to his heir Eka Daishi,[16] saying that this sutra was the statement of his teaching. The *Vimalakirti*,[17] the *Mahaprajnaparamita*,[18] the *Vajracchedika*,[19] the *Nirvana*,[20] and even the abstruse *Avatamsaka*[21] were among those known to and studied by Zen men. This is not to say that from their study of the sutras they attained their enlightenment. Enlightenment stands by itself. It is not dependent upon the sutras, any sutras. Enlightenment is the awakening of man's own true mind, it is his own seeing into his own true nature. When that fact is established, however, Zen does not deny the value of scriptures, does not throw them into the trash can. In the scriptures the enlightened man finds the attempts of others to describe or elucidate in words the experience of awakening, to probe in words the experience of awakening, to probe the implications lying within awakening, and he, in his turn, finds his own awakening to be the key to the understanding of the sutras. Many of the Mahayana sects were founded upon the teachings of one or more sutras: for instance, the Sanron,[22] the Tendai,[23] the Shingon,[24] the Jodo[25] sects. Zen is founded upon no sutra, as Bodhidharma said. It takes no written words as the foundation of its teaching and its discipline. Its priests in the past and today do not give lectures in commentary upon the traditional Buddhist scriptures. The lectures, or *teisho*[26] as they are called in Japanese, given by Zen masters to their monks and students, are lectures upon the recorded sayings and writings of Chinese and Japanese Zen masters of the past. But though the traditional non-Zen scriptures are not used as the basis for lectures, many are daily chanted in whole or in part in Zen monasteries and temples and studied today by Zen monks in Zen colleges and universities before they enter the monasteries, or after they have completed their Zen study and discipline, or both.

One of the last and greatest Mahayana scriptures to be brought from India to China was that known, under its Sanskrit name, as the *Avatamsaka-sutra*. Upon the teachings of this sutra there developed in China a great school of Buddhism, known in Chinese as the *Hua-yen*, in Japanese as the *Kegon*, school.[27] In this school Chinese Mahayana Buddhism reached the apex of its development. The Hua-yen school, as a school, was short-lived. Perhaps its doctrines were too profound and abstruse for it to become popular with the general public. And support of the general public, though this public has little comprehension of the real teachings, is essential for the existence of any religious sect. But the doctrines and philosophy of the Hua-yen entered into and became an important part of those of other Chinese Buddhist sects. The teachings of this sect reached Japan during the Nara period, when they were embraced by the

Emperor Shomu.[28] The temple in Nara known as Todai-ji,[29] which shelters the Great Sun Buddha, the largest of the bronze Buddha images in Japan, was built by the Emperor Shomu to be the sanctuary of the Kegon doctrines and the headquarters of the Kegon sect in Japan. But in Japan, as in China, Kegon as a sect or school did not flourish long or widely. Today, though only Todai-ji and perhaps twelve other temples belonging to the Kegon sect still remain active, the philosophy and doctrines of Kegon still constitute one of the major studies in all the Buddhist schools and universities of Japan.

The Kegon philosophy and doctrines formed a magnificent structure, immense in conception and intricate in detail. From them Zen has taken and made its own use of one concept, that of the Fourfold Universe.[30] According to Kegon teaching, the universe in which we live is a fourfold universe and is to be observed or, better, realized under four aspects. The subject is somewhat technical, but I shall try to be as simple in my statement of it as my understanding permits.

The total universe—earth, sky, sun, moon, planets, stars, infinite space—is known in Buddhist-Sanskrit terminology as the *Dharmadhatu*,[31] in Japanese as the *hokkai*. The word *dhatu*, Japanese *kai*, means "field" or "realm," and the word *Dharma*, Japanese *ho*, has two meanings: the Absolute Truth and also the individual elements which constitute the universe. So the *Dharmadhatu*, the *hokkai*, is the "Realm of Absolute Truth" and also the "Realm of All Elements."

Kegon and Zen, as I have said, observe this *Dharmadhatu* or *hokkai* in four ways:

First it is observed as the actual world in which we live every day, the world of phenomena. The universe under this aspect is termed *ji hokkai*[32] in Japanese. *Ji* means "things," "phenomena." So this first way of observing the universe is as the world of things, the actual, factual world, the phenomenal world as such. Of this world as it appears to us ordinary men, Zen at first has nothing to say. Later, however, when we are prepared to understand its real nature, we shall have to make a thorough investigation of its every phase.

The second way of viewing the *hokkai*—and when I use the English word viewing or observing, it is always with the deeper meaning of realizing—is as the Absolute World, the world of Reality. The world under this aspect is termed the *ri hokkai*,[33] the Realm of the Absolute Principle. This is the undifferentiated world, the world of complete Oneness, Emptiness, Sunyata. To enter this world, to realize this world, and to make this world our permanent abiding place, the place where we stand, this is the *sine qua non* for the Zen student. This is the world entered by many artists and mystics, and by people who go through some personal religious experience, the world of cosmic consciousness, as it is sometimes called. I was interested to read some time ago the following quotation from the famous European art critic Berenson: "It was a morning in early summer. A silver haze shimmered and trembled over the lime trees. The air was laden with a caress. I remember . . . that I climbed a tree stump and felt suddenly immersed in Itness. I did not call it by that name. I had no need for words. It and I were one." In this world the individual self or ego vanishes. One becomes merged with, one with, the Great Self. Too often, unfortunately, this vision fades with time and is forgotten, its profound significance never penetrated or understood. But when this realization is completely achieved, never again can one feel that one's individual death brings an end to life. One has lived from an endless past and will live into an endless future. The problems of heaven and hell, of individual sin and individual salvation, are ended once and for all. At this very moment one partakes of Eternal Life— blissful, luminous, pure. This experience is salvation in Zen.

It is this world that we wish to enter into when we begin our Zen studies. The first koans given to the Zen student—Joshu's "Mu,"[34] Hakuin's "Sound of the Single Hand,"[35] the Sixth Patriarch's "Before your father and mother were born, what was your original face?"[36]—these are the koans, penetration into which will lead us through the Gateless Barrier into the Absolute World, the Realm of the Absolute Principle, the *ri hokkai*. But since a first satori is often merely a glimpse into this world, a getting of one's foot inside the gate, as it were, the Zen student studies many koans in order that this world may become a never extinguished reality to him.

But we live and function in the everyday world, the phenomenal world, the world of relativity, the world of separated things. Of this Zen is well aware. The next step is to bring us to the realization that noumenon and phenomena, the Absolute and the relative, are but two aspects of the one Reality. Therefore, when the Zen student has thoroughly realized the *ri hokkai*, the world as the Realm of the Absolute, he is asked, *standing in the Absolute*, to look again at the relative, phenomenal world which he previously believed to be the only world.

This, the third way of viewing the universe, is that known as the realization of the universe as the *riji muge hokkai*,[37] that is, the world in which the Absolute and the particular, the noumenal and the phenomenal, the Principle and the manifested are realized to be completely harmonized and united. The particular, the relative, the phenomenal, the manifested, are but the aspect under which we observe the noumenon, the Absolute, the Principle. The actual words *riji muge hokkai* translated literally mean: *ri* "Principle," *ji* "things," *mu* "without," *ge* "hindrance" or "obstruction." That is, the Absolute and the relative completely interpenetrate one another without any obstruction or hindrance. Or, to use another term, they are completely united. In truth, they are one and the same thing.

When we attain this realization we come to know everything in the world about us, every tree, every rock, every star, every bit of dust and dirt, every insect, every animal, every person, including ourselves, *as they are* to be a manifestation of the Absolute, and every function performed by every one of these as the functioning of the Absolute. Every existing thing, sentient or non-sentient, is holy in essence. From this realization arises the certainty that everything and everyone, no matter how lowly or how depraved, intrinsically is Buddha, is destined for salvation, will ultimately realize Buddhahood.

But there is a still more profound realization to be attained. This is known as the realization of the *jiji muge hokkai*,[38] the realization of the realm of the completely harmonious and unobstructed interpenetration and interconvertibility of all things with one another. *Ji*, we know, means "things," so *jiji* means "things and things"; *muge* means "without hindrance," "without obstruction." So the *jiji muge hokkai* is the realm in which all things, which we have already come to realize as the Absolute manifested, together form one complete and total whole by means of harmonious and unobstructed penetration, interconvertibility, and identification with each other. The realization of the *jiji muge hokkai* is the realization that everything in the universe is constantly and continuously, freely and harmoniously interpenetrating, interconverting itself with every other thing. It is the realization of the universe as the expression of the eternal self-recreating play of the Absolute. Thus experienced, the universe is seen to be one in time and one in space, or, rather, to be timeless and spaceless.

When my teacher was speaking to me about this he said: "Now think about yourself. You think you are a separate and independent individual. But you are not. Without your father and mother you would not be. Without their fathers and mothers they would not have been and you would not be. And without their fathers and mothers, your fathers and mothers would not have been. And so we can go back endlessly to the origin of the human race and before that and before that. You, at this moment, are the apex of the great triangle formed by all these previous individual lives. In you they all exist today. They live in you today as truly as they lived individually in what we call time.

"But, in addition, just as you live today by virtue of all the other individuals and existences in the world at this moment—your body is sustained by the food cultivated and processed by innumerable persons throughout the present world, your body is covered by clothing produced by innumerable persons throughout the present world, your activities are conditioned by the activities of innumerable persons living in the present world, your thinking is conditioned by the thinking of innumerable persons living in the present world—so the bodies, the actions, the thinking of all your ancestors who form the great triangle of which you are the present apex, have in their turn been dependent upon and conditioned by the innumerable persons existing in the world at the time they individually lived. So, if we consider that all past time is concentrated in you at this moment, we must also consider that all past space is also concentrated in you at this moment. Therefore you and every other being in the world at this instant actually each stand at the apex of a great cone rather than a triangle.

"But this is not all. From you will come your children and their children's children; from your actions will come the results of your actions and the results of those results; and from your thoughts will come the future thinking and the thinking resulting from that thinking, *ad infinitum*. You hold within yourself the seed from which the future will spring. Just as much as you at this moment are the entirety of past time, so you are the entirety of future time. Just as you at this moment represent the concentration of all past space, so you at this moment represent the concentration of all space in the future. And this is true for each sentient or non-sentient existence in the universe. In you and in each one of them at this moment is all time and all space. In other words, this moment is all."

Kegon and Zen each have their own symbols for illustrating this *jiji muge hokkai*. In Kegon the symbol used is known as Indra's net. It is described as being a great net extending throughout the universe, vertically to represent time, horizontally to represent space. At each point where the threads of the net cross one another is a crystal bead, the symbol of a single existence. Each crystal bead reflects on its shining surface not only every other bead in the net but every re- flection of every other bead upon each individual bead—countless, endless reflections of one another.

For the Zen Sect, when Shakamuni held up the single lotus flower before the assembly he was showing the *jiji muge hokkai*, he was manifesting the totality of the universe in time and space, he was illustrating the complete and harmonious interpenetration of all things with each other, he was expounding his complete teaching in its minutest detail and demonstrating its most profound and mys- terious principle: that each single existence is the totality of Life, beginningless, endless, ever self-creating, Infinite Life.

That is what we are. That is what you are, that is what I am, that is what everything in the universe is—beginningless, endless Life, infinite, boundless, eternal Life. This is what we must realize. And to this realization Zen practice leads us step by step. This is the aim of Zen. This is true satori.

When we first enter the great and wondrous world of the *Dharma-dhatu* we are like babies who open their eyes for the first time to the world they are to live in. In the beginning they can distinguish little, but gradually their eyes make out the form of the mother's breast, the bed, the room, the playthings. Just so, when with our first awakening we push open the gate and enter the Absolute World, we can at first distinguish little about it. But gradually, with our Dharma-eye, as it is called in Zen, we come to see more and more clearly. That is why a first satori is not enough, why Zen study must continue, and continue. And though our formal Zen study may reach its conclusion, real Zen study never ends. For Zen study is the ever continuing and deepening realization of this one ever-renewing-itself Eternal Life.

As a matter of fact, Zen goes one step farther than the realization of the fourth view of Kegon. The last step in Zen is what may be called "the return to the natural." Though we may have realized the *jiji muge hokkai*, we must now demonstrate our realization in the practice of our everyday life, whatever that everyday life may be. If we must wash dishes, we wash dishes; if we must be the president of a country, we are the president of a country; if we must teach, we teach; if we must be students, we are students. But as we wash dishes, as we act as president, as we teach, as we study, we know that this act is a holy act, an act indispensable to the total universe; upon its being done and done when and as it must be done the entire future of all existences depends. Then, as our realization becomes deeper and more profound, when we have thoroughly digested and assimilated it, as it were, we do not need to think about the philosophic or religious implications of our activities. Naturally and spontaneously we respond to the moment. Without thinking about anything we naturally act. This is the "freedom" of Zen. This is also what is known as "having no thing in the mind and no mind in things."[39] This is the ultimate in the Zen way of life. It is then only that we may say with Master Nansen, "The everyday mind is Tao."[40]

Such understanding as this is the true enlightenment of Zen, the way to which Shakamuni blazed the trail. Now we are prepared to carry out the implications of this enlightenment—our responsibilities to others. These responsibilities to others are envisaged in Zen under three aspects, three important attitudes, which make of Zen a complete religion. They are infinite gratitude to all beings in the past, infinite gratitude and infinite service to all beings in the present, and infinite responsibility to all beings in the future. Not that we should wait for true enlightenment before undertaking these responsibilities. From the beginning they are ours. But since we can fulfill them only in so far as we have wisdom or understanding, Zen emphasizes the necessity for our attaining complete awakening in order that we may carry out these responsibilities with fully enlightened wisdom. In no Mahayana school is love or compassion alone sufficient. Wisdom must be pervaded with compassion, but just as truly must compassion be pervaded with wisdom.

Therefore the Zennist each morning stands before his Buddha-shrine with his hands in reverent greeting and, for a moment, awarely realizes his oneness with the Real World, then silently offers his gratitude to Shakamuni Buddha, who made this teaching known to us of this time, to all the Buddhas of the past and the present, to his ancestors, to all the members of the Buddha's Great Sangha, that is, to all beings who have ever existed and are existing, and reminds himself of his responsibility to the present and the future by repeating the Four Vows:

> Sentient beings are numberless;
> I take a vow to save them all.
> Delusions are inexhaustible;
> I take a vow to destroy them all.
> The gates of Dharma are manifold;
> I take a vow to enter them all.
> The Buddha-way is supreme;
> I take a vow to complete it.[41]

And when his morning meal is served, he offers reverent and grateful thanks to the lower forms of life that are giving their lives that his body may be nourished and sustained, and again vows that, in gratitude to them for their sacrifice, he will strive his best to carry out the Four Vows he has taken.

This is the Buddhist life and the Zen life, as I understand it; a life lived in full realization of who we really are and what this world we live in really is; a life lived simply, naturally, spontaneously, and awarely; a life dedicated to infinite gratitude to the past, infinite gratitude and service to the present, and infinite responsibility to the future. Such a life is truly a religious life, and toward such a life Zen teaching and discipline lead us. Yes, truly, Zen is a religion.

NOTES

1. 悟, Ch. *wu*: Enlightenment or Awakening.
2. 小乘, J. *shojo*; Ch. *hsiao-ch'eng*: The "Lesser Vehicle," the name given to the form of Buddhism which after Shakamuni's death developed on strictly orthodox lines; also known as Southern Buddhism. It is represented today by the Buddhism of Ceylon, Burma, and Siam.

3. 大乘, J. *daijo*; Ch. *ta-ch'eng*: the "Greater Vehicle," the name given to developed Buddhism, also known as Northern Buddhism. It is the Buddhism of Tibet, China, Mongolia, Korea, and Japan today.

4. Sasaki Sokei-an Roshi, founder of the First Zen Institute of America.

5. 臨濟, Ch. Lin-chi (d. 867), founder of the Rinzai Sect of Zen. For his life and teachings see Dumoulin and Sasaki, *The Development of Chinese Zen* (New York: The First Zen Institute of America, 1953), pp. 20–24.

6. 真正見解, J. *shinsho no kenge*; Ch. *chen-cheng chien-chieh*.

7. 見性, Ch. *chien-hsing*.

8. 維摩詰 or 維摩, Ch. Wei-mo-chieh or Wei-mo.

9. 傳大士, Ch. Fu Ta-shih (497–569).

10. 龐居士, Ch. P'ang Chu-shih (d. 813?). He sank his wealth in Tung-t'ing Lake 洞庭湖 (J. Doteiko) and became a maker of bamboo baskets, wandering from place to place with his family and visiting the great Zen masters of his time, with whom he held witty and profound conversations. His conversations and poems are contained in the *Ho koji goroku* 龐居士語錄, Ch. *P'ang chu-shih yu-lu*.

11. 馬祖道一, Ch. Ma-tsu Tao-i (d. 788).

12. 石頭希遷, Ch. Shih-t'ou His-ch'ien (700–790).

13. 教外別傳, 不立文字, J. *kyoge betsuden, furyu monji*; Ch. *chiao-wai pieh-ch'uan, pu-li wen-tzu*.

14. 六祖, J. Rokuso; Ch. Liu-tsu (638–713). Also known as Eno Daishi 慧能大師, Ch. Hui-neng ta-shih. He was the real founder of Chinese Zen, from whom all the major Zen schools of China and Japan trace their descent. For the story of his life as recorded in the *Keitoku dento roku* 景德傳燈錄, Ch. *Ching-te ch'uan-teng lu*, see "The Transmission of the Lamp," *Cat's Yawn* (New York: The First Zen Institute of America, 1947), pp. 22, 26, 30, 34, 38, 42.

15. 愣伽經, J. *Ryoga kyo*; Ch. *Leng-chia ching*; Engl. transl., *The Lankavatara Sutra*, translated by Daisetz Teitaro Suzuki (London: Routledge and Kegan Paul Ltd., 1956); the same, edited by Dwight Goddard, *A Buddhist Bible*, ed. by Dwight Goddard (2nd ed., rev. and enl., New York: E. P. Dutton and Co., Inc., 1952), pp. 277–356.

16. 慧可大師, Ch. Hui-k'o ta-shih. For the story of his life from the *Zoku koso den* 續高僧傳 Ch. *Hsu kao-seng chuan*, see "The Transmission of the Lamp," *Cat's Yawn*, p. 10.

17. 維摩經, J. *Yuima kyo*; Ch. *Wei-mo ching*, a sutra which consists largely of

conversations between Vimalakirti and various Bodhisattvas and disciples of the Buddha. Engl. transl., "Vimalakirti's Discourse on Emancipation," translated by Hokei Idzumi, *The Eastern Buddhist*, Vol. III (1924-25), pp. 55-69, 138-153, 224-242, 336-349; Vol. IV (1926, 27, 28), pp. 48-55, 177-190, 348-366.

18. 大般若波羅密多經, J. *Dai hannya haramitta kyo*; Ch. *T'a pan-jo po-lo-mi-to ching*; "Great Perfection Wisdom Sutra." A great body of sutras described as discourses delivered by Shakamuni on the Vulture Peak and other places, and devoted to an exposition of the doctrine of the Void or Sunyata. The most famous translation from the original Sanskrit into Chinese is the 600-volume version made by Genjo 玄奘, Ch. Hsuan-tsang. The short *Hannyashin gyo* 般若心經, Ch. *Pan-jo-hsin ching*; "Heart of the Perfection of Wisdom," is said to be an epitome of the 600-volume sutra. For an Engl. transl. of the *Hannya*, see Daisetz Teitaro Suzuki, *Manual of Zen Buddhism* (Kyoto: Eastern Buddhist Society, 1935), pp. 27-32.

19. 金剛經, J. *Kongo kyo*; Ch. *Chin-kang ching*; "The Diamond Sutra," a short scripture within the Mahaprajna-paramita sutra. There are several English translations, among them, from the Chinese, *The Diamond Sutra*, translated by Wai Tao, in Goddard, *op. cit.*, pp. 87-107; *The Diamond Sutra*, translated by William Gemmell (London: Kegan Paul, Trench, Trubner and Co., Ltd., 1912).

20. 大般涅槃經, J. *Dai hatsunehan kyo*; Ch. *Ta pannieh-p'an ching*; "The Sutra of the Great Decease." This is a Mahayana sutra, and is not to be confused with the sutra of the same name belonging to the Hinayana Canon. It contains discourses said to have been given by Shakamuni just before his death. There are three versions in Chinese, but no part of this sutra has, to my knowledge, been translated into English.

21. 華嚴經, J. *Kegon kyo*; Ch. *Hua-yen ching*. The title is generally translated as "The Wreath (or Garland) Sutra." Goto Roshi reads *gon* 嚴 as meaning "dignity" or "majesty," and *Kegon* as "Flower (i.e., the lotus) Dignity." He interprets the title as the name of the state of he who has realized the sutra, that is, such a man has the dignity or majesty of the lotus flower. There are three versions of this sutra of varying lengths in the Chinese Canon. None have been translated into English, though D. T. Suzuki has written several essays on that version known as the *Gandhavyuha*, which appear in his *Essays in Zen Buddhism*, *Third Series* (London: Luzac and Company, 1934). The

sutra is represented as being a sermon or sermons preached by Shakamuni immediately after his enlightenment and containing his complete doctrine as he had experienced it in his Great Awakening.

22. 三論宗, Ch. San-lun tsung; "The Three Treatise School." It was founded upon the *Madhyamika sastra* (J. *Chu ron* 中論, Ch. *Chung lun*; "Treatise on the Mean") and the *Dvadasa-dvara sastra* (J. *Junimon ron* 十二門論, Ch. *Shih-erh-men lun*; "Treatise on the Twelve Gates"), both attributed to Nagarjuna (J. *Ryuju* 龍樹, Ch. Lung-shu), and the *Sata Sastra* (J. *Hyaku ron* 百論, Ch. *Po lun*; "The One Hundred Verse Treatise") by Aryadeva (J. Daiba 提婆, Ch. T'I-p'o). The school was founded in the 5th century by Soro 僧朗, Ch. Seng-lang, and developed during the 6th century by Horo 法朗, Ch. Fa-lang (507–581), Kichizo 吉藏, Ch. Chi-tsang (549–623), and others. J. Takakusu, in his *Essentials of Buddhist Philosophy* (Honolulu: University of Hawaii, 1947), describes the school as one of "negative idealism."

23. 天台宗, Ch. T'ien-t'ai tsung, named for the mountain in southern China which was its headquarters. Its basic text was the *Saddharama-pundarika-sutra* (J. *Myoho renge kyo* 妙法蓮華經, Ch. *Miao-fa lien-hua ching*), in Japan more often shortened to *Hokke kyo* 法華經, Ch. *Fa-hua ching*. In English it is known as "The Lotus Sutra," or "The Lotus of the True Law." The classic English translation is that from the Sanskrit: *The Saddharma-Pundarika* or *The Lotus of the True Law*, translated by H. Kern, Sacred Books of the East, Vol. XXI (Oxford: Clarendon Press, 1909). Its most famous exponent was Chigi 智顗, Ch. Chih-i (538–597), founder of the Chinese T'ien-t'ai Sect and probably the finest of all Chinese Buddhist scholars. The doctrine admits of graduated truth being contained in the various Mahayana scriptures, but contends that the final and complete truth is revealed only in the *Lotus Sutra*. The ultimate teachings of the sect, as described by Takakusu (*op. cit.*), is that "there is no noumenon besides phenomenon; phenomenon itself is noumenon."

Dengyo Daishi 傳教大師 (767–822), founder of Japanese Tendai, during his stay in China, studied the Vinaya (J. *ritsu* 律, Ch. *lu*), Shingon (眞言 Ch. Chen-yen) mysticism, and Zen, in addition to Tendai, and incorporated various elements from these into his teachings. The headquarters of Japanese Tendai on Mount Hiei near Kyoto, together with its numerous sub-temples, is still in a fairly flourishing state.

24. 眞言宗 Ch. Chen-yen tsung; "True Word Sect." The major text of this school is the *Mahavairocana-sutra* (J. *Dainichi kyo* 大日經, Ch. *Ta-jih ching*; "The Great

Sun Sutra"). The esoteric doctrines and practices of the sect, brought from India to China by several teachers during the 7th and 8th centuries, seem to have had some relation to Tantrism and Tibetan Buddhism. These were combined and systematized by the Japanese priest Kobo Daishi 弘法大師 (774–835), who had studied in China under the last of the Indian teachers. Kobo Daishi's headquarters on Mount Koya, some distance southeast of Osaka, still flourishes as the main center for the mystic doctrine. According to this teaching, the entire universe is the manifestation of the Great Sun Buddha. By the recitation of mantras (esoteric words or phrases), use of mudras (esoteric hand positions and movements), and mystical concentration, man can perfect communion with Buddha and thus attain Buddhahood in this life.

25. 淨土宗 Ch. Ching-t'u tsung; "The Pure Land Sect." It has three basic texts: the large and small *Sukhavati-vyuha sutras* (J. *Daimuryoju kyo* 大無量壽經, Ch. *Ta-wu-liang-shou ching*, and the J. *Amida kyo* 阿彌陀經 Ch. *A-mi-t'ou ching*) and the *Amitayur-dhyana sutra* (J. *Kammuryoju kyo* 阿彌陀經, Ch. *Kuan-wu-liang-shou ching*). English translations of these are: "The Larger Sukavati-vyuha" and "The Smaller Sukavati-vyuha," translated by F. Max Muller, and "The Amitayur-Dhyana Sutra," translated by J. Takakusu in *Buddhist Mahayana Texts*, Part II, Sacred Books of the East, Vol. XLIX (Oxford: Clarendon Press, 1894).

Several lines of transmission of Amida doctrines came into China between the 4th and 8th centuries with Indian teachers or Chinese monks who had studied in India. The main tenet of the Pure Land School is that birth into the Pure Land, or the Western Heaven, over which the Buddha Amitabha or Amida, to use his Japanese name, presides, and ultimately the attainment of Buddhahood, can be gained through perfect faith in the saving grace of Amida Buddha and the repetition of his name. "A strain of Amida pietism," to use Takakusu's phrase, has run through almost all sects of Chinese Buddhism. Today the main exponents of this school in Japan are the Jodo ("Pure Land") Sect, founded by Honen Shonin 法然 上人 (1133–1212) and the Jodo Shinshu ("True Sect of the Pure Land"), founded by Honen's disciple Shinran Shonin 親鸞聖人 (1173–1262), the former emphasizing the necessity of both faith and the repetition of Amida's name, the latter of faith alone. Jodo Shinshu is the most flourishing of all present-day Buddhist sects in Japan.

26. 提唱, Ch. *T'i-ch'ang*.

27. 華嚴宗, Ch. Hua-yen tsung. It was founded by Tojun 杜順, Ch. Tu-shun (557–640), and its doctrines and philosophy were developed and systematized by its third patriarch Hozo 法藏, Ch. Fa-tsang (643–712). For a detailed exposition of the tenets of this important sect of Chinese Buddhism, see Takakusu, *op. cit.*, pp. 108–125. Hozo was a famous and brilliant cleric. Once, when he was ordered to lecture on Kegon doctrines before the Empress Wu 武后 (J. Bu Ko) of T'ang, to illustrate the Brahmajala or Indra's Net doctrine (cf. p. 17 of the text), he had a single candle placed in the center of the palace hall and around the room tens of mirrors arranged in such a way that, when the candle was lit, the Empress saw not only its reflection in each individual mirror but also the reflections of the reflections in every other mirror, repeated endlessly. It is said that through this graphic representation she was able to grasp the significance of the doctrine immediately.

28. 聖武.

29. 東大寺.

30. 四法界, J. *shihokkai*; Ch. *ssu fa-chieh*.

31. 法界, Ch. *fa-chieh*.

32. 事法界, Ch. *shih fa-chieh*.

33. 理法界, Ch. *li-fa-chieh*.

34. A monk asked Master Joshu, "Has the dog Buddha-nature or not?" The Master answered: "Mu!" *Mumonkan* 無門 關, 1.

35. Hakuin Osho 白隱和 尚 used to ask his disciples, "What is the sound of the single hand?" *Transmitted*.

36. The monk Myo pursued the Sixth Patriarch and reached the mountain range of Daiyurei. Seeing Myo approaching, the Patriarch threw the robe and the bowl down upon a rock and said: "This robe symbolizes our faith. How can it be contended for with force? I give you leave to take it."

    But when Myo tried to lift it, it was as immoveable as a mountain. He stood disconcerted and shivering with fear. Then he said: "I came to seek the Dharma, not the robe. I beseech you, O Anja, to disclose it to me."

    The Patriarch replied: "Thinking neither of good nor of evil, at this moment what was your original aspect [face] before your father and mother were born?"

    At these words Myo was suddenly enlightened. *Katto shu* 葛藤集, 2.

37. 理事無礙法界, Ch. *li-shih wu-ai fa-chieh*.

38. 事事無礙法界, Ch. *shih-shih wu-ai fa-chieh*.

39. The words of Tokusan Senkan 德山宣鑑, Ch. Teshan Hsuan-chien (780–865): *Kokoro ni ji naku, ji ni shin nashi.* 無事於心, 無心於事, Ch. *Wu-shih yu hsin, wu-shin yu shih. Keitoku dento roku* 景德傳燈錄, 15.

40. 南泉普願, Ch. Nan-ch'uan P'u-yuan (748–834). *Byojoshin kore do* 平常心是道, Ch. *P'ing-ch'ang-hsin shih tao. Ibid.,* 10.

41. *Shujo muhen seigando*   衆生無邊誓願度
    Bonno mujin seigandan   煩惱無盡誓願斷
    Homon muryo seigangaku   法門無量誓願學
    Butsudo mu jo seigan jo   佛道無上誓願成

ZEN: A METHOD FOR RELIGIOUS AWAKENING

by RUTH FULLER SASAKI

KYOTO, THE FIRST ZEN INSTITUTE OF
AMERICA IN JAPAN, 1959

FOREWORD

IN THE AUTUMN OF 1958 I was invited by Dr. Huston Smith, Professor of Philosophy at the Massachusetts Institute of Technology, Cambridge, to deliver a lecture on comparative religion to faculty members, students of the Institute, and their friends. During his visit to Kyoto the previous year, Dr. Smith had become acquainted with the work of the First Zen Institute of America in Japan, of which I am the Director, and with my long association with Japanese Rinzai Zen.

When I received Dr. Smith's invitation I had only recently returned to the United States after an absence of nearly four years, and was quite unaware of the degree of interest being taken in Zen in the West and even less aware of the various interpretations to which Zen was being subjected and the uses to which it was being put. I was happy, therefore, to have the opportunity Dr. Smith's invitation afforded me of clarifying certain important points in Rinzai Zen and of correcting some of the mistaken views so obviously rife.

The text of my lecture that evening is here reproduced with a minimum of change. Perhaps I might have written another more interesting and comprehensive study of Zen but, since I find that clarification and correction are needed among a far broader audience than that before which I had the pleasure of speaking that evening, I have decided to let the text stand as it is.

This much I should like to add, however. In Japan today there are two major Zen sects, the Rinzai and the Soto. The Rinzai Sect represents the Zen current in the Chinese Lin-chi school of late Sung, at which time (13th century) it was brought to Japan by a number of Chinese masters and Japanese monks who had studied under Lin-chi masters in China. At that period the *koan* system, which I have described in the text, had already become the distinguishing teaching method of the Lin-chi school. Present-day masters in Japanese Rinzai Zen, the lineal descendants of those early teachers, in instructing their students continue to use approximately the same method as that used in the Chinese Lin-chi school in the days of Sung.

On the other hand, Japanese Soto Zen represents the Ts'ao-tung school of Zen, also current in China in the Sung dynasty. The masters of the Ts'ao-tung school, however, did *not* use the koan as a means of bringing their disciples to enlightenment, but depended almost entirely upon the practice of *zazen* (meditation). The great Japanese priest Dogen Zenji, after studying under a Ts'ao-tung master in China, brought the method of this school back to Japan, also in the 13th century. Moreover, Dogen greatly modified both the teaching and the teaching method of the school to accord with his own highly personal views, so that the Japanese Soto Zen of today has lost much of its resemblance to the Zen of the Ts'ao-tung Sect in China from which it sprang.

The goals of both the Soto and Rinzai sects in Japan today are not different, but the teaching methods in use in the two schools are, and should not be confused. It is in the method of Rinzai Zen that I myself have had many years of training and which I have described in the following text.

I sincerely hope that, after reading this short exposition, much about Rinzai Zen teaching that has seemed difficult to understand may have become somewhat more clear. Other aspects of Zen, including its relationship to Buddhism as a whole, as well as to the Kegon (Hua-yen) school of Chinese Mahayana, have already been taken up in *Zen—A Religion*, an earlier publication of mine which the present lecture in some ways supplements.

> Ryosen-an, Daitoku-ji
> Ruth Fuller Sasaki
> Kyoto, Japan
> May 15, 1959

ZEN: A METHOD FOR RELIGIOUS AWAKENING

ZEN IS A WORD which, unfortunately, seems to have been much bandied about in the West of late. I think it rather too bad that the term "Zen" should have been given such wide currency here without the accompanying word "Buddhism," for, correctly speaking, we should say "Zen Buddhism." In China and Japan, where Buddhism was, and to some extent still is, the prevailing religion, there has been little or no need to emphasize what everyone understood, namely that the words *Ch'an* and *Zen*, as the case might be, were convenient short forms of the Chinese or Japanese words *Ch'an-tsung* and *Zen-shu,* meaning "Meditation Sect," and referred to the meditation school or sect of Buddhism. In the West, however, for many people the word "Zen" alone does not immediately call up this reference, with the result that the teachings of the Zen Sect have been laid open to a variety of interpretations, many of them personal and equally many far-fetched, and these interpretations have come in some quarters to be accepted as standard for Zen. If some of what I am about to say does not accord with what you have heard or conceived about Zen, please understand that I am speaking about the sect of Mahayana Buddhism known as the Zen Sect. I am acquainted with no other Zen.

Perhaps I should first introduce myself to you. I am a Zen Buddhist and have been one for over twenty-five years. So I speak from within Zen, not as one who observes it from the outside. Though brought up in a strict Presbyterian family, I became a Buddhist in my twenties. The study of early Buddhism, into which I soon plunged, brought me to the conclusion that the pivot of that religion was Awakening and the Buddhist life a life lived in accordance with Awakening. Meditation was the means through which Sakyamuni, the historical Buddha, had come to his enlightenment. The forty-nine years of his life after his great experience were spent in trying to show other men how they, by following the path he had pursued, might attain this awakening for themselves. Therefore, to find a teacher who could give me correct instruction in how to practice Buddhist meditation became my aim. Also, I wanted to see if meditation methods that eastern people had for centuries found successful would work equally well for a westerner. At forty I first had the privilege of practicing under a famous Rinzai Zen master or *roshi,* Nanshinken of the Nanzen-ji monastery in Kyoto, Japan. Later, as the obligations of a normal family life permitted, I continued my practice and study in Japan under Nanshinken, and in America under the late Sokei-an Roshi. For the past ten years, free of household responsibilities, I have lived almost continuously in Kyoto, devoting myself to Japanese and Chinese language studies as they relate to Zen, and to Rinzai Zen practice under my third Zen teacher, Goto Zuigan Roshi. Though I have not yet completed my Zen study, perhaps I can share with you a little of what I have learned. But please do not expect a learned discourse. During these years, I have had little time to keep up with the latest developments in philosophy, psychology, and science. Furthermore, though Zen does not necessarily outlaw books—contrary to what you may have heard about it—gradually I have found that just living life every day, fully and awarely, is so fascinating and rewarding that the majority of books that come my way hold little of interest for me.

Many people say to me, "Zen is so difficult to understand. I have read a lot about it, but, though I think I understand what it's about while I am reading, afterwards I realize I haven't understood at all." Of course there are others who, without having read a single primary Buddhist or Zen text, think they know all about it. How many hours have I not spent in my Kyoto temple listening to people, usually Americans recently come to Japan, tell me just what Zen is! To such visitors I have nothing to say; to those who do not understand, I am always searching for a way to give a clue to what Zen is about.

Perhaps for westerners the primary hindrance in understanding Zen, even intellectually, lies in the fact that the great verities that Zen, with Buddhism, takes as basic are diametrically opposed to those the Hebraic-Christian religions have always assumed to be absolute. It is difficult to put aside one's way of looking at even an inconsequential matter and to observe it from a totally new and different standpoint. How much more difficult to do so with religious concepts and beliefs with which we have been inculcated from earliest childhood! But unless you can put aside your usual viewpoint, you will never be able to understand what Zen is concerned with, and why, and who. Try, now, for a few minutes to clear your minds of all your previously held notions and read what I am going to say with what, in Buddhism, is called a "mirror mind."

Zen does not hold that there is a god apart from the universe who first created this universe and then created man to enjoy, or even master it—and these days it seems not to be enough to master the planet Earth; we must now master the universe as well. Rather, Zen holds that there is no god outside the universe who has created it and created man. God—if I may borrow that word for a moment—the universe, and man are one indissoluble existence, one total whole. Only This—capital This—is. Anything and everything that appears to us as an individual entity or phenomenon, whether it be a planet or an atom, a mouse or a man, is but a temporary manifestation of This in form; every activity that takes place, whether it be birth or death, loving or eating breakfast, is but a temporary manifestation of This in activity. When we look at things this way, naturally we cannot believe that each individual person has been endowed with a special and individual soul or self. Each one of us is but a cell, as it were, in the body of the Great Self, a cell that comes into being, performs its functions, and passes away, transformed into another manifestation. Though we have temporary individuality, that temporary, limited individuality is not either a true self or our true self. Our true self is the Great Self; our true body is the Body of Reality, or the Dharmakaya, to give it its technical Buddhist name.

Buddhism, and Zen, grant that this view is not one that can be reasoned about intellectually. Nor, on the other hand, do they ask us to take this doctrine on faith. They tell us it must be experienced, it must be realized. Such realization can be brought about through the awakening of that intuitive wisdom which is intrinsic to all men. The method for awakening this intuitive wisdom is meditation. Zen, among the various schools of Buddhism, is the one which has emphasized over everything else the attainment of this realization in this very body, here and now, and provided a method, tested through centuries, for accomplishing it.

It is the generally accepted view today that, as far as doctrines are concerned—and, as you see, Zen does have them, contrary to what you may have heard—Zen is developed Mahayana Buddhism as the Chinese mind, steeped in the Chinese world view and classical Taoism, realized it. In fewer words, we might say that Zen is Indian Buddhism dyed with the dye of Chinese Taoism. Japanese Zennists, however, while conceding this, consider Zen to be rather a return to the Buddha's Buddhism. By that they do not mean a return to Hinayana or Theravada Buddhism, the Buddhism of the monkish schools that arose after the Buddha's death, but rather a return to Sakyamuni's basic teaching that every man can and should attain this transforming religious experience of awakening for himself. Sakyamuni, as the embodiment of his total teaching, is the central figure for Japanese Rinzai Zen, and Sakyamuni's image is always the main image in its temples.

From the very beginning of its history the first aim of the followers of the Zen Sect has been the attainment of awakening. The founders of the sect left to other schools the writing of dissertations on methods, descriptions of progressive stages along the way, discussions and treatises on the doctrinal implications of the experience. The old Zen masters said: "Get Awakening yourself! Then you'll know what it is." In other words, if you want to know the taste of water, drink it!

Meditation, the method the Buddha had followed, was the method the old masters of Zen themselves pursued and urged upon their students. It is not too clear whether the meditation practices of developed Chinese Zen were those directly transmitted from Indian teachers to their Chinese disciples, or whether they owe something to the Taoist meditation practices current in China in the earlier days. It has been stated by the eminent scholar Dr. Hu Shih that Chinese Zen discarded the classical sitting meditation of Indian Buddhism as a method of attaining enlightenment, and that Chinese Zen monks practiced, rather, "walking meditation," that is, they preferred to gain their realization through contact with nature on long walking trips from one mountain temple to another and through their sharp verbal give and take with the Zen masters they visited. While I do not deny that Chinese Zen monks were great travelers afoot, my own reading leads me to believe that the younger monks undertook these pilgrimages in order to search for a suitable master, one with whom they had *innen*, as we say in Japan, true rapport or true relationship; and that the older monks set out upon their pilgrimages after they had, or thought they had, attained enlightenment, in order to test their own understanding against that of the famous masters of the day. I am inclined to believe that classical sitting mediation was as basic a practice in Zen throughout its history in China as it is in the monasteries of Japan today.

In the early days of Zen in China, that is, in the seventh and eighth centuries, an enlightened Zen monk would settle himself on a remote mountainside in a little hut, often made by his own hands. There earnest students would seek him out and, having built their own huts close by, pass their days meditating, serving the master, and receiving such instruction as he deigned to give them. As the group of disciples increased in number, permanent buildings to house them would be constructed. Thus a temple was founded. Or, a master accompanied by his immediate disciples would take up residence in some already well-known temple. If he was famous, student-monks would flock from everywhere, their numbers sometimes swelling to two or three thousand. Such a body of monks lived in their own quarters and their mode of life was ordered by fixed rules and regulations. Meditation and physical labor were the main forms of activity. At regular intervals the master gave talks to the monks, talks called in Japanese *jodo*, meaning literally "ascending the hall." For this talk the master seems to have taken a raised seat in one of the temple halls or in a courtyard. There he discoursed on Buddhism in a decidedly informal way, often employing the colloquial speech of the district. At the conclusion of the talk, the master's own students or a visiting monk would come forward and question him about the problems that troubled them. The ensuing exchange of question and answer between master and monk was known as a *mondo*, literally "question and answer." The mondos seem always to have taken place in the presence of the assembly of the monks. The master appears to have given little private instruction except to his more immediate disciples.

During this jodo or talk, the master was accustomed to hold a stick in his hand, three feet long or thereabouts. This he flourished from time to time to emphasize important points in his sermon. Sometimes he would deal the questioning monk a blow with it. Perhaps he recognized that, through his meditation, the monk had reached a state where his mind was frozen, as we say. At such a moment there is nothing like a good hard whack to break the mental impasse. Perhaps the monk was just plain stupid, or perhaps he was trying to show off before everyone. Then the blow might be given in hope of waking the stupid monk up or to indicate the master's displeasure with the smart aleck.

Far too much has been made of the Zen stick in some western expositions of Zen. In the hands of the old masters it served primarily as a teaching device, as it still does in the hands of the Japanese masters today. As for the long stick held by the head monks as they patrol the meditation hall during the periods of sitting, all practitioners of zazen, or Zen meditation, regard it as the sword of Manjusri, the Bodhisattva who represents the doctrine of intuitive wisdom. After the head monk takes the stick from its customary hook, he bows deeply before the shrine of Manjusri, a shrine in every meditation hall. From that moment on until he bows again and lays the stick on the altar before the Bodhisattva, the head monk represents Manjusri, himself. If the head monk must use the stick to rouse a drowsy or inattentive monk, after the blow has been struck both bow politely to one another. There is no personal rancour on the part of he who strikes the blow and only gratitude on the part of he who has been struck.

In the early days of Zen, the monks and laymen who came to the mountain temples to receive instruction from the master had burning spiritual problems to solve. They strove with the greatest ardor to attain awakening. For many the attainment of awakening was a life and death matter and they gave themselves over body and soul to it. The students' zeal and the profound religious understanding of the great masters of T'ang and early Sung produced a body of brilliant mondos, "questions and answers," which cover the entire range of Zen doctrine and experience. These mondos were recorded in writing by the close disciples of the masters, as were also many of the masters' talks and sermons.

But as time went by, the fires of enthusiasm began to die down. Though hundreds and hundreds of monks still surrounded the masters, and laymen in large numbers continued to come for instruction, the urgency to solve spiritual problems came to seem less pressing and the spontaneous exchanges of question and answer took place less often. The masters, their own originality flagging, began to use the sermons and mondos of the great masters of earlier days as texts for their sermons, commenting upon these as they had heard their teachers comment before them. To spur on students who lacked their own strong "spirit of inquiry," the masters gave the old mondos as problems to be solved through meditation. To these were added statements from some of the sutras (scriptures) and stories from the lives of the masters of the past, stories containing seed words or phrases the masters had uttered. Thus was gradually built up a body of "problems for meditation"—in Chinese *kung-an*, in Japanese *koan*—a large part of which the Japanese Rinzai masters use today with identical intent. At what period the masters ceased instructing their disciples through public interchanges before the assembly of the monks and placed full dependence upon the somewhat artificial device of the koan, I do not know. Today, however, all instruction in Zen takes place in private interviews between the student and the master, and what transpires during *sanzen*, as this interview is called in Japanese, is considered a matter for absolute secrecy on both sides.

The word "koan" was originally a Chinese legal term meaning "case," that is, a legal case that had been decided and thereafter was used as a precedent for decisions in cases of the same kind. In Zen, koans are used both as a means of opening up the student's intuitive mind and as tests of the depth to which it has been opened. Koans are not solvable by the rational mind or intellect. To solve a koan the student, through meditation upon it, a particular kind of meditation we call in Japanese *kufu*, must reach the same level of intuitive understanding as that from which the master spoke the words of the koan. When the student has reached this level of understanding, his understanding and, therefore, his answer to the koan will be approximately the same as that of all the Zen students who have solved it in the past. Each koan has what may be called a "classic" answer. Against this classic answer the master tests the student's answer. When the two agree, the student may be said to have "solved" or "passed" the koan.

Originally there seems to have been little system in the sequence in which koans were given to a student. Each master had mondos and stories that had come down in this teaching line or "house," as it was called, and apparently gave to each student such of these as he felt were needed at the time to awaken or deepen the student's insight. But already in *Mumonkan*, the late Sung collection of koans known to many of you as *The Gateless Gate*, a definite progression is discernible to one who has studied them.

In the Sung period, Japanese Buddhist monks began going to China to study under Zen masters there and Chinese Zen masters began coming to Japan. Both the Chinese masters and the returning Japanese monks brought to Japan with them the koans they had studied under their respective masters, and in their turn used them in instructing their Japanese disciples. Toward the end of the seventeenth century, by which time Japanese Zen had suffered a serious decline, Hakuin Zenji, a brilliant and energetic Japanese Rinzai priest, journeyed from one part of the country to the other, studying under all the remaining authentic teachers the Chinese koans previously transmitted to them. These he made into a collection which he arranged in a systematic progression. To the perhaps seven or eight hundred Chinese koans he had gathered, Hakuin Zenji added a few of his own making, the only koans in modern use that did not originate with Chinese masters. Hakuin Zenji transmitted these

Portrait of Ruth Fuller Saski, circa 1940s

From left to right: Philip Yampolsky, Gary Snyder, Donatienne Lebovich, Ruth Fuller Sasaki, Miura Isshu Roshi, Vanessa Coward, Manzoji Yoko, Walter Nowick, Seizan Yanagida. Spring 1957.

Ruth Fuller Sasaki at Daitoku-ji, circa 1950s

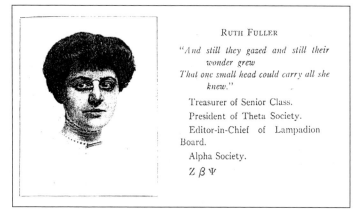

RUTH FULLER

"And still they gazed and still their wonder grew
That one small head could carry all she knew."

Treasurer of Senior Class.

President of Theta Society.

Editor-in-Chief of Lampadion Board.

Alpha Society.

Z β Ψ

Ruth Fuller's senior year photo from the
Lampadion Yearbook, 1911

Ruth Fuller (front row, center) as the editor of the
Lampadion Yearbook, 1911

Ruth Fuller Sasaki
giving donation for
takuhatsu, circa 1934

Ruth Fuller Sasaki
standing in front of
the rocky wall
Empuku-ji, circa 1930

Interior view of Ryosen-an zendo, shrine at the far end

The current Ryosen-an zendo altar (butsudan) with a framed
photograph of Ruth Fuller Sasaki at the far left

The view from the Ryosen-an library of the Ryosen-an graves,
where half of Ruth Fuller Sasaki's ashes are kept

The Woodlawn Cemetery, in New York, with a special
memorial stone for Ruth Fuller Sasaki.
Sokei-an Sasaki's ashes are also buried here.

The group sitting on the veranda at Daitoku-ji, circa late 1950s.
Ruth Fuller Sasaki is the third from the right, front row.

Entrance gate to Ryosen-an

Current gardens within Ryosen-an

Ryosen-an courtyard, zendo is at far left

koans to his numerous immediate disciples, and it is they that make up the body of koans used by all Japanese Rinzai masters today. Though present-day Zen roshis do not slavishly follow the order Hakuin Zenji established, since individual students have individual needs and the masters individual preferences, on the whole, koan study today follows the ordered, progressive system handed down from him.

Now who are these Zen masters or teachers and what is the role they have played throughout the long history of Zen and continue to play today? From the very beginning, as strongly as it has emphasized meditation as the basic practice, Zen has emphasized the necessity for the direct transmission from teacher to disciple of the intuitive understanding of THIS. Traditionally it is said that Sakyamuni Buddha transmitted his Dharma—his understanding of THIS or of Ultimate Truth, to use the technical Buddhist term—to his disciple Kasyapa; Kasyapa, in his turn, transmitted his understanding to Ananda, and so on down through a long line of Indian teachers and disciples until, through Bodhidharma, it was eventually transmitted to Hui-neng (Eno), known as the Sixth Patriarch of Zen in China. Hui-neng had a number of immediate disciples to whom he transmitted his Dharma. To two of Hui-neng's Dharma-heirs can be traced back all the major lines of Zen teaching and Zen teachers throughout the history of Chinese and Japanese Zen up to the present day.

What is this transmission? When the disciple has reached the same profound depth of intuitive understanding and realized completely the same deepest truth as his master, when both see inner eye to inner eye, or when they "lock eyebrows together," as the old texts put it, then only does the master put his seal on the disciple's attainment, guarantee it, as it were. And only when the disciple has had his attainment "sealed" is he properly prepared to teach others and may he, in turn, transmit the Dharma to another, "transmit" meaning, of course, "acknowledge the attainment of his disciple."

The same holds true in Japanese Rinzai Zen today. The only person who is considered to be a teacher of Zen is he who has received the authentic transmission from his teacher. Teacher or disciple may be either monk, priest, or layman, provided that the transmission is authentic. In Japan such teachers have the title *roshi*, "old master." It is such a teacher only who is called a Zen Master. Today, the authentic Zen roshi, or master, guides his students to the experience of awakening by means of koans and the special type of Zen lecture or sermon known as *teisho*. Monks or priests or laymen who have studied and practiced Zen but have not received the transmission, who are not authenticated roshis and therefore never called by the title "Zen Master," often write and lecture and talk about Zen, but they may not give koans to their students or followers. If people go to hear them talk or read what they write, it is with the knowledge that such a person is talking or writing from an incomplete understanding of Zen. So, in Japan today, all men and women who wish to study authentic Zen in the authentic way study it under a roshi or teacher belonging to a direct line of transmission. It is quite easy to determine who these authentic Zen masters are.

As I have said before, the student may be a monk who hopes to become a temple priest, if not a Zen master; or he may be a layman or laywoman who seeks no more than personal religious experience. Though there may be some difference in details of procedure, the study and practice are identical in every case. I might add that today—and perhaps the same has been true throughout Zen history—not everyone whose understanding of Dharma has been acknowledged by his teacher becomes a roshi or Zen master. Some disciples may have attained true enlightenment yet lack certain qualifications necessary for teaching others. In actual practice, permission to teach koans is a step beyond acknowledgment of attainment, and is a matter on which the teacher has final decision. Not a few persons receive the master's seal on their attainment but do not receive the title of roshi.

Now how does one go about studying and practicing Zen today? A would-be student goes to a Zen roshi, one for whom he has deep respect, in whom he has faith, and with whom he has a distinct feeling of relationship. In a polite and humble manner the student requests to be accepted as a disciple. If the roshi consents, he will turn the student over to his head monk or senior disciple to be instructed in zazen, or meditation practice. The student will be told how to sit and how to breathe; he will be given certain concentration exercises to practice. For a considerable period the student pursues these elementary practices at home several hours a day, or sits with a group of other students who meet for zazen practice at certain specified times. When the head monk or senior disciple decides that the student has acquired a "good seat," that is, can sit in the correct posture for a considerable length of time and is proficient in concentration, he will inform the roshi that the student is now prepared to begin his koan study.

The student then goes to the roshi and, during the private interview known as *sanzen*, an interview conducted in a formal and specifically prescribed manner, the master gives the student a koan which he is now to meditate upon. At definite times from then on the student is expected to go to the roshi for a like interview, and during each interview to express to the master his view at the moment of the inner meaning or content of the koan on which he has been continuously meditating. When the student attains correct insight into the koan, the master, to test his understanding still further, will ask him to bring a word or phrase, preferably from some old Chinese proverb, pithy saying, or poem, that conveys in secular words the inner meaning of the koan. These words or phrases are known in Japanese as *jakugo*. I have yet to find a suitable English word for this expression, though perhaps "capping verse" might do. When the student has brought the correct jakugo—and almost every koan has a fixed jakugo—the master will give him another koan to meditate upon. And thus the student's Zen study will continue—hours and hours of meditation upon koan after koan for years and years. The constant supervision of the master throughout the course of this study assures that the student's own personal views and his mistaken and deluded notions are discarded one by one, for, in order to pass a koan, he must reach the traditionally correct understanding of it. No other understanding is acceptable or accepted. It is undoubtedly due to this teaching method that Rinzai Zen has continued to flow in so pure a stream in spite of the many hands it has passed through in the course of so many centuries.

Since each koan deals with some aspect of Truth as it is held in Zen Buddhism, little by little the student is brought to realize the total of Zen doctrine which is wholly concerned with the THIS, of which I have spoken earlier, and its relative, or manifested, aspects. The doctrines of Zen are not stated specifically either in written or spoken words, but, through long-continued meditation upon the succession of koans, deeper and deeper levels of the student's intuitive mind are opened, levels where these unspoken doctrines are realized as truths. For the Zen master teaches his student nothing. He guides him in such a way that the student finds everything he would learn within his own mind. As an old Chinese saying has it, "The treasures of the house do not come in through the gate." The treasure of Truth lies deep within the mind of each one of us; it is to be awakened or revealed or attained only through our own efforts.

You may be somewhat surprised that I have spoken at such length and not once used the word "*satori*." This word, I fear, has suffered as much abuse as the word "Zen," and what it connotes and implies has been as much misconstrued. Recently, after a conversation with an American visitor who considered himself a well-informed Zennist, a conversation in which the word "satori" had appeared innumerable times, I said to my old teacher, Goto Roshi: "I have studied Zen for nearly thirty years under three Zen masters, and I don't believe I have ever heard any one of them use the word 'satori'!" "Well," Roshi replied, "I doubt if you have ever heard it from my lips."

The Chinese character for "satori" is composed of the character for "mind" and the character for "myself." When "myself" and "mind" are completely united, there is satori. Really, the solution of each and every koan implies a satori. For without becoming one with the koan, without attaining the state of mind of which the koan is an expression, one cannot solve it. To be sure, satori is sometimes experienced without formal meditation upon a koan, or by persons not engaged in Zen study. But every satori is unquestionably the result of intense occupation of the mind with some deep problem. In the case of Zen students it seems seldom to occur while actually practicing formal meditation; most often it takes place when least expected.

There are, however, greater and lesser satoris. Some of the koans of Zen are great or basic koans, through which realization of great basic truths is attained. The satori that usually accompanies the solution of one of these great koans is termed "Great Satori." Around each of the basic koans are many, what I like to term, satellite koans. Since their underlying truth is the same as that of the great koan with which they are associated, when the great koan has once been realized, the dependent koans can be fairly easily solved. My first teacher, Nanshinken Roshi, once told me that when, after spending three years of meditation upon his first koan, the koan "MU," he finally attained the realization of it, he was able to pass through forty minor related koans in a few days.

The attainment of the realization of the first koan is undoubtedly the most difficult and usually takes the longest time to accomplish. Two or three years, or even more, is not unusual. The satori accompanying the realization of this first koan is often so momentous and transforming an experience that many people consider this to be THE satori, the one and only satori, beyond which there can be nothing more. How wrong they are! The old masters were constantly inveighing against this idea. Ceaselessly they urged their students to continue on and on. Ta-hui (Daie), a famous master of Sung, used to say: "I have had eighteen great satoris and lost count of all the small satoris I have had." It is only after the first satori that true Zen study may be said to begin. Please do not forget this!

Though you have now heard something about Zen and Zen practice, undoubtedly you still wonder why, throughout the centuries, people have continued to pursue this curious study. What can they hope to get through all this effort? The classic Zen answer, and the Buddhist answer as well, is "Nothing."

I don't profess to know clearly what is causing so many Americans and Europeans to interest themselves in Zen today. In fact I should like to have someone tell me. I know they are said to be unable to have faith in traditional religious doctrines, to find in scientific materialism poor nourishment for their spirits, to feel that modern life, with its multitude of machines, is an exhausting and unrewarding way of life for them as human beings. And, of course, there are always the few who don't like to conform and who seem to think that perhaps in Zen they will find justification for their own personal interpretations of freedom.

I have indicated to you why I began to study Zen. Certainly, however, many persons in the past, and in Japan today, have been driven to this practice by a consuming urge to discover the answers to such difficult and profound questions as: What is the nature of man and of the universe? What is life? What is death? I don't know if you will find satisfactory answers to these problems through Zen or not. Certainly you will not unless, through your Zen practice, through seeing into your own deepest mind, you attain intuitive insight into the THIS within which all the answers lie.

To the three basic questions that men have always asked: Who am I? Where am I? Why am I? strange as it may seem, the answers have been spelled out in the writings of the Zen masters and in the Buddhist scriptures as well.

To the question, "Who am I?" the answer is, "Buddha."

To the question, "Where am I?" the answer is, "In Nirvana."

To the question, "Why am I?" the answer is, "For no purpose."

The realization of these answers is left to you to attain.

In the course of studying and practicing Zen for a long, long time, and in the course of realizing for oneself the answers to these questions, the small personal self gradually dissolves and one knows no self but the Great Self, no personal will, only the Great Will. One comes to understand the true meaning of the term *wu-wei*, or in Japanese *mui*, "non-action," for one knows that, as a separate individual, there is nothing further to do. One does not cease to act, but one's actions arise spontaneously out of the eternal flow of the activity of THIS, which one is not only in accord with, but IS. The man of Zen is clearly aware that he is abiding in, and will eternally abide in,

THIS AS IT IS; that the world in which he is living his everyday life is indeed THIS in its myriad of manifestations, forever changing, forever transforming, but forever THIS. In the words of the sutras: "Nirvana is none other than Samsara; Samsara is none other than Nirvana."

But in Zen, when we must speak, everyday words are preferred to quotations from the scriptures. So, in conclusion, let me put more simply what I have just said. The aim of Zen is first of all awakening, awakening to our true self. With this awakening to our true self comes emancipation from our small self or personal ego. When this emancipation from the personal ego is finally complete, then we know the freedom spoken of in Zen and so widely misconstrued by those who take the name for the experience. Of course, as long as this human frame hangs together and we exist as one manifested form in the world of forms, we carry on what appears to be an individual existence as an individual ego. But no longer is that ego in control with its likes and dislikes, its characteristics and its foibles. The True Self, which from the beginning we have always been, has at last become the master. Freely the True Self uses this individual form and this individual ego as it will. With no resistance and no hindrance it uses them in all the activities of everyday life whatever they are and wherever they may be. This is true self-mastery; this is true freedom; and this only is truly living. Now have the long years of Zen study and practice come into full flower.

RINZAI ZEN STUDY
FOR FOREIGNERS IN JAPAN

by RUTH FULLER SASAKI

KYOTO, THE FIRST ZEN INSTITUTE OF
AMERICA IN JAPAN, 1960

CONTENTS

Foreword   180

   I. Zen—Present, Past, and Future   181

  II. Why Do You Want to Study Zen?   184

 III. Zen for the Sightseer   192

 IV. A Whiff of Zen   198

  V. The Zen Monastery and the Zen Master   204

 VI. Monastery Life   208

VII. Adapting to Monastery Life   218

VIII. Accomplishment in Zen Study   223

 IX. Study at Ryosen-an   231

Appendices

 Visas   234

 Expenses   236

 Preparations   240

FOREWORD

D URING THE YEAR 1957, in answer to various inquiries from Americans and Europeans as to how they might study Zen in Japan, I devoted seven of my "Letters from Kyoto" to describing in some detail how foreigners might carry on such practice and what the problems involved were. So many requests were made to The First Zen Institute of America in New York for additional copies of those issues of *Zen Notes*, the Institute's monthly publication, in which these letters appeared, that a second printing was made. This, also, has now long been exhausted. Since the interest in how Zen may be studied in Japan still continues and has, perhaps, even increased during the two years that have passed, a reissuing of these letters in the more convenient form of a pamphlet has seemed warranted.

In the course of these two years the New York Institute has opened a Japanese branch at Ryosen-an, a subtemple within the precincts of the Rinzai Zen headquarter temple of Daitoku-ji in Kyoto. Here the Institute has built a small meditation hall for the exclusive purpose of training foreign students in the practice of Zen meditation and preparing them for further Zen study under a Japanese Zen master. Since the opening of this meditation hall, a number of westerners have come to the Kyoto Institute for study. Thus an opportunity has been provided for further understanding of the aims and needs of occidentals who wish to study Zen in Japan.

All the material appearing in the "Letters" mentioned above has been included in the present publication, though in somewhat different arrangement, and new material added as well. If the advice seems at times overdetailed and tedious, it is offered only in answer to questions already asked or situations already encountered.

The chapter setting forth the study program of the Kyoto Institute is new. A copy of the pamphlet *The First Zen Institute of America in Japan* will be sent gladly to those wishing to know more about all the activities being undertaken here.

I should like to thank the older students of the Kyoto Institute for their many helpful suggestions toward the improvement of the manuscript, and also Mrs. Donatienne Lebovich for the drawings accompanying the instructions for zazen practice.

> Ryosen-an, Daitoku-ji
> Ruth Fuller Sasaki
> Kyoto, Japan
> October 31, 1959

I. ZEN—PRESENT, PAST, AND FUTURE

ONE OF THE INTERESTING phenomena of the last twenty years in the intellectual scene in the West has been the rapid and widespread rise of interest in Zen Buddhism. Thirty years ago, except for a few historians of Far Eastern art and religion, scarcely anyone in Europe or America had even heard the word Zen or its Chinese equivalent *Ch'an*. Today, due in large part to D. T. Suzuki's voluminous writings in English on Zen—many of them translated into other European languages—Zen is known *about* in almost every part of the civilized world. Furthermore, Dr. Suzuki's numerous followers have written on Zen from almost every possible angle. Zen has always been credited with influencing various forms of Far Eastern art and culture, and quite correctly. But now the discovery has been made that it was existing all along in English literature.

Ultra-modern painting, music, dance, and poetry are acclaimed as expressions of Zen. Zen is invoked to substantiate the validity of the latest theories in psychology, psychotherapy, philosophy, semantics, mysticism, free-thinking, and what-have-you. It is the magic password at smart cocktail parties and bohemian get-togethers alike. Radio and television comedians consider it a natural for spoofing. Zen jokes appear in the daily papers, and a recent magazine contains an excellent satire on it, really long overdue.

How far away all this is from the recluse Gautama sitting in intense meditation under the Bodhi-tree trying to find a solution to the problem of human suffering! How far from Bodhidharma, the traditional founder of Zen, sitting in absolute silence for nine years before the rocky face of the soaring cliff in order to demonstrate the profound principle of the teaching! And, if we follow the legend, how far from the Second Patriarch Eka, knee-deep in the snow, cutting off his left arm and presenting it to Bodhidharma as proof of his sincerity!

The origin of Zen in Sakyamuni's awakening to truth, and the supreme efforts made by many men through the centuries to transmit this truth to following generations—all this seems either to have been forgotten or passed over as of little importance by the self-styled western Zennist of today. Fortunately, however, regardless of what we may think about Zen, actually it remains just what it always has been: a way successfully pursued by many to realize within themselves the essential truths of Mahayana Buddhism and the living expression of this realization in daily life. Practice and living in accordance with the understanding reached through the practice—this is what Zen is. That many by-products useful in various fields accrue from this practice goes without saying. But the mistake should never be made of confusing the by-products with Zen itself.

It is true that a few western people have had the eye with which to see through to the real purpose and value of Zen from the beginning of the West's acquaintance with it. As the fad subsides, it is to be hoped that more will do so. However, it is not very likely that occidentals in any number will ever sit down to practice Zen and realize its final goal. For that, first of all, much time is needed. Time for personal development is at a premium today. If we are fortunate enough to have it, the outside world, mechanical and human, seems to resent this and redoubles its efforts to demand our attention. Sustained will power, determined purpose, and willingness to put aside what the world values for what we value more—these are the only effective weapons in this combat. Without them we are defeated before we begin. This was as true in the past as it is today.

For myself, I believe that Zen practice is one of the most remarkable religious disciplines men have devised, and that the fruits of the practice are beyond price. Therefore, though real Zen students may be few, for those few it seems to me important that this discipline be preserved and made available.

But are, then, the many men and women whose religious yearnings are not being fulfilled and for whom life will never provide time for prolonged study and practice to be cut off from any relationship with living Zen? This question is asked me very often. In the past, those who have sought to attain enlightenment have either retired from the householder's life or within it had the means and leisure to pursue their aim. For those who were not so situated there were other paths in Buddhism. But this is the present. Just as firmly as I believe in the value of Zen practice, I believe—unorthodoxly, no doubt—that the basic principles of Mahayana Buddhism as they are interpreted in Zen can be put into words. To present these principles accurately, the first and most important thing is the realization of them through practice, then clear intellectual understanding of what has been realized, and lastly ability to express this understanding simply and straightforwardly in words and terms that are as exact as possible. Only thus can arbitrary, fuzzy, and mistaken interpretations be obviated. When this has been successfully accomplished and when the basic Zen texts have been made available through the translations of those who have prepared themselves for their work by Zen practice as well as linguistic studies, I feel sure that such westerners as have a natural relationship with Buddhism and with Zen will find they have been provided with an unparalleled foundation for abstract thinking and a guide for daily life as well. Please do not mistake what I have said. These westerners will not gain through reading that realization which is the pivot of Zen today, as in the past. But perhaps through the expedient of words, the import of which they can grasp, they may achieve a clearer view of the depth and breadth of Zen teaching, and from there be led on to undertake such of the practices as their way of life permits.

To accomplish this presentation of Zen we need those rare occidentals who can enter completely into the oriental mind, linguistically, historically, culturally, and spiritually, and who can as completely transmute their understanding into an expression that is fully comprehensible to the western mind. Such persons we look for as we scan the face of each new student.

II. Why Do You Want to Study Zen?

IN THE MEANWHILE people write to ask how they can study Zen in Japan now. Some plan to come for only a few weeks, some want to stay several months, and some inquire about study over a period of years. Each letter requires an individual reply, of course. However, there is much to be said in general that may aid people in making up their minds for or against embarking upon Zen study, and in preparing themselves in advance for the facts they will be face to face with once they come to Japan. For, though coming here to study Zen is a dream well worth cherishing, like all dreams it can suffer a rude awakening when it is not based upon thorough acquaintance with reality. If, therefore, in the course of the following pages, the problems seem to be stressed, it is not because they are insoluble, but because they must be understood and accepted, and what is to be gained must be gained within the limitations they impose.

But before I go further, let me reiterate what the title of the pamphlet states quite clearly, namely that Rinzai practice only is being discussed. As many readers already know, there are two schools of Japanese Zen, the Soto and the Rinzai. The Soto Sect takes *zazen* (Zen meditation) as its basic practice. The few Soto masters who employ *koans* (the words and phrases of the old masters used as subjects for meditation) in instructing their students seem to regard them as an auxiliary study and to handle them in ways that vary with the individual teacher. The procedures and regulations in Soto Zen monasteries also are different from those in Rinzai monasteries.

In Rinzai Zen, with which we are here concerned, though zazen is the basic practice, the study of koans is equally important. As a matter of fact, Rinzai Zen study, after the student has become proficient in zazen, is essentially koan study. Koans are studied in an order that, though sufficiently flexible to allow for the individual preferences of the master and the individual needs of the student, is a more or less established sequence. The student meditates on his given koan while practicing zazen. The insight into the import of the koan achieved through his meditation he conveys to his teacher at the daily, or at times more frequent, private interview between them known as *sanzen*. During this interview, which is conducted in a definitely prescribed manner, the master rejects, corrects, or accepts the student's view.

Now let me ask those who would like to undertake actual Zen practice: What attracts you to Zen? How ephemeral is your interest, or how serious? What do you think Zen is? Why do you want to study it? What do you think it can give you? How much are you willing to pay—not necessarily money—to study Zen? It is of the utmost importance that those who want to come to Japan for Zen study should think out these questions carefully even before beginning to think of coming.

Merely to want to have a strange and exotic experience is not a valid reason for attempting Zen study. On the other hand, to want to be better informed about a little known foreign religion—one in which there is considerable general intellectual interest at the moment—is commendable. But so many books and articles about Zen have already come out that, though all that can be said about Zen has by no means yet been said, enough has appeared in print to satisfy normal intellectual curiosity.

To want to get something from Zen is a somewhat different matter. There are those who seem to believe that Zen has a "technique" that can be useful in fields outside that of religion—writing, art, psychiatry, for instance—and are interested in having some degree of knowledge or experience of this technique in order to apply it in their own work. To some extent their belief is justified. However, I am personally inclined to think that the several arts in Japan usually associated with Zen—tea ceremony, archery, fencing, sumi painting, calligraphy, haiku—basically are neither expressions of Zen nor derived from it, as seems to be the popular opinion, but rather that the practitioners of these arts found in Zen discipline an aid to the more expert handling of their own individual art. I do not deny that, in addition, Zen practice deepened their insight and made their intuitions more acute. Nor do I deny that there have been true Zen men, skilled in one or more of these arts, who have given expression to their Zen understanding through them. But it is also true that others did not hesitate to take various Zen doctrines from their Buddhistic context and reinterpret them so as to make them conform to and justify purely Japanese cultural patterns. For this reason I cannot agree with the often expressed opinion that the occidental can best approach Zen through the study of one of the traditional arts of Japan.

To such persons as are interested in the techniques of Zen for their own purposes I should like to say this: Though Zen has a technique, Zen is not a technique. Real Zen is first and foremost a religion. Zen is one of the currents in the great ocean of Buddhism, specifically in that part of the ocean to which we give the name Far Eastern Mahayana Buddhism. Zen has definite doctrines, or views, if you prefer. These doctrines or views are based upon what the ancient Zen patriarchs and their successors realized through their own experience to be the core of total Buddhism, from its origin in the life and teachings of Sakyamuni until it reached its final development centuries later in China and Japan. All Buddhism is based upon Sakyamuni's Awakening and his demonstration of the meaning of that experience in the life he lived after it. Whatever technique Zen has, has been developed for the sole purpose of bringing men to the experience of this Awakening in order that thereafter they may live a life in accordance with its deepest meaning. Therefore, if you approach Zen study to "get" from it something you can adapt and use for your own purposes, you may get something, but what you get will be merely the outer husk of Zen. You will never know its living heart.

To those of you who, though wholly or partially committed to some western religious persuasion, feel they might reach a deeper understanding of their own faith through Zen study, I should like to say this: If you approach Zen treasuring and clinging to your orthodox religious beliefs, beware! For a time you may find them clarified, even illumined by your Zen practice. But the day will inevitably come when you will have to choose. You may delude yourself into thinking you can make a satisfactory synthesis. But real Zen is ruthless and uncompromising. It is a two-edged sword that destroys life and gives life. Before the Great Life arises the Great Death must be experienced. And when the Great Death strikes, nothing remains. Only when all you have believed, clung to, supported yourself by, cherished, is swept away, do you come to know what the Great Life of Zen is.

The lively interest taken in Zen by psychiatry has given rise in some quarters to the view that Zen is a kind of psychotherapy. Here again a warning is necessary. The beneficial effects of the practice of zazen, the primary discipline in Zen, have long been known to medical men in Japan. To sit in a quiet place for some length of time each day without moving, breathing in a certain rhythm and practicing certain concentration exercises—this unquestionably both quiets and energizes body and mind. But further than that Zen as a therapy should not be expected to go. True, all religions are in some wise therapies, soul therapies or, as one psychiatrist put it to me, "Great Therapies." But they are not because of that necessarily suited to deal with the neuroses afflicting so many in the modern world. For those, specialists are needed. The role of the Zen master is to assist you to awaken to profound religious experiences. He will have insight into your deepest nature, but do not expect him to have insight into your private neurosis or to be able to cure it for you through koan study. Zen practice will strengthen your body and mind, but a strong body and mind are essential in beginning it and in carrying it on.

Of all the reasons people have for wanting to embark upon Zen study, perhaps the one most fraught with danger is the desire "to get satori." It has been truly said that *satori* (enlightenment) is the heart of Zen, that without satori there is no Zen. But the mere fact that so much glib talk about satori is going around seems to have given people the impression that to attain it not much more is needed than the desire.

Satori is not attained the moment you put your feet on the soil of Japan, as one student who came unannounced expected. Nor is it a ripe persimmon just waiting for you to get under the tree to fall into your lap. In the history of Zen, and Buddhism, satori has come only after long, painful, determined, and dedicated striving to awaken to truth and, most important of all, with no aim to "get" anything. Moreover, do not think there is only one satori which, when it comes, will bring your Zen study to an end. The first satori, as I have said elsewhere, opens the door to the world of Zen just a crack. To know that world, many more years of practice and many more satoris will scarcely suffice.

So do not bring with you, if you come to Japan, your preconceived notions of an instantaneous and total enlightenment that can be experienced in a few weeks or a few months at most and that will give you "all knowledge" once and for all. If you do, you will be easy prey for the "Fox Zen" teachers who throughout Zen history have been lying in wait for those gullible ones who believe there is an easy and quick way.

There is one thing more the westerner is warned to denude himself of before embarking on Zen study in Japan. That is his own view of what Zen is. Of all the difficult things to discard, this is perhaps the most difficult. It is extraordinary how much the foreigner who has set foot on Japanese soil only a few days previously and whose Zen comes entirely from his reading can tell old Zen hands about Zen. An incident that took place some little while ago will illustrate this point.

A western Zen enthusiast was being shown around a monastery by the *Roshi* (Zen Master). With increasing surprise he watched the Roshi bow before a stone here, a gate there, a shrine a little farther on in the garden. Finally, when they reached the main Buddha-hall and the Roshi bowed reverently before the Buddha-image enshrined in it, our western Zennist could restrain himself no longer.

"I thought you were a Zen man!" he exclaimed. "And I thought that Zen people had discarded all forms and rituals. In the past didn't they smash Buddha-images and burn them! But you, you go on bowing here and bowing there. I don't understand you. I, on the other hand, have gone beyond such nonsense. I'm through with it. Why, I wouldn't even mind spitting on the Buddha-image!"

"Very well," said the Roshi quietly in his inadequate English, "You spits, I bows."

All of which is not to say that we foreigners must avidly and thoughtlessly swallow all of Japanese Zen Buddhism just as we find it and, after we leave the monastery or finish our Zen training, conscientiously carry out all its forms in the minutest detail. But when the foreigner enters the Japanese Zen world he must be prepared to enter a world that differs from his own in that it is Buddhist and in that it is Japanese. He must be prepared, temporarily at least, to strip himself as far as is humanly possible of his previously held beliefs and opinions and enter not only with an unbiased mind but with a mind willing to accept a new bias if this agrees with his reason. Always he will have to be on guard against the tendency to judge and criticize what he sees and what he hears by the standards he has brought with him and is still clinging to. Often he will find himself resenting the activities he is expected to participate in, refusing, or wanting to refuse, to follow the customs and manners that are the mode of daily life in this new world he has entered and, after they have lost their first strangeness, to consider them ridiculous or even obnoxious.

Zen Buddhism as we find it in Japan today is heavily incrusted with the Chinese culture that produced and nurtured it, and heavily enveloped in coverings of the Japanese culture that has preserved it for us. But under these incrustations and wrappings the living heart of Zen, which is the heart of Buddhism, still beats strong and true. The important work for future western Zennists is to scale off these external coverings and, reaching that true living heart, to make it clearly visible again. Since these Zennists will be westerners, they in their turn cannot help but envelop this living heart in some of their own cultural wrappings. That is at once inevitable and correct, for the living heart can never be exposed just as it is. It must be made visible to men of today and the future—to the extent it can be made visible—through the forms and terms they can understand, just as it has been made visible to the men of the past in the forms and terms intrinsic to their cultures.

But before we westerners boldly begin tearing off the old wrappings, we must first be able to clearly discern what are merely cultural accretions and what is the living heart. To do this we must not only penetrate to the living heart itself, but we must try sympathetically to understand the forms themselves under which Zen is presented to us, to understand what they have meant and why they have persisted. Only when we have done that can we begin throwing them away. Perhaps we shall find that there are not so many to discard as we first thought, that there are many which fulfill a real purpose for men of all cultures and times and which, with some adaptation to modern minds, are unrivaled in their efficiency in producing the man Zen has always been striving to produce.

III. Zen for the Sightseer

GENERALLY SPEAKING, the occidentals who come to Japan with an interest in Zen or Zen study fall into four categories: those who come for three or four weeks; those who come for three or four months; those who can remain a year; those who can remain several years. From now on I shall take up the conditions those in each category will find themselves faced with, suggest how these conditions can best be adapted to, and indicate what degree of accomplishment may be anticipated. Everything said about the problems of those who come for shorter stays will, of course, apply to those who remain longer and, to some extent, vice versa.

It cannot be too often reiterated that we are still at a very early stage in the great movement of Buddhism—and Zen—from the East to the farther East, that is the West. Japanese Zen people are only beginning to be aware of the interest Americans and Europeans have already taken in their religion and, therefore, have made few if any preparations for the reception of either superficial or serious students. Of course they are pleased that the foreigner admires this aspect of Japanese culture, but they have difficulty in grasping just what it is he wants to know about it and why he wants to study it.

With Zen, as with the traditional Japanese arts, there has long been the instinctive feeling that real insight and accomplishment in this field lie outside the capacity of one not born a Japanese.

I am not quite sure that I know what people, particularly those with no knowledge of the Japanese language, have in mind when they say they are coming to Japan for three or four weeks and want to find out as much as they can about Zen. It is somewhat as if a Japanese person, who had no knowledge of English but had read some books and heard some lectures in Japan on the Episcopalian faith, were to go to England and say that he wanted to find out as much as possible about Episcopalianism during the few weeks of his stay. He would be shown a number of cathedrals and churches, be taken to various types of services; he would look at religious paintings in galleries and museums, talk through an interpreter to a few Anglican priests, and perhaps even be permitted to make a tour of an Anglican seminary or monastery. In the end he would have seen what is visible to the eye and have felt something of the mood of this branch of the Christian Church, both valuable experiences, to be sure, but certainly falling far short of his hopes and dreams for coming to a closer and more intimate understanding of it.

The case of Zen in Japan offers more difficulties to the occidental than does that of Episcopalianism in England to the Japanese visitor. Most temple buildings and gardens can easily be seen, and they are both strange and beautiful. Services, however, in the sense that they are held in any Christian sect, are not to be found in Zen. In the big headquarter temples a gorgeous ceremony is held annually on the Founder's Day. In addition, there may be one or two special ceremonies held during the year. Other than these, such services as take place are attended only by the priests connected with the headquarters, and at them only the chanting of sutras (scriptures) takes place.

In the smaller temples the situation is almost the same. There is a
Founder's Day Ceremony, ceremonies at the time of the spring and
autumn equinoxes, and at O-bon in August, these latter three being
in the nature of masses for the dead. Lay believers in large numbers
attend these services, which usually consist first of sutra-chanting,
then dinner, then perhaps a short sermon, and finally a tea ceremony
party. There are no daily or weekly services open to the adherents
or the public. In the smaller temples the priest chants a few sutras
before the image on the altar morning and evening, but no one other
than himself is expected to be present. Some of the higher ranking
priests have small private groups of lay adherents who gather once
or twice a month to listen to a talk on Zen. These meetings are held
either in temple rooms or in private houses. In some cases they include a short period of meditation and, for the more serious members of the group, sanzen with the priest, should he be a roshi.

As for seeing paintings, though Zen temples own some of the
most famous paintings in Japan, they are kept in the storehouses,
except when a few are displayed on the occasion of one of the ceremonies, or when all are taken out and hung up to be aired during
one or two dry days each autumn. The exceptions to this are usually
the greatest paintings, ranked as National Treasures and turned over
to the care of the big museums of Tokyo and Kyoto. There they are
occasionally put on exhibition, perhaps once or twice in five or ten
years. To get special permission to see the paintings either in the
temple storehouses or in the museums is extremely difficult, and in
all cases they are taken out only when the weather is suitable. Damp-
ness, which characterizes the climate of Japan most of the year, is
extremely hard on the old Chinese and Japanese paintings.

Images are less difficult to see. They are usually on the altar, often
in closed cases, but these latter will readily be opened on request.

The Zen Sect, however, does not emphasize the cult of images, so aside from those of the Founder—often life-sized—there are not many important examples of the art of sculpture to be found in Zen temples.

To visit a Zen monastery offers still more problems. The monasteries are not monasteries in the Catholic or western sense of the word. They are primarily what might be called "theological seminaries," to which monks—and monks are today either students for the priesthood or such priests as do not yet wish to undertake the duties of caring for a temple—come to engage in Zen study and practice under the direction of a Zen master. After two or three years, the majority of these monks will be ordained as priests and go to their own temples. Only a few of the more serious stay the fifteen or more years necessary to complete their Zen study.

Monastery studies are carried on during two terms each year: a summer term beginning usually the first of May and continuing until the end of July, and a winter term beginning the first of November and continuing until the end of January. The remaining months are vacation periods, during which the majority of the monks return to their home temples in other cities or villages, leaving only a skeleton staff to keep the monastery running, to recite the sutras morning and evening, and to attend the roshi when he is in residence. Many roshis use these vacation periods for travel to temples in various parts of the country, where they conduct ceremonies, give lectures, and instruct groups of lay students.

Foreign visitors to Kyoto often ask if they cannot stay a night in a monastery, or at least sit with the monks for a time in the *zendo* (meditation hall). If the monastery is in session, the head monk is sometimes kind and will put them up as overnight guests in one of the monastery guest rooms, for all temples have one or two such rooms. Occasionally, if the visitor insists he can sit in the meditation posture, he will be permitted to sit with the monks for a short time during the evening meditation. But sitting at home for fiteen or twenty minutes with freedom to move or shift one's position is very different from sitting immobile in a zendo for even one of the required thirty or forty minute periods. And, since any unusual movement is distracting, the monks are loath to have a guest in the meditation hall unless they are convinced he can sit almost as well as they. For zazen is the heart of Zen practice and, at least to the more serious monks, a matter of life and death. To sanzen, of course, no visitor is admitted. This is a meeting between the roshi and the student only.

During the summer and winter terms the roshi gives a special type of lecture designed primarily for koan students and called in Japanese *teisho*. To these lectures normally only the monks and the roshi's lay students are admitted, though it is not impossible for a visitor to obtain an invitation to attend. These lectures are very interesting to watch as they are conducted in a fashion that has varied little since Sung times in China.

Foreign visitors should remember that Japanese temples, except in the rare instances where one of the buildings has been designated a National Treasure, no longer have any government support whatsoever. Also, though the largess of the feudal lords, who in olden days took pride in building and sustaining fine Zen temples, came to an end almost a hundred years ago, the individual temple adherent has not yet come to feel that responsibility for its support that is understood by even the most humble member of a Christian congregation. Moreover, the lands remaining in the possession of the temples after the Meiji Restoration were practically all taken away under the new land laws promulgated at the time of the Occupation.

Therefore, when a westerner goes to see temple buildings, gardens, or works of art, if a regular sightseer's fee is not posted at the entrance, on leaving he should make a small donation of money to the priest, the amount depending upon the courtesies he has received and the number of persons in his party. A somewhat larger donation should be made when visiting a monastery or if the visitor is permitted to sit in the meditation hall. If he spends a night in a temple or monastery, the gift should be the equivalent of the cost of a like stay in a hotel. Money gifts should always be placed in the white paper envelopes sold by all stationers for that specific purpose. Money is a very common form of gift in Japan, but to be offered such a gift in any other way than in one of these envelopes is offensive to any Japanese person, and particularly so to a priest.

As to interviews with distinguished Zen priests or Zen masters, these are not impossible to arrange. How rewarding they are will depend in large part upon the visitor himself. Many Zen priests are excellent tea masters and enjoy making thick tea for their guests, though not always in the stiff style of the traditional *cha-no-yu*. One can best see that demonstrated in the tea room of a professional tea master. At such times an adequate interpreter is necessary and, unfortunately, there are very few of these. I know of only two or three in Kyoto—one a priest, the others scholars—capable of interpreting at such a conversation. Ordinary interpreters are practically useless, since they are not acquainted with the idiomatic Zen speech Zen priests customarily use.

Another problem is to get the Zen man, either priest or learned lay adherent, to talk about Zen. In the first place, since Japanese Zen people are not accustomed to analyze their religious thinking as we in the West are, it is difficult to find a common intellectual ground for discussion. Furthermore, Zen men do not like to talk about Zen.

When they are questioned about it they are apt to reply, "There is nothing to Zen," or "There is nothing to study in Zen," or "Zen is daily life," remarks that smack of being clichés and, unfortunately, too often are just that. Sometimes, however, just drinking plain *bancha* with an old teacher in his shabby room will have a meaning deep beyond words to describe.

IV. A WHIFF OF ZEN

I ASSUME THAT those who come to Japan for only a few weeks and hope to find out something about Zen in that time will come to Kyoto, for only in the old capital can at least the outer expressions of Zen still be found in abundance. Here are seven of the great Rinzai Zen headquarter temples, each with its monastery. Here are the finest examples of Zen gardening. Here the old arts of Japan—Noh, tea ceremony, flower arrangement, sumi painting, calligraphy, pottery, among others—can best be enjoyed or studied. And here is the only Rinzai Zen university.

The first actual problem is, of course, a place to live. Ryosen-an will never be able to provide guest accommodations for either longer or shorter periods. The house is too small and the ground with the compound walls is now completely given over to buildings and gardens. A temple building within the Daitoku-ji area where a small number of students can live together in a manner approximating monastery life is a dream we hope some day to make a reality. But when, we do not know.

Kyoto's two first-class foreign-style hotels are fairly expensive; with three meals a day the cost is from $10 upward for one person. There is a less expensive second-class hotel, and, though the location near the railroad station is not too desirable, many people seem to find this hotel adequate. Several new western-style hotels are either under construction or planned for the next two or three years.

First-class Japanese inns are as expensive as foreign-style hotels of the same rank, often more so. Second-class inns are also relatively expensive and, furthermore, usually noisy. Japanese people who patronize Japanese inns are almost invariably on an excursion. They are apt to get up early and go to bed late, and to have little or no consideration for the tired fellow guest who might like a night's sleep. The larger second and third class inns cater almost exclusively to the big—sometimes mammoth—groups of country people and school children who come to the old capital for sightseeing.

Chotoku-in, a temple within the precincts of Shokoku-ji, one of the Rinzai Zen headquarters, is a very pleasant and convenient place to stay and enjoy some temple atmosphere. Sohaku Ogata, its priest, has been one of the forward thinking Zen men in Japan. Several trips to America and one to Europe have given him facility in English, and his acquaintance with western ways of living has made it possible for him to arrange rooms in Chotoku-in that combine Japanese temple atmosphere and certain comforts westerners consider indispensable. Mr. and Mrs. Ogata can receive five or six foreign guests for a few days or for several months. They give preference to those who have come to study Zen or subjects related to it. Breakfast is provided at Chotoku-in, but not other meals. Though Mr. Ogata is not a Zen master, he is extremely kind and helpful in explaining Zen to his foreign guests and introducing them to Zen temples. I know of no other Zen temple where westerners may stay for a short period of time.

The Kyoto YWCA has rooms for women for shorter or longer stays. Breakfast only is served there. The YMCA has no rooms. In addition, Kyoto now has three youth hostels where young men and women can find accommodations for a short period under the conditions usual at such hostels everywhere. Three meals a day are served and charges are minimum. Furnished apartments do not exist in Kyoto. Unless you have friends here to help you, finding a room in a Japanese house for a short period is practically an impossibility.

Kyoto is the sightseeing center of Japan and tourism one of its greatest sources of income. In the spring and autumn especially, the hotels and inns are crowded to overflowing. So my advice is, if and when you decide you are coming, and if you want to stay at a hotel or inn, to consult your travel agent and make your reservations through him before you leave on your trip. If you think of Chotoku-in or the YWCA, write to them well in advance.

There are many foreign-style and Japanese restaurants in Kyoto, but except for the deluxe ones, none are too good, especially the foreign-style ones, and all are rather expensive considering the quality of food offered. Kyoto is famous for *not* providing good eating. From olden days Kyotoites have been said to deprive their stomachs in order to decorate their backs.

Naturally you will want first to visit the most famous places for sightseeing in and near Kyoto. Three or four days should suffice for that if you leave the Zen temples until later. If you want to buy souvenirs, to prowl in the byways of the city, or to visit some of the numerous coffee houses and cabarets—none of them very glamorous, I warn you—do that during your sightseeing period. Satisfy the tourist in yourself first. Then you will be prepared to surrender yourself to the Zen atmosphere without any hankerings.

When you are ready for this, there are a few rules you should lay down for yourself. The first is to put your camera away. You can buy plenty of photographs that are better than any you can take yourself.

If you want colored slides, the shops sell literally thousands of different ones. Rather, let all your senses register what you are experiencing. Then all will become part of yourself—the scene, the movement, the fragrance of the pines, the feel of the wind as it brushes your face. You will not have to open an old album or set up a projector to recall your experiences.

Secondly, do not plan to do more than one major thing in one day. Do not try to see lots of Zen temples and lots of Zen gardens. One headquarter temple and two or three small ones and a few gardens will be enough for your entire visit if you assimilate these thoroughly. It is not how much you see but *how* you see what you see that matters. The ability to retain sense impressions is greatly diminished by trying to absorb too much and too many things too quickly.

Thirdly, take your time and go leisurely. It is only when you have no sense of time and no special aim or intention that you can really open up all your senses. The willful urge to experience will hinder your capacity to experience. Give yourself lessons in *mushin* (no-mind). Here is a way to begin your Zen study. Zen study is not learning about Zen but making use of Zen principles and letting them work on you. It is for the purpose of making you into a Zen man. It is not to give you the ability to astound your friends with your profound knowledge, but to cause you to become him whom you truly are.

Don't hesitate to go anywhere alone. Going alone is preferable to going with an unsympathetic companion. Comprehension of what true aloneness means is an important part of Zen understanding. It is only when one is alone, whether it be in a crowded city street, in a quiet garden, or walking along a mountain path, that one begins to share in the vivid living quality of each and every one of Nature's manifestations, in their simplicity, their directness, their just-as-they-are-ness. Practically speaking, it is quite easy to go about Kyoto and its environs without a guide, especially if you approach the man in the street for directions with a smile and don't become annoyed by an occasional failure in communication.

Never take a taxi to get anywhere if you can help it. Take a tram or walk. Or, if you like to bicycle, rent a bicycle for the period of your stay. Don't have a luncheon date you must get back for. When you go to Nanzen-ji, for instance, go for the day. Explore leisurely all the corners of that lovely headquarter temple. Sit long in the rooms with the gorgeous gold *fusuma* (sliding wall-panels) painted by the Kanos, and long before the austere Kobori Enshu garden. Wander up one of the mountain paths back of the temple buildings and, resting on a rock under a pine, listen to the sound of the rushing stream or breathe in the color of the masses of mountain flowers. Then walk slowly back to the little bean-curd shop within the temple enclosure and, sitting in the bark-thatched hut, eat your thirty-yen *tofu* and watch the insects playing hop-scotch on the leaves of the lotus in the adjacent temple pond.

If it's a rainy day, take your sandwiches and go up to Ryoan-ji. The stone garden is never more beautiful than when seen through the veil of water that falls from the spacious roofs. You can sit for hours on the verandah by the garden and no one will disturb you. No one but the hordes of sightseers that come in groups of a hundred or more at a time. But they remain only long enough to take some pictures and buy a few postcards. Then they go on. And the stillness and beauty of the garden are the more intense for their having come and having gone. When the sun appears in the afternoon, perhaps you will want to walk up the mountain behind the temple and look for the tomb of Lady Murasaki or for the wild orchids that abound there in the early summer.

Or go to Arashiyama and hire a boat. Let the boatman pole you around the better part of the day. Take a plunge from the prow into a cold pool in one of the deeper parts of the river, then lie on the cushions at the bottom of the boat and snooze and dream. I can tell you lots of things to do. All will have to do with putting your feet on the bare earth, letting your skin feel the sun and the wind, and your eyes drink up the landscape.

Perhaps one day you will go to see a Noh play, or perhaps another there will be a big ceremony to attend, depending upon the time of the year you are here. On another, perhaps, you will visit one of the Daitoku-ji temples and, after viewing the paintings the priest has hung up for the annual airing, enjoy the unbelievable red of the autumn maples while drinking tea with him on the verandah.

Then every night, if you wish, you may come to Ryosen-an and sit with us in the quiet of our zendo. You will sit on your cushion on the *tan* (raised platform), awkwardly at first, no doubt, but gradually with more ease. You will hear the sharp clack of the clappers and the ching of the bell; you will smell the incense, and you will share in the deep silence that envelops this most wonderful of rooms. Later, you will join us in drinking the bitter zendo tea with Manjusri, the Bodhisattva of Intrinsic Wisdom. And at the end the evening, you will find your heart strangely moved as the men and women students chant the vow to devote whatever they may gain in walking the Buddha's path to the saving of all sentient beings.

When you return home and your friends ask you what you have learned about Zen in your three or four weeks' stay in Kyoto, probably you will have to say, "Not much." Not much you can speak about, perhaps, but much you will never forget.

V. THE ZEN MONASTERY AND THE ZEN MASTER

NOW THERE ARE THOSE who are fortunate enough to have three or four months for study in Japan and who look forward to spending this time in a monastery presided over by the Zen master of their choice. Before their dreams carry them too far, they should inform themselves about the problems that lie ahead. Disappointment is likely to be in store for those who insist upon clinging to the idealized picture of monastery life most westerners have built up in their minds through reading books about it. Since the basic problems will be the same whether the foreigner stays in a monastery a few months, a year, or longer, in the next chapters I shall speak of these problems in some detail, later relating them to the length of the student's stay.

The first thing for the would-be foreign student to consider is the time of his visit. As I have said, the monasteries are open for Zen study approximately six months during the year: from May first to the end of July, and from November first to the end of January. Anyone who wants to enter a *sodo*—literally "monks hall," the Japanese name for the monastery—should be ready to do so shortly before one of the terms opens and should plan to remain for the duration of the term. Even monks, except those returning from a sick leave, are seldom permitted to enter the monastery after the term has begun. On the other hand, during the vacation periods when the majority of the monks are away, the few who remain are too busy to bother with a new guest. The meditation hall is closed; there is no group zazen and, except in rare instances, no sanzen and no teisho. Three or four weeks before the opening of the new term, the monks begin to come back. This is the best time for a newcomer to enter.

All monasteries have rooms where they can put up men and

women guests for a night or two, but only men are accepted in the sodos for a longer stay. Among Rinzai monasteries, that of Naka-gawa Soen Roshi—about whom more below—is the one exception to this rule that I know of.

Now what monastery shall the foreigner go to? No one can just present himself at any Zen monastery and expect to be taken in. He must be introduced to a sodo by responsible persons who will act as his sponsors. Even Japanese Zen monks cannot enter any monastery they wish; they must have recommendations from their home temple, their personal teacher, and their previous Zen master if they have had one. Since monastery life is a communal life, the head monks, upon whom the final decision in these matters largely rests, are careful to accept only such persons as they feel assured will fit into their group or those who have a definite relationship with that particular monastery or teaching line.

Nor can the foreigner ask any Zen master he may happen to fancy to take him as his disciple. Here it is even more important to be personally introduced. Whether the would-be student speaks Japanese or not, not many Japanese Zen masters will be eager to accept him for koan study for a long term, much less for a few months. Still fewer are as yet themselves prepared to take him.

Soen Nakagawa, the roshi of Ryutaku-ji Monastery at Mishima, is in many ways the best prepared. Soen Roshi twice visited Nyogen Senzaki, who for many years had a group of Zen followers in Los Angeles. After the old monk's death about two years ago, the group invited Soen Roshi to come again to America, this time to instruct them for two months. He is now reasonably at home in English and his contacts with American people have given him some understanding of their natures. In the past ten years he has been most kind about receiving foreign guests at Ryutaku-ji. Some have stayed only a few days, others have become his disciples and remained several months or longer.

Though Sogen Asahina, the roshi of Engaku-ji, Kamakura, does not speak English, he, also, has had considerable acquaintance with foreigners. He made a trip to America after the war, and numerous westerners visited his temple during the Occupation and still continue to visit it. Ever since the days when the great Shaku Soen wielded the stick at Engaku-ji, this temple has been especially hospitable to Americans and Europeans. Asahina Roshi has accepted a few western students for koan study, but, except in the one or two rare cases where they were well acquainted with the Japanese language, he has had to call upon one of his monks to act as interpreter.

Zuigan Goto Roshi, the teacher of a number of the members of our Kyoto Institute, speaks remarkably good English. He studied the language as a university student and later spent four years in America when his teacher, Sokatsu Shaku Roshi, had a Zen center in San Francisco in the early years of this century. Thus, those of us who had the great good fortune to be accepted as Goto Roshi's disciples have had the invaluable experience of taking sanzen in English without an intermediary. Now just eighty and rather frail, Goto Roshi lives in retirement in a small temple on the outskirts of Kyoto. He no longer accepts new students.

Oda Sesso, roshi of the Daitoku-ji Monastery, has so far limited himself to such Japanese-speaking foreign students as our Kyoto Institute has recommended to him.

There are a few other roshis in Kyoto and elsewhere who might be persuaded to take a foreign student, provided a suitable interpreter were available. However, since the only person permitted to act in such capacity at koan interviews is one whose koan study is far in advance of that of the student for whom he is interpreting, all but the older monks or lay students are ruled out. In most cases, unfortunately, these have insufficient English or none at all.

And here a word of caution must be given. In China, in olden times at least, it would seem that a Zen student was free to go to a Zen master for a time, remain perhaps several years, then go on to another master, and later to still another. In the end, the student seems to have been considered the disciple or heir, as the case may be, of the teacher under whom he completed his attainment.

Such freedom as this does not exist in Japanese Rinzai Zen today. Once a student is accepted as a disciple by a Zen master, he remains that master's disciple until the relationship is terminated by the death of one or the other, or by some unusual circumstance. For instance, the master or the student may come to feel that there is no deep *innen* (spiritual relationship) between them. Then the roshi will suggest that the student go to another teacher, or the student will ask to be released from the relationship. Or, if the student must move to a place too far distant for him to continue studying under his master, he will request the teacher to recommend him to another roshi. In that case, the new teacher will probably be of the same or a related teaching line. Though the old intimacy between teacher and disciple may never again be resumed, relations will in any case remain most friendly. But if, for some reason or other, unknown to his master the student goes to another roshi to "try him out," or if he just "walks out" on the master with no explanation, when the master becomes aware of what has taken place, the student may expect never again to be allowed to enter the master's room and to find the rooms of other masters of the same line closed to him as well.

Sometimes one of the headquarter temples will hold a great meditation meeting which all the roshis and monks of the temples belonging to that headquarter attend. At such a time, a monk is free to test his Zen understanding by taking sanzen with any of the roshis present. Or, during the vacation period, a roshi will sometimes hold a special meditation meeting lasting a week or more outside his own temple or monastery. With his master's permission, a monk or lay student may take part in this meditation week. He may wish to have his understanding tested by a master other than his own; or it may be that he wishes to study some special koans that have been handed down only in the teaching line of this roshi.

Few westerners understand the rigid etiquette governing the master-disciple relationship in Japanese Rinzai Zen. Some have quite unthinkingly taken sanzen with a roshi for a short time; then, on hearing of another they believe they might like better, gone on to him. The second roshi may accept them because he does not yet know of their earlier relationship, or for some reason of his own. Such foreigners, if they do not remain long in Japan, in all probability will go home blissfully ignorant of the firmly closed door behind their backs. Where they have stayed longer or returned and attempted to resume friendly relations with their original teacher, they have soon been made aware of their earlier error.

In short, before he begs any roshi to accept him as a disciple, the foreign student should consult with other westerners who have studied under Japanese Zen masters, then go to visit several monasteries and have interviews with their roshis. Once he has asked to be accepted as a sanzen student and the roshi consents, the die is cast.

VI. Monastery Life

THE FOREIGN GUEST-STUDENT in a sodo during the months it is in session presents many problems to the monks: Can the foreigner put up with the general living conditions in the monastery? Can he and will he follow the daily schedule? Can he keep well during the extreme cold of the winter in buildings that are unheated and have only paper-covered windows and doors? Can he take the extreme heat and the insects in the summer? Can a foreigner live on monastery food? Can he sit in zazen posture? Can he speak enough Japanese to communicate with the monks regarding at least simple matters? Can a suitable interpreter be found if he stays long enough to take sanzen with the roshi?

What follows is a general description of present-day monastery routine, in large part based upon the regulations of the Daitoku-ji Sodo. Each sodo, however, has some traditional regulations peculiar to it; also, the character and personal views of the roshi presiding over a monastery usually influence that sodo's policy, for the period of his regime at least.

During the summer and winter terms, the monks adhere to a rigid daily routine. They rise in summer at three in the morning, in winter at four. After they have dressed and put away their bedding, there is a period of meditation in the zendo, during which they go to the roshi for their individual sanzen. A sutra-chanting service follows, then breakfast. By eight they are working in the fields or gardens, cleaning the temple, or going *takuhatsu* (begging). Dinner is at ten-thirty, followed soon after by a short rest, then more work. At four-thirty supper, a rest, then meditation from six until nine, broken by evening sanzen. A half-hour is devoted to preparing for the night. Then the lights are put out and, theoretically, the monks go to bed. Actually, however, all are expected to slip into the garden or onto the verandahs for night meditation out of doors.

This regular program is somewhat changed on the days the roshi gives teisho, or when special ceremonies are held, and it is made more arduous in the one week each month devoted especially to meditation. During these week-long periods of meditation known as *sesshin*—one interpretation of the characters with which the word is written is "searching the heart"—the monks devote themselves to zazen from early morning until late into the night, and the roshi hears sanzen from three to five times each day. For the entire week the monastery gate is closed to all outsiders except those laymen who live at home but come regularly to the sodo for sanzen under the roshi.

When a foreigner first goes into a sodo to live, usually he is not permitted to sleep in the zendo with the monks, but is given a small separate room in one of the various buildings within the monastery compound. He is expected to join the monks in their meals, in listening to the Zen master's lectures, and in the general ceremonies that take place from time to time. He must do his zazen practice by himself in his own room or in one of the halls where the services are held. He is not permitted to sit with the monks for meditation in the zendo until such time as he can sit well. He is not given a koan until he has proven his sincerity as well as his ability to sit, and unless an interpreter is available for his sanzen. Occasionally he will be invited to have tea with the roshi in his room, or with the older monks who have a few English phrases at their disposal and who will come to chatter, satisfy their curiosity, improve their small English, and eat cakes and drink tea. Until he has proven himself a serious Zen student, the guest will not be invited to assist in the monastery work, such as gardening, cleaning, and cooking, though he will be asked to help with outside sweeping. In other words, he will remain in every sense a monastery guest.

All living conditions in Japan, except those in foreign-style hotels or houses, from the westerner's standpoint are primitive and uncomfortable. Whether or not one adapts oneself happily to this change in living habits depends primarily upon flexibility of both body and mind. One must sleep on a pad and sit on a pad, though at first one's back and legs protest loudly. Yet in time a thin mat becomes the most comfortable of beds, and legs will adapt themselves to being continuously crossed or folded back.

Monasteries always have extra *zabuton*—the thin cushions ordinarily used by Japanese for sitting—which the foreigner can use folded over for zazen practice in his room or in the zendo. If he wants one of the especially thick pads known as *tanbuton*, which the monks all use for meditation, he must purchase this for himself.

The monastery can usually provide the guest with bedding such as is given to the monks. This is a double-width cotton-stuffed pad; one half serves as a mattress, the other half, folded over, serves as a quilt. Any additional covering such as blankets or quilts must be individually supplied. Sheets and pillow cases are unknown in the monastery. For sleeping, the monks merely remove their *koromo* (monk's robe) and lie down inside their folded bed pad. The type of koromo they may wear is fixed by regulation, as are the number and kind of kimonos and the amount of underwear permitted under the robe. In accordance with an old and still generally prevailing Japanese custom, everyone provides himself with his own soap, towels, and toilet paper.

The foreign guest-student may, of course, have what he thinks he needs in the way of clothing. For wear in winter he should have heavy long underwear and wool socks, enough of each so as to be able to put on two or three sets, one over the other. Then plenty of sweaters, a heavy bathrobe for sleeping in, and, above all, a wool stomach band. He will need a windbreaker for out-of-door work, and may often find it comfortable when sitting in his room, though it cannot be worn in the zendo.

In the winter the temperature in most of Japan reaches at its lowest about 15 degrees above Fahrenheit. The atmosphere is extremely damp most of the winter and the cold very penetrating. Normally there is no heat of any kind in the monastery except a *hibachi* (brazier) with charcoal in the roshi's private room and one in the room of the head monk. If the guest is in a separate room and needs heat, a hibachi can probably be provided, but he must be careful to supply his own charcoal for it, and must be prepared to find that it will do little more than warm his hands or boil a small kettle of water.

In summer the temperature is often close to 100 degrees Fahrenheit and the air very humid. Then the student will need the lightest of clothing. At all times clothing may be most casual, except when attending services or sitting in the zendo, when certain regulations must be conformed to. In the meditation hall, for instance, everyone must have bare feet and use a certain type of straw sandal; overcoats are not allowed. After he has remained a considerable time and been accepted as a sanzen student, occasionally the foreigner is permitted to buy his own monk's robe to wear while sitting in the zendo and attending services, but such permission is at the discretion of the roshi and should not be expected.

Baths are taken in the communal bathroom, Japanese style, five or six men bathing together at a time. The westerner will be expected to do his own laundry work. Only cold water is used for washing clothes. Hot water is a luxury most Japanese people, let alone monks, do not permit themselves, except for cooking and bathing. Insects are a great nuisance in summer and autumn. There are no screens in the monastery. Mosquito incense, which he must purchase for himself and may use only in his own room, is the sole available defense and a not very efficient one.

The question of food is a most important one. The usual fare at the monastery consists of rice and barley boiled together, salted radish pickles, and tea for breakfast; seaweed soup with greens and some bean-curd in it, rice, pickles, and tea for dinner; cold rice, into which hot tea is poured, and pickles for supper.

The monks, in groups of two or three, are invited out quite often, several times a month on the average, to the homes of supporters of the monastery. There they are given a huge dinner of meat, fish, vegetables, and sweets, and they depend upon this extra food to supplement their usual monastery diet. Also, they often receive gifts of bean-flour cakes, or buy them for themselves from the small donations occasionally given them by the believers. With these they piece out between meals, a generally prevalent Japanese habit.

Any regular Japanese diet is, from the western standpoint, seriously lacking in protein and fat. No foreigner can subsist for any length of time and keep well on monastery food alone. He may be invited to accompany the monks to a dinner at the house of a supporter on occasion, but he cannot expect this to happen often. Furthermore, Japanese people are accustomed from childhood to eating great quantities of rice. Zen monks are famous rice eaters, and can easily consume at each meal three or four bowls of rice piled up high. The westerner's stomach, on the other hand, has not been trained to be elastic enough to accept sufficient rice to supply his body with adequate nourishment.

The foreign guest-student must therefore be prepared to supplement monastery food with meat, milk, butter, fish, eggs, and cheese. In Japan these are the most expensive foods. Prices are on a par with or higher than in New York City for the same things, while the quality is usually inferior. Some monasteries are not averse to the guest taking eggs and milk products in his own room privately, but all draw the line at meat or fish being brought into the monastery precincts. Though outside the temple gate most Zen monks and priests eat what is offered them regardless of whether or not it is "pure food," all monasteries and the stricter temples will not permit fish or meat to be brought in. In a city the size of Kyoto, the guest may slip away for a good steak dinner without causing comment. Where the monastery is situated in a smaller town or in the country, the fact that the foreigner must take food outside becomes a subject for considerable comment among the townspeople or villagers, comment not always favorable to the monastery. Great care has to be taken in this matter.

If the westerner has a tendency toward weak lungs, he must be particularly careful about adequate food. The strain of unaccustomed exposure to damp cold in the winter, coupled with inadequate nourishment, can have grave results in a country where tuberculosis is still a serious menace to the health of a large percentage of the population. If he pays attention to his diet, however, the simple regular life in what amounts to the open air and the continuous practice of zazen with its regular deep breathing will improve his general physical condition greatly.

Sitting is the next question. Few foreigners when they first come to Japan can sit even cross-legged, not to speak of sitting in half-lotus or full-lotus posture. To learn to sit and sit well takes continuous practice over a long period. Even Japanese monks are traditionally said to need one year of zazen practice in the monastery before they can sit well enough to meditate upon a koan. The famous Zen master Shaku Soen of Engaku-ji is quoted as having said: "To attempt to go into a Zen koan without first tranquillizing and refining the mind (that is, without being proficient in zazen) is like going after a fish with a hammer or looking for birds in a thunderstorm."

One who is serious about Zen study should from the very beginning devote at least eight hours a day to the practice of zazen. During these hours, periods of sitting accompanied by breathing and concentration exercises should be interspersed with periods of walking, the best antidote for cramped legs. While walking, the regular breathing and concentration of mind should as far as is possible continue without interruption. If the student will conscientiously and persistently follow this program, he will be surprised at the progress he will make.

In all this, the attitude of mind toward the practice is of the utmost importance. If the student keeps thinking how difficult it is to sit, how ill-adapted the structure of his particular body is to sitting, and so forth, he will never be able to sit well, though he practice for years. From the first moment he sits down on his cushion he must be convinced that he *can* sit, that if he asks his body kindly to sit—if he takes into consideration that he is demanding of his body that it train itself in new habits and that becoming habituated to new physical habits takes time, not the time he would like, but Nature's time—then gradually his body will sit. He must, in most cases, anticipate severe pain at times. At first he will give in to the pain and get up and walk about, then come back and sit again. But little by little, as his mind becomes quieter through the continued practice of the breathing and concentration exercises, he will find that he can sit through the pain. Then one day suddenly he will "give up sitting and just sit," as one of our students has very aptly put it. With that the sitting problem is over for good.

The next problem is that of language. Daily life in a monastery, when one's only language is English, presents difficulties, but no insurmountable ones. Almost every monastery has one or two young monks with a few ready phrases, remnants of high school English studies. These few phrases and a two-way dictionary will do much to bridge the gap. With good will on both sides and, on the part of the foreign student, eagerness to understand, communication can be established.

However, if the foreign student has some Japanese language before he comes to Japan, no matter how little it may be, this will be a great help. If he keeps his ears open to the speech around him, gradually he will be able to recognize, within the thick fog of strange sounds in which he is groping, a familiar word or two here and there and to piece them together into some kind of meaning. But he must always be prepared to have missed the point, not to have caught the negative at the end of the sentence, or the double negative in it, and to find that he has totally misunderstood what was said to him and "pulled a terrible boner." He must be prepared always to be wrong and, with a smile, to apologize and start all over again.

The young monks will, on their side, be most helpful and kind with what English they have, though the foreign student must guard against letting himself be pushed into the position of being an English teacher, a position that will waste his time and that of the young monks. For in the sodo, especially during the summer and winter periods, Zen study and practice must come first and nothing must interfere with them or distract the mind from them.

Koan study under the Zen master presents more and greater language problems than does daily life. I have already spoken of the fact that among the roshis only Nakagawa Soen and Goto Zuigan are fluent enough in English to give sanzen in it, and that for the student who speaks no Japanese to take sanzen with any other roshi than these two, either in or outside of a monastery, necessitates an interpreter. One of the older monks, if he knows some English, is the person usually called upon to undertake this role. In two or three cases, priests, who at one time studied in a given monastery and now reside in nearby temples, have been induced to return to the monastery during the meditation weeks to act as interpreters.

The interpreter must, in every case, be a person who has himself had long experience in sanzen. He must be far in advance in koan study of the person for whom he is called upon to interpret. The reasons are obvious. To find a monk or priest of greater experience is not too difficult when the foreign student is just beginning his koan study. And for some time to come we are not likely to be faced with the problem of advanced foreign students who do not know Japanese. But even for the beginning student it is difficult enough to find an interpreter who can quickly seize the meaning of the foreign student's words as well as just the words themselves—to say nothing of their intonation and the feeling behind them—then translate these immediately into Japanese that will convey to the roshi everything the student wishes to convey, then do the same in reverse for the roshi's reply, provided always that he makes one. Further, the interpreter must guard against stating for either teacher or student what he, the interpreter, *thinks* either means to say, rather than their actual words. The good interpreter translates as literally as possible, then leaves the interpretation of the meaning to the teacher or the student, as the case may be.

Under the best of circumstances, the interpreter's responsibility is a heavy one. Also, the presence of a third person at sanzen is a serious impediment to the roshi and the student, and a nervous strain as well. So taking and giving sanzen in this way, even when an interpreter is available, is far from ideal. But again I must remind you that these are pioneer days in the transmission of Zen to the West. We have to content ourselves with the possible, and not demand more.

VII. ADAPTING TO MONASTERY LIFE

I HAVE SPOKEN about the obvious problems facing both the monks and the foreigner when the latter goes to live in a Japanese Zen monastery. For the monastery, two less obvious, though no less important, problems remain: What effect will the guest-student's being there have on the monks, especially the younger monks? Can and will the foreigner adjust to his new life and environment? From the foreign student's standpoint, there is only one remaining problem: How can he best adapt himself to this new life?

The majority of present-day sodo monks are country boys or the sons of small temple priests. It would seem that at this late day everyone in Japan must have had some contact with foreigners, especially Americans, but that is really far from being the case. Though one may say that all Japanese people have been subjected to foreign influences, many people, especially those living in small towns and villages, have never actually come into personal contact with a foreigner. Curiosity regarding the strange and unusual is a highly developed characteristic of the Japanese people. So when a foreigner first enters a monastery he becomes, particularly for the younger monks, an object of the greatest interest. Everything about him is subject to intensive investigation—his hat, his shoes, his belt buckle, his underwear, his possessions, his daily habits, the characteristics of his physical body. These are endlessly commented upon, admired, criticized, and joked about, sometimes to a degree that demands a good deal of a sense of humor on the part of the newcomer.

Japanese life on all levels permits of little or no individual privacy of any kind. Only in exceptional cases does anyone ever knock or speak before pushing open a closed door or *shoji* (paper-covered sliding door panel). Japanese guests, at least when they visit foreigners, expect to comment upon every item of food, every dish set before them, every object in the room in which they are being entertained, every article of dress worn by the host or hostess, and the comments made are apt to be straightforward and uninhibited. So the younger monks, mercilessly investigating the new foreign member in their midst, are acting quite within their own code of manners.

But from the standpoint of the practice they have come to the monastery to engage in, this new and fascinating object is an undesirable distraction. The older monks, who are responsible for the training and behavior of the younger ones, do not like new and disturbing influences to come into the sodo. This is perhaps a minor reason for their disinclination to take in a westerner, particularly for a few months, but it is none the less a real one. Unfortunately, the foreigner himself is quite helpless in this dilemma. He cannot do much to diminish his strangeness, and he may be called upon to exert considerable patience until the curiosity dies down of itself. Good humor and adaptability to the ways of sodo life are about all he can do about it.

This matter of adapting to the ways of monastery life is of the utmost importance if the western student is to make any kind of success of his stay. Even Japanese people consider Zen monastery life to be a life of rigid discipline. If it is difficult for Japanese to accept, how much more difficult for occidentals, all of whose lives are known to be freer, easier, and more comfortable. The monks will be watching for and expecting the foreign student to fall down on the job. There is almost a sense of cultural rivalry in this—"You can't take what we can take." But if the foreigner shows he is making a sincere effort "to take it," no one will be more pleased than they. The kindness and sweetness that, for all their severity, are distinguishing qualities of Zen monks will then become more and more apparent.

As a matter of fact, however, most western students do not find Zen training as such so difficult to undergo. It is, rather, Japanese temple life that is hard to adapt to, life in which, of course, most of the monks have been brought up since earliest childhood. So for westerners there is a double challenge.

What is necessary from first to last is to accept sodo life just as it is. The daily routine of a monastery is strictly fixed. One person's dawdling over dressing or toothbrushing in the morning throws the program out of gear. So does not being exactly on time for meals, eating too slowly, taking a long time to get settled on the zazen cushion or to get off it. The disturbance to the pattern made by just such small things is felt by everyone in the group.

Occasionally the monks are given a holiday when they may go out to make small purchases, to see an art exhibit, or visit a friend. Except in unusual circumstances, the foreign student would do well to limit his city-going to these days. This is the time for him to treat himself to a thick steak and apple pie à la mode. If he wants to see a movie, there is no reason why he shouldn't do so. But he should have a clear understanding with the head monk as to when he is expected back. Being late for supper once may be excused. More often will not be. And when the monastery gate is closed for the night it remains so until the morning.

One more adaptation problem remains to be spoken of. The monks' schedule during the time the sodo is in session allows them few if any free hours during the day. But, since he cannot participate in such duties and activities as are the province of the monks only, the foreigner may find himself with time on his hands and nothing to do with it. Such time can too easily give rise to depression. If he has entered the monastery fairly recently, he has no koan to spend the extra time puzzling over. He has no letters to write since, if he is wise, he will previously have arranged to receive and answer none except in an emergency. News from relatives and friends is always distracting when it isn't disturbing. As completely as possible he should cut off contact with and even thinking about the world outside the monastery. He has nothing interesting to read for he will have brought no books with him for general reading and, least of all, books about Zen. (Two exceptions will be mentioned in a moment.) There is no one to chatter with for all the monks are busy elsewhere. His body is full of pains and his stomach complaining. So there is little left for him to do but think: How alone I am, an alien in an alien land, with no one to talk my language, share my thoughts, explain to me the meaning of what is going on! Why did I come here anyway? Is it worth the pain and discomfort? Is there anything in this practice after all, or is it just humbug? Why don't I chuck it all and go back to my own people and my own culture where I really belong?

I am sure that there is no westerner to whom sooner or later these thoughts do not come. To stop them is difficult. But you must not "give them a chair." If your body is too tired for more zazen in your own room, this is the time to begin memorizing sutras. Perhaps you have already questioned in your own mind the usefulness of this old practice and think it isn't necessary for you, a foreigner, especially since you cannot understand what you are reciting. Put such thoughts away with all the other doubts and questionings. Get out the two books you should have taken to the monastery with you—aside from your dictionary, of course—Suzuki's *Manual of Zen Buddhism* (the first edition only is useful) and *The Training of the Zen Buddhist Monk*, recently republished. Ask one of the monks which of the sutras in the *Manual* they chant as a group in the dining hall and in the meditation hall, and get him to mark the rhythm in which these sutras are recited. Most monasteries have their own traditional way of chanting. Then sit down and memorize these sutras one by one. The monks will be pleased to have you join with them, and their respect for your earnestness and sincerity will be increased. For yourself, gradually you will find the sutras a potent weapon against thoughts of self-pity and doubt, and their silent recitation the greatest possible help in quieting your mind when you first sit down to do zazen, and many other times as well.

Accepting and entering into the spirit of monastery life without questioning, at least while you are living there, is even more important than adapting to the rules and regulations. Sensitivity runs high in a monastery. Spoken words and overt actions are not needed to convey the visitor's feelings. For all the monks the monastery is a sacred place and the life lived there a religious life. If it is the Zen Buddhist life lived in the context of the Japanese cultural patterns— something different from the western or Christian conception of the religious life—it is none the less a religious life and their religious life. They do not want it to be misinterpreted or its aims misunderstood and held up to ridicule. The older monks do not want the younger monks infected by an outsider's ill-considered, critical appraisal. One who stays in a monastery for some time gradually comes to understand the reasons for and the deep meaning behind the unwestern forms in which this religious life expresses itself. It is important for all foreign students, but especially so for those who come for only a few months, to enter the monastery with an open mind and a pure heart.

There have been instances in the past where western students have not been able "to take" monastery life, where they have become antagonistic to the discipline and tried to find ways of getting around it or "beating it." This, also, the older monks know, and they don't want it to happen in their sodos. Since the war a few American students have done much to increase the respect of the roshis and older monks for foreign students. But each visitor who comes to stay has on his individual shoulders the responsibility of proving over again that the westerner is sincere in his efforts to study Zen to the point where he not only can take the daily discipline, however severe physically or however restricting to his personal freedom it may seem, but that he can enter into the deeper meaning of the Zen life with appreciation and with understanding. The adapting will have to come from him, however; it will not come from the monastery.

VIII. Accomplishment in Zen Study

ALL FOREIGNERS who think seriously of coming to Japan for Zen study are at once faced with two questions: How long can I stay? Have I the necessary funds available for such a stay? The sightseer, of course, once he has determined to make a trip to Japan, without unduly stretching his overall budget, can include in it the few special expenses he might incur in finding out about Zen. Those who come for three months, a year, or several years will each have different financial situations to consider. From the information in the section of the Appendix entitled "*Expenses*," the prospective student should be able to judge fairly closely what he can or cannot afford.

A third question will certainly soon follow in every would-be student's mind: In the time I have at my disposal, how far can I go in understanding Zen? Of course that question cannot be answered. Every person is an individual case. What one may achieve in a shorter time may take another much, much longer. The best attitude of mind is to determine to do one's best. That's all. Don't aim for results. The results will be just what they are. What is important in the end is what you make of the results. However, from the experiences of those who have already come to study Zen in Japan we can arrive at a general idea of what may be expected.

The student who comes for three or four months and goes almost directly into the monastery will learn to sit, of course. How well will depend upon how much practice in sitting he has done before he comes and how much time he devotes to it each day while he is living in the monastery. If his progress has been good, before his stay comes to an end he is sure to be sitting with the monks for the regular daily meditation periods in the zendo. He will learn to accept order, discipline, simplicity, even frugality. He will learn about Japanese Zen monastery life; he will make the acquaintance of Japanese Zen monks; he will participate in Japanese Zen rituals and ceremonies. The stark simplicity of Zen life and thought may bring him to dispense with some of the clutter in his own. The moments of reverence felt during the sutra-chanting or when bowing he may long remember and cherish. If he practices zazen earnestly, he will be aware of a sharpening of all his senses that will remain with him for some time. If he has gone beyond mere sitting to some progress in concentration, he may have glimpses of a deep and quiet mind he had no inkling of before. This is the most he can hope for.

The foreigner who has one year to give to Zen study and wants to experience as much of monastery life as possible will also probably go into a sodo soon after his arrival. If he enters just before the summer or winter term begins and becomes well adjusted to the life during those three months, by the time the term ends, undoubtedly he will no longer be considered a guest, but rather one of the group of monks. When the vacation period comes, they will be glad to have him remain on with them and let him share in all their daily tasks.

Since, as I have already said, the meditation hall is always closed during the vacation, the monks who remain sleep here and there in other buildings. There is no group meditation and the roshi gives no formal lectures. Nor is there any sanzen, except in the monasteries belonging or related to the Myoshin-ji line. Traditionally, in the sodos of this line, when the roshi is in residence during the vacation period he gives sanzen once a day, in the early morning. This is a great advantage for, if the foreign student has already begun koan study, he does not have the long break of three months without any formal Zen practice at all, something very frustrating to those whose time is limited.

Under any circumstances, however, the three vacation months afford the western student much free time. First of all he should devote this to his meditation practice, perfecting his posture and lengthening his sitting periods in preparation for the sesshins that will follow the coming term. If he has advanced to the point where the roshi has given him a koan, he should work hard on it, whether he can meet the roshi or not. But for two or three weeks he ought to get entirely away from the monastery, going to the mountains, the seashore, or the lakes, forgetting all about the routine of Zen study. Perhaps one of the monks will invite him to go back with him to his home temple. Living in a country temple is an interesting experience, and there are sure to be places of historic or other interest to visit nearby. He will feel much refreshed by this short break with sodo life and in much better spirits to resume it again.

Of course, if he has the means, he may prefer to spend the entire three months in traveling and sightseeing. Or he may want to take a room outside the monastery for that time and read and amuse himself as he will. But if he has only one year for Zen study, such a long and complete break is not to be recommended. In addition to getting out of practice physically, a long interruption in Zen practice causes a mental sagging that takes some time to overcome, with the result that he is likely to find the first weeks of the new term almost as difficult to go through as those when he first entered the monastery.

With the second term the student will find himself completely integrated into the community of monks. He will sleep in the zendo with them, help in the garden, the kitchen, and with the general cleaning. The monks will call on him to assist in various ways at the larger ceremonies attended by lay adherents of the monastery and by priests from other temples. Such ceremonies usually include a dinner that the monks themselves cook and serve. They may even invite him to go takuhatsu with them, loaning him a robe, a big hat, leggings, and straw sandals.

A year's stay in the sodo will give the westerner complete familiarity with Japanese Zen monastery life and some insight into the deeper meaning behind many of the formalities insisted upon. If he has enough Japanese, or if an interpreter is available, he will probably have begun sanzen, and thus to work seriously on his first koan, though he shouldn't expect to have made much real progress toward solving it. He should be proficient in zazen and in concentration, this latter being an accomplishment he will find of great value in his life, whatever the field he may later enter. Certainly he will carry away memories he will always treasure of the kindness, simplicity, and quietude of Zen monastery life.

But for those who really want to get a firm hold on Zen, to get their teeth into it, difficult as it is for most people to undertake, a stay of two or three years is really necessary. The economic problems involved in such a stay I shall take up a little farther on. But this I want to state at the beginning. *During the early period of Zen study*, to earn one's living and study Zen at the same time is practically impossible. Everyone who has come here with any other idea has found this to be true. Where it has become necessary during the *early* period to earn a living, serious and continued Zen practice has had to be curtailed or temporarily put aside.

There are two courses open to the long term student. One is to enter the sodo immediately on arrival and, in spite of language and other difficulties, to devote oneself only to Zen practice during the entire stay. Perhaps this is the way for some, but experience would seem to indicate that, on the whole, this is not an advisable course for the majority of foreigners. That a period of monastery life is necessary goes without saying. But, as I have said, many aspects of sodo training are specific preparation for the positions the monks are later to assume as priests of smaller or larger temples. They are unnecessary for the western Zen student unless the very unusual situation were to arise where he decided to take the vows and devote himself to being a full-fledged monk or priest.

The best plan for the two or three year student is to live outside the sodo for the first year, dividing his time between intensive study of the Japanese language and the practice of sitting. During this time he will have the opportunity to visit several monasteries and several roshis. If he should decide upon a monastery in Kyoto, when he sits well enough he would probably be invited to sit with its monks for meditation from time to time, even though he was not living in the monastery itself. In addition, this program will give him time to get acquainted with the Japanese way of life.

Even if the student has had a year or two of Japanese in a university, when he reaches Japan he will find the spoken language as it is used every day almost impossible to understand or to speak. Attending classes at a Japanese language school five days a week continuously for a year usually results in making communication with Japanese people fairly satisfactory. During this time he can also familiarize himself with the special Zen words and terms in daily use in the monastery, without knowledge of which he is at a great disadvantage in his relations with the monks and utterly unprepared for koan study under the roshi.

It may seem strange to say that one needs a year in which to get used to Japanese life, and everyone, when I tell them so, says: "Oh no, it won't be so in my case!" But one and all at the end of the year admit that they have just then begun to get adjusted to the climate, food, living habits, different social customs, to say nothing of the different ways of thinking. All students, no matter how long their stay, should always remember that, however much it may superficially resemble western countries, Japan is, nevertheless, a part of Asia and its people Asiatic people, long conditioned in ways of thinking and in behavior patterns that are the antithesis of those in which Americans and Europeans have been brought up.

When the student comes for a few months only, he is treated as a distinguished visitor, and, on his part, he is fascinated by all that is new and strange around him. But when he stays longer he finds he must willy-nilly conform more or less to the ways of Japanese life. This conforming, no matter with what good will it is undertaken, is a mental and physical strain. An added strain is the impossibility of usual human communication, for very few Japanese have English adequate to convey more than the most superficial facts, and the newcomer's Japanese is more than likely to be on the same level or below. So, except when he is with foreign friends, conversation is reduced pretty much to the kind that takes place between children. Only one who has experienced the sense of frustration that can come to an adult from not being able to exchange ideas over a long period of time can realize what a strain this is.

But really the most important reason for the year of preparation is that it gives the foreign student time to perfect himself in zazen practice. Roshis usually will not take a student for sanzen who does not have a "good seat." A "good seat" includes being able not only to sit for long periods of time in half-lotus or full-lotus posture, but also to concentrate the mind so that it can handle a koan. In cases where the roshi has, under urging, taken a student not yet proficient in zazen, our experience has been that he later stops the sanzen until such time as the student has learned to sit well, or the student stumbles along as best he can until, discouraged, he himself gives up.

Very few westerners, particularly men, find it easy to sit in zazen posture. They must be prepared to stick doggedly at it, enduring the pain for some months before they achieve a modicum of success. Those who naturally sit with more ease usually find the concentration practice difficult. If, therefore, in addition to his language studies the western student practices these basic preparatory exercises for three or four hours each day, by the end of the year he should be well equipped to enter the sodo and begin his koan study immediately. Also, during that time he will have learned much about the external facts of Zen monastery life and come to know some of the monks in the sodo he is to enter.

Thus, when at the beginning of his second year in Japan he enters the sodo for strict Zen practice, the foreign student can pack away all his books except for those I have already mentioned, and give himself up totally to his practice. It is difficult to stress sufficiently the necessity for having the mind completely free from ordinary concerns during the initial stages of Zen koan study. Simply stated, the reason is that meditation on the first koan, at least, should develop a kind of mental tension, without which even a mild first satori cannot be experienced. To gain this tension, mind and body must be concentrated in the koan twenty-four hours a day. Simple physical tasks that entail no special mental activity can be engaged in without interfering with the building up of this tension. Family responsibilities, studies, money worries, breaking in and taking the student's attention from concentrating on the koan, can seriously hinder the building up of it, even to the point of inhibiting it entirely. A person long experienced in Zen concentration is able to carry on his usual life and still study koans, for he has opened up deeper levels of his mind where koans are solved. His deep mind will continue to work on a koan even though his usual mind is busy with studies, work, or other concerns. But years of practice are needed to develop this capacity fully. The beginner needs to direct every ounce of will power and determination to conscious concentration on his koan.

At the conclusion of this year spent in the sodo, the student should have a reasonably well trained mind and body, and he should be familiar with what constitutes real Zen practice. How to meditate on a koan should no longer puzzle him, and he should have a fair idea of what is expected of him in sanzen and how to prepare for it.

The third year of the westerner's stay in Japan may also be passed in the sodo or, if he feels he has had enough monastic Zen training as differentiated from pure Zen practice, he may live outside the monastery, going there morning and evening for sanzen and participating with the monks in their long evening meditation periods and their sesshin weeks. If he has conducted himself correctly and earnestly, whether he remains in the monastery or lives outside it, he will find himself considered not only a welcome guest but a member of the body of the monks.

At this time, if the student's intention is to continue his Zen practice indefinitely, either in Japan or elsewhere when a teacher is available, whether he is living in the sodo or not he should again take up his Japanese language study. Now he should turn his attention to the written language as it appears in Japanese translations of the koans. Better still, he should begin to study Chinese. Though here at Ryosen-an we have already made considerable progress in the translation into English of koans and verses used in answering them, every serious Zen student, at this period at least, will find it advantageous to have sufficient familiarity with Chinese characters to make rough translations of his own koans. If his year of intensive Zen practice has been successful, he should now be able to carry on these language studies without disturbing his ability to handle his mind in the fashion necessary for zazen and sanzen. But until he is thoroughly grounded in the way Zen practice demands that he handle his mind, he should not attempt any intellectual work together with it. If he does, his Zen progress will suffer sadly.

After two or three years of practice, will the western student go home an enlightened man? That is a difficult question to answer. Undoubtedly he will have passed his first koan and perhaps some other koans as well. If he expects to have become what at present he conceives an enlightened man to be, then the answer is "No." But the man who returns will be a different man from the one who came. That I can promise.

IX. Study at Ryosen-an

IN THE PRECEDING CHAPTERS more or less typical programs for Zen study for foreigners in Japan have been outlined. That none of these programs will fit any individual case or be quite suitable for it, I am quite well aware, but I have attempted to suggest most of the possibilities. Each would-be student will have to think over in advance what he would like to do and then what he can do.

When The First Zen Institute of America established its Kyoto Branch at Ryosen-an, one of its aims was to assist foreigners who came to Japan to study Zen to orient and prepare themselves for their study. The student program at Ryosen-an is limited to this aim.

Since the primary practice in Zen is zazen, the Kyoto Institute places special emphasis upon this. The Ryosen-an zendo, though smaller than the Zen meditation halls of most of the monasteries, conforms in construction to the traditional style of these halls. The regulations followed are those of the Daitoku-ji Monastery, to which Ryosen-an is closely related. Meditation is held in the zendo five evenings a week from seven until nine o'clock throughout the year, with the exception of the week before and the week after the New Year and two weeks during the month of August. Friday evenings the meditation period is somewhat shortened in order that students may attend a lecture on Zen in the library. This is followed by a question and answer period.

The meditation hall is in charge of western and Japanese Zen students who have had long training in Zen. These older students first instruct the newcomer in sitting, then in breathing, and lastly in concentration exercises. During the zazen periods the new student is closely observed and his posture and attitude corrected when necessary. The meditation hall is open from early morning for those who wish to use it for personal practice during the day.

Some westerners have come to the Kyoto Institute especially for instruction in zazen practice. Among these have been artists as well as university professors with a part of their sabbatical leave to devote to Zen study. The latter have found a completely new view of Zen through personal practice, through reading the translated manuscripts in the Institute library, open to all students, and through the personal contacts with Zen priests and scholars that their relation to the Institute has made possible. Artists have come primarily to train themselves in deeper concentration for their work.

Other westerners have come to prepare themselves to enter a Zen monastery. The Institute's being open all the year gives them the opportunity to begin their practice at any time of the year without taking the monastery schedule into consideration.

As I have repeatedly said, considerable time and practice are necessary to gain proficiency, or even ease, in zazen. Therefore, except in special cases, the Institute does not accept students for less than two months, and unless they are willing during that time to attend the zazen sessions regularly and, in addition, practice an hour or two daily either at home or by themselves in the Ryosen-an zendo. The instructors have found two months to be the minimum period of practice necessary for any grasp of the essentials of sitting.

For the student who plans to enter a sodo, regardless of the length of time he will remain there, unless he has learned to sit before coming to Japan the Institute recommends from four to six months of preliminary practice at Ryosen-an. In such cases, when the student can sit reasonably well, at certain times an invitation is arranged for him to sit for a few nights with the monks at the Daitoku-ji Sodo. Still later in his practice, he is sometimes invited to live in the sodo for one of the meditation weeks. In this way he becomes at home in a monastery meditation hall and conversant with its etiquette, a very important requirement. Such a program permits time for reading background material on Zen, in which the library abounds, and for private instruction in Japanese, should the student desire it.

The Ryosen-an program is also well suited to the requirements of the westerner who has a year for preparation before going into a sodo. With a year of practice under the Institute's instructors, he will find himself completely ready to enter into every aspect of monastery life. If he prefers a private teacher in language study to the Japanese Language School, the Institute can recommend an excellent one who has had experience in preparing other foreigners to enter a sodo. The associations with the Zen world that he will make through his connections with the Institute will provide him with a rich background for his new Zen life. And finally, the Institute members who have long been studying Zen in Japan and with whom he will be in daily contact will share with him personal experience that will never be written down in books.

When the foreign student is fully prepared to enter a monastery and study with a Zen master, the aim of the Institute is accomplished. There is no roshi at Ryosen-an. The Institute feels that at this period at least all foreigners who want seriously to study Zen in Japan should go to the source and drink from it directly. Only thus can they really prepare themselves to assist in the movement of true Zen to the West.

APPENDICES

VISAS*

Those persons who come to Japan for a few weeks and want to get a whiff of Zen while they are here should apply to the nearest Japanese Consulate for a Tourist Visa. This is good for sixty days. Such a visa is usually issued soon after the application is made.

* Editor's note: This information was current in 1960 and is not applicable now.

Those who come for three or four months of study also need only a sixty day Tourist Visa. This can easily be renewed two or three times at the Japanese Immigration Bureau nearest to or in the city where they are living. More than three renewals are difficult or impossible to obtain. If, after being in Japan some time, such a student should decide to remain a year or more, at present it is likely that he would have to leave the country and re-enter from Hongkong or some other port in a nearby country, having applied at the Japanese Consulate in the foreign port for a one year or three year visa, and complied with the necessary requirements for such visas.

Students who wish to come for one or more years of study should apply for a one year or three year visa before leaving their home country. These visas, in the case of American citizens, are rather difficult to obtain and entail the presentation of many documents including: an invitation to come to study, or a letter of acceptance as a student from the school or monastery where the applicant is to study, or from the teacher under whom he will study; a bank guarantee of his ability to support himself while in Japan; a letter from a responsible person, either foreigner or Japanese, residing in Japan, who will guarantee the applicant's support and his good conduct in accordance with the Japanese law during his stay, and his return to his home country at the expiration of the term of the visa. Such a guarantor will probably be called upon to give certified proof of his financial ability to act as guarantor. Application for such visas should be made at least four months before the student intends to leave for Japan.

Such, in brief, are the present requirements for citizens of the United States. Japanese visa requirements are not the same for all countries, however. Naturally they are subject to change at any time and in any way. This information is intended merely as a guide to prospective students. Only Japanese Consulates can give the latest definitive information.

Expenses*

Most of those coming to Japan for only a few weeks need no special information beyond that given in Chapter IV. However, the student with very limited funds should expect that room and food alone will cost at the very least ¥750 ($2) a day, even at a hostel. The YWCA charges at present are ¥750 a night, and breakfast is ¥150 additional.

The student coming for three or four months should have a minimum income of ¥35,000 ($100) a month. If he lives at an inexpensive student hotel, he should anticipate that his expenditure for room and food will be more than the amount mentioned above for a hostel, since living in Japan for that length of time, he will find it necessary for his health to supplement the usual meals served with extra milk, fruit, cheese, and meat.

If he wishes to live in more pleasant surroundings and to eat adequately where he lives, he must be prepared to spend $90 to $100 a month for room and meals alone.

If he can go into a monastery immediately, his expenses will be less. He should make a gift to the sodo of not less than ¥3,000 ($8) a month to cover his room and food, and a gift to the roshi of ¥1,000 ($3) a month whether he is taking sanzen or not. If he begins koan study, he should double his gift to the roshi. If one of the monks acts as interpreter for his sanzen, that monk should have a gift of money from time to time. In addition, gifts of cakes, tea, fruits, or candy should be given to the monks occasionally. On the whole, they

* Editor's note: These prices reflect figures accurate in 1960.

will share with him gifts of this kind when they receive them from outside friends, and he should return their kindness by sharing with them all such presents given to him.

The monastery usually has an extra sleeping pad and cushions for zazen practice that will gladly be lent to the foreign student. If he comes for the winter term, he would be well advised to bring his own blankets or sleeping bag, as the single pad supplied is inadequate against the winter cold. He must supply all his own towels, soap, and toilet paper. He must be prepared to buy extra food outside the monastery and vitamin pills to take regularly.

All temples and monasteries in Japan, regardless of their appearance, are poor. Funds for daily necessities in the sodo are provided for through money or food stuffs obtained by begging, supplemented by gifts from the parents or home temples of the monks. Historically Japanese lay people in any number have never supported Zen temples or monasteries. The Hinayana doctrine that the layman can store up merit for himself in a future life by giving generously for the support of monasteries and their monks during this life has never taken root in Japan. The foreign guest, whether his stay be for a night, a month, or a year, must be prepared to make gifts, of money preferably, adequate to cover completely the expense to the monastery of having him there.

To rent a single room outside the monastery for three or four months is not easy, in Kyoto at least. Kyoto has a number of colleges and universities, the students of which take over practically all the available cheap rooms except for the vacation months of July and August. To find such a room the foreign student needs to have friends on the spot, and even then he must plan to devote several weeks to the search. When he finds a room, the chances are that it will be totally bare of furniture and he will be forced to supply what he needs. Japanese university students customarily bring their own bedding, hibachi, desk, sitting cushions, electric stove, etc. The cost of such a room runs from ¥3,000 to ¥6,000 ($10 to $20) per month.

One other pertinent bit of information. Most houses that rent rooms close the gate at 10 P.M. Since there are no keys to Japanese gates or houses—all are bolted from the inside—the house mistress must sit up to wait for the late-returner. This she will do from time to time with a smile, but the foreigner is warned that it is better to try to conform than to take too frequent advantage of her kindness.

The long-term student, also, should plan for a fixed minimum income of $100 a month for his stay, more if he plans to buy clothing, books, or go sightseeing. Of course, if he has made arrangements to enter the monastery as soon as he arrives, he can get along on somewhat less.

The foreigner who decides to spend his first year in language study and the practice of zazen will need a room or rooms. What has been said above on this subject will, of course, apply here. This much may be added, however. When the student's stay is to be a long one, kitchen privileges are often available. If he is able to do at least some of his own cooking, his food costs will be considerably reduced. In many cases, bath privileges are also included. When not, the westerner must go to the public baths, relatively cheap and clean here, and used by a large percentage of the population. In the case of long-term tenancy, it is the general practice for the landlord to ask for what is known as "key money." Such "key money" may range from ¥10,000 to ¥30,000 ($30 to $85) and must be paid by the tenant before he moves in. In some instances this money is returned when the tenant leaves, in some instances not, according to the initial contract. The long-term tenant is usually expected to make any and all repairs to the room he rents, such as new shoji paper, fusuma paper, *tatami* (straw mat covering), etc.

Tuition at the Japanese Language School in Kyoto is approximately ¥25,000 ($70) for a term of three months. Classes are held for three hours each morning, five days a week. Three hours of outside study are expected of the student each day. The courses cover conversation, reading, and writing. Private lessons may be had with teachers from the school or independent teachers. The present charge for private lessons runs from ¥350 to ¥500 ($1 to $1.50) per hour. The student who wants to make real progress in Japanese language study is warned against exchanging English lessons with a Japanese student in return for lessons in Japanese. In the beginning a trained instructor is an absolute necessity. Too often westerners, wanting to curtail expenses this way, find to their grief that, though they have saved money, they have wasted what is more precious, lots of time.

Visiting Membership in The First Zen Institute of America in Japan, entitling the member to instruction in zazen, the use of the library, attendance at Institute lectures, and other activities, is ¥2,000 ($5.50) a month.

If an English or French speaking student needs supplementary income, he will not find it too difficult, after he has been here a time—that is, in Kyoto or Tokyo—to pick up some tutoring to do in one or the other language. But he must be prepared to find that giving such lessons makes inroads on his time hardly commensurate with the amount he earns from them. For instance, if he teaches three hours one evening a week in an Osaka night school, he will need at least three hours more each time to go from his home to the school and back again, since Osaka is a forty minute train ride from Kyoto. For this he may expect a salary of ¥5,000 ($15) a month.

Positions as English teachers in Japanese high schools or colleges can sometimes be found, provided the foreigner has a university degree and has been here long enough to make the acquaintance of some of the professors in the English department of the school. Though the teaching duties are usually not arduous—they are likely to be frustrating, at least in the beginning—the salary is small, ¥20,000 to ¥30,000 ($65 to $85) a month at the most.

The real problem, however, is to adjust a teaching time schedule to a Zen study time schedule. Morning sanzen is held at 4 A.M. in the summer, 5 A.M. in the winter; evening sanzen is held at 6:30 P.M. in the winter and 7:30 P.M. in the summer. If the student wants to live in the monastery for the sesshin weeks, he will find that these seldom if ever take place during the school vacations. To have a regular position of any kind outside the monastery while living in it is utterly impossible.

Before he plans to study Zen while supporting himself, the westerner should read again carefully all that has been said above about Zen study. To the degree that he must support himself, to a like degree he will interfere with or slow down—even, perhaps, nullify—his progress in Zen understanding.

The figures given in this section on expenses are based upon prices current in the autumn of 1959. Those who are planning their budget should take into consideration the fact that the cost of living is slowly but surely going up in Japan as elsewhere.

PREPARATIONS

Perhaps some westerners who hope to come to Japan to study Zen would like to know how they may best prepare themselves in advance. Here are a few suggestions.

If possible, begin to study the Japanese language at a school, university, or with a private teacher. If no one of these is available,

Spoken Japanese by Bernard Bloch and Eleanor Harz Jordan (2 vols., New York: Henry Holt and Co.), with records, is excellent for study by oneself. There are many, many Japanese language books on the market, but the Ryosen-an staff feels that the book mentioned above, particularly if studied in combination with the records, gives the English-speaking foreigner who must work by himself the quickest and best approach to everyday spoken Japanese.

Next, the prospective student should begin to practice sitting. The best way is for him to join a group who are practicing zazen. If this is not possible, he should try to find someone to help him, a person who has already had some instruction in zazen, or a Zen priest of either the Rinzai or Soto sect. Failing that, he should be able to train himself to sit fairly well if he will follow these simple instructions. He will not be practicing zazen, but at least he will be making preliminary preparations to do so.

The student should get two flat but thick cushions about 2½ feet square. He should place one on the floor, then double the other in two and place it on the back half of the first cushion. (Fig. 1) He should then seat himself on the folded cushion with his legs crossed before him on the lower cushion. (Fig. 2)

The back should be straight except for a slight curve inward at the waistline; the abdomen should be slightly distended;

FIGURE 1

FIGURE 2

the shoulders thrown back a little so that the back of the shoulders is in a straight line with the back of the buttocks.

The head should be held erect with the chin pulled in slightly so as to relax the neck. (Fig. 3)

The hands should be on the lap, the left hand, palm upward, on the right palm, with the tips of both thumbs touching. (Fig. 4)

FIGURE 3

FIGURE 4

The eyes should fall, unfocused, on the floor about 15 to 18 inches in front of the lower cushion; the eyelids should be kept half shut, never under any circumstances allowed to close entirely. If an incense stick is lighted and placed in a stand just a little beyond where the eyes fall, the tiny red light will serve to help the student unconsciously to be aware of whether his eyelids have closed or not.

As the next step, the student should put the left foot in the knee-crotch between the right thigh and leg, bringing both knees down on the lower cushion by putting the left knee beyond the right foot, which has been brought in close to the body. (Fig. 5) To get the knees down firmly on the under cushion

FIGURE 5

FIGURE 6

FIGURE 7

may take considerable time, but this is absolutely essential for a solid and immoveable base for the body. To make bringing the knees down easier, in the beginning another single cushion may be placed upon the doubled cushion. This will raise the buttocks up and throw the knees forward and down.

When the student is able to sit for half an hour or more in this position without moving he should begin to sit in the *hanka fuza* (half-lotus posture), that is, to draw his left foot up onto his right thigh (or vice versa), still keeping both knees on the lower cushion. (Fig. 6)

Then gradually he should try to sit in the *kekka fuza* (full-lotus posture), that is, with the left foot still on the right thigh, to draw the right foot up onto the left thigh (or vice versa). (Fig. 7)

From the very first, even when sitting with the legs merely crossed, the student should breathe through his nostrils in the following rhythm, keeping his mouth always closed:

He should exhale slowly and evenly, concentrating his attention on his breath and trying to control it as it is exhaled so that it does not wobble and flicker, but is smooth and even. When the breath has been exhaled to a comfortable degree, he should let it remain out for a few seconds; then let the inhalation take place spontaneously and naturally, its speed and duration depending upon what his body asks for.

In Zen breathing there is no fixed relation between the length of time given to the exhalation, leaving the breath out, and the inhalation.

The student's attention must be kept on the breath always. He should not concentrate on any object or thought.

Zazen practice should always be approached with a relaxed body and a quiet mind. The body should never be forced to assume a position; rather, it should be asked to cooperate. This is a very important first principle.

Sitting ten minutes at a time is sufficient in the beginning. The student should always continue sitting a little beyond the point where he is sure he cannot sit any longer. This is the best way to make progress.

When he can sit in half-lotus position for half an hour, with his knees firmly fixed on the lower cushion and always breathing quietly and rhythmically, his mind concentrated in his breath, the student will have accomplished the first fundamental steps in zazen practice.

Finally, it is an absolute necessity for every student to have some acquaintance with both Hinayana and Mahayana Buddhism as a background for his Zen study. The books listed below are recommended. Unfortunately a few of the more important are out of print. These have been starred. Perhaps by searching in accessible libraries or second-hand bookstores they can be found.

References

Thomas, Edward J.

The Life of Buddha as Legend and History (London: Kegan Paul, Trench, Trubner, 1931)

Early Buddhist Scriptures (London: Kegan Paul, Trench, Trubner, 1935)

The History of Buddhist Thought (London: Kegan Paul, Trench, Trubner, 1933)

Rhys Davids, T. W.

Dialogues of the Buddha, translated from the Pali of the *Digha nikaya* (3 vols., London: Henry Frowde, 1899–1938)

McGovern, William Montgomery

**An Introduction to Mahayana Buddhism*, with especial reference to Chinese and Japanese phases (London: Kegan Paul, Trench, Trubner, 1922)

**A Manual of Buddhist Philosophy* (London: Kegan Paul, Trench, Trubner, 1923)

Conze, Edward

Buddhism, Its Essence and Development (New York: Philosophical Library, pref. 1951)

Buddhist Texts Through the Ages, ed. by Ed. Conze (New York: Philosophical Library, 1954)

Buddhist Wisdom Books (London: George Allen and Unwin, 1958)

Takakusu, Junjiro

The Essentials of Buddhist Philosophy (Honolulu: The University of Hawaii Press, 1947)

Yamakami, Sogen

**Systems of Buddhist Thought* (Calcutta: University of Calcutta, 1912)

Suzuki, Daisetz Teitaro

An Introduction to Zen Buddhism (2nd ed., London: Rider and Co., 1957)

Essays in Zen Buddhism, First Series (2nd ed., London: Rider and Co., 1949)

Essays in Zen Buddhism, Second Series (2nd ed., London: Rider and Co., 195)

Essays in Zen Buddhism, Third Series (2nd ed., London: Rider and Co., 1953)

A Manual of Zen Buddhism (2nd ed., London: Rider and Co., 1957)

The Training of the Zen Buddhist Monk (1st Amer. ed., New York: University Books, 1959)

Blofeld, John

> *The Zen Teaching of Huang Po*, on the Transmission of Mind (An Evergreen Original, New York: The Grove Press, 1959)

As for the publications of The First Zen Institute of America, the full list of which will be found at the back of this book, all are recommended. For a beginning, *Zen—A Religion* and *Zen—A Method for Religious Awakening* are suggested, followed by *Cat's Yawn*, and last of all *The Development of Chinese Zen*.

But the student is urged to do his reading at home. When he comes to Japan, except for his language study books, dictionaries, and Dr. Suzuki's *Manual of Zen Buddhism* and *The Training of the Zen Buddhist Monk*, he should leave all his books behind. From the day he begins his real Zen study he should put his brain on the shelf, for a time at least, and learn how to know without learning.

Acknowledgments

Researching the interconnectedness of Ruth Fuller Sasaki's life and work has been a fascinating and rewarding project. Over the past several years, many, many people connected with Ruth in some way have assisted me. The idea for the book grew out of conversations with Matsunami Taiun Osho, the priest of Ryosen-an for the past several years; Victor Sogen Hori, professor at McGill University and longtime monk and priest at Daitoku-ji; and Maya Hara, a friend of Matsunami Osho's visiting Ryosen-an when I happened to be staying there. I am very grateful for the hospitality of Matsunami Taiun Osho in encouraging my visits to Ryosen-an, and in helping me find material in the Ryosen-an Library.

These three helped considerably in the early phase of this book, and we had many interesting meetings in Kyoto with Professor Iriya Yoshitaka at his home on Mount Hiei; with Professor Yanagida Seizan, who came to Ryosen-an; with Mihoko Okamura Bekku, former assistant to D. T. Suzuki; and with Professor Furuta Kazuhiro, as well as others at Daitoku-ji who still remembered Ruth.

The retired kancho of Daitoku-ji, Fukutomi Settei Roshi, thought the idea of a book about Ruth was an interesting and worthwhile endeavor. I will never forget his kindness and his calligraphy. He said he had good memories of Ruth.

Following the initial phase, I forged ahead through the tremendous good fortune of connecting with people who knew Ruth and were very supportive in providing me with information. These especially included Gary Snyder, Haru Yoshida, Carlton Gamer, Joanne Kyger, Janwillem van de Wetering, and Richard Leavitt.

I am thankful for the many phone conversations, correspondence, and visits with people, including William Regnery and Mrs. Ann Grube (whose family bought and lived in Swan House in Hinsdale); Michael Gamer, Joan Watts, and Ann Watts Andrews; Michael Hotz of the First Zen Institute in New York; Donatienne Lebovich Sapriel of Paris; Fielder Schillinberg, one of the early First Zen Institute students; Judith Laws Hoyem; Al Klyce, who was married at Daitoku-ji; Wayne Yokoyama, a researcher working on the D. T. Suzuki papers in Japan; and Jessie Duff-McLauren, whose parents worked in Hinsdale for the Everetts in the 1930s. Sandy Williams of the Hinsdale Historical Society provided me with great information about Swan House. Lewis Lancaster gave me information about Nyogen Senzaki's work in addition to Ruth's impact, particularly with *Zen Dust*.

I am deeply grateful for the invaluable assistance of Robert Felsing, Linda Toenniessen, and Jim Carlton in providing feedback on my writing and storytelling as this book took shape—as well as encouraging me through the lengthy process. I am also grateful to Mack Horton for his valuable comments and suggestions on the manuscript. I would also like to thank Julie Wrinn for her invaluable editorial assistance, and Roxanna Font at Shoemaker & Hoard. A very special and deep thank-you to Jack Shoemaker for his support and vision. There are many more people out there who knew Ruth, and for one reason or another I was unable to make good connections with them. I would like to thank Burton Watson, Donald

Richie, Walter Nowick, Irmgard Schloegl, and Washino Akiko for their direct and indirect comments about Ruth and her life, and their ability to look back over the years with a perspective; I hope that our paths will cross someday.

I am sorry I was not able to meet Philip Yampolsky, Kanaseki Hisao, or Lindley Hubbell, who had passed away before this book was started. They elicit my deep admiration for their contributions and character during the years of working with Ruth in Kyoto.

I am deeply indebted to all of these people, and I am grateful for having had the chance to research and share the life of a woman who exemplifies resourcefulness, dedication, perseverance, and generosity.

Ruth's life of meeting challenges has provided a valuable legacy for subsequent generations of those interested in Zen Buddhism's mid-century emergence in the West.

Chronology

Year		Narrative Comment
1892		October 31. Ruth Fuller born in Chicago, Illinois, to Clara Elizabeth and George E. Fuller. They live at 6 Scott Street, Chicago.
1895	Age 3	Brother, David Fuller, is born in Chicago.
1911	Age 18	Ruth graduates from Kenwood Institute and Loring School, both private schools in Chicago. Goes to France and Germany for two years of language tutoring.
1917	Age 25	April 7. Ruth marries Edward Warren Everett, Plymouth Congregational Church, Chicago. Honeymoon in Honolulu.
1918	Age 26	December 30. Ruth gives birth to her only child, Eleanor Everett.
1924	Age 31	Ruth visits Clarkstown Country Club in Nyack, New York, meets Pierre Bernard, learns yoga, and becomes interested in Eastern religions.
1924	Age 32	Ruth and Eleanor stay at the Clarkstown Country Club, run by Pierre Bernard.

1927	Age 35	Ruth and Edward build and move into Swan House, Hinsdale, Illinois.
1927		Ruth enrolls in Sanskrit and Indian philosophy courses at the University of Chicago for two years.
1930	Age 38	Ruth becomes a member of the American Oriental Society.
1930		Summer. Ruth, Edward, Eleanor, and governess travel for three months to Japan, Korea, and China. In Japan, Ruth is introduced to D. T. Suzuki by William T. McGovern. Suzuki teaches Ruth basic zazen sitting.
1931		Ruth and Edward donate a rare Ming Chinese painting to the Field Museum, Chicago (school of carp in a pond, painted on silk).
1931	Age 39	May 11. Sasaki Sokei-an incorporates Buddhist Society of America, 63 W. 70th Steet, New York City.
1932	Age 40	April 1–end of June sesshin. Ruth returns to Japan in the spring and begins studying at Nanzen-ji with Nanshinken Roshi. She rents a house near the Kamo River.
1932		Late summer. Edward meets Ruth and Eleanor in Kyoto—they make another visit to China, returning to the U.S. in November.
1933	Age 41	April 7. Ruth meets Sasaki Shigetsu (Sokei-an) in New York City.
1933		October. Ruth returns to Kyoto (with Eleanor) to continue studying at Nanzen-ji until June 1934.

Receives Buddhist name "Kuge" from Nanshinken Roshi.

1934   Age 42   Edward joins them in Kyoto. They revisit Beijing.

1935   Age 43   Ruth's husband, Edward, retires due to ill health.

1935   Nanshinken Roshi of Nanzen-ji dies.

1936   Age 44   Ruth takes Eleanor to London, and they meet Alan Watts at the Buddhist Lodge.

1937   Age 45   Alan Watts accompanies Eleanor to the Everetts' in Hinsdale for Christmas.

1938   Age 46   Eleanor and Alan Watts marry in London.

1938   Ruth moves to New York City (Park Crescent Hotel, 87th and Riverside Drive). Edward in sanitarium in Hartford, Connecticut. Ruth starts studying with Sasaki Sokei-an. Receives Buddhist name, Eryu ("Dragon's Wisdom"), after taking vows, December 10. Takes over editorship of *Cat's Yawn*. (Alan and Eleanor live next door at Park Crescent Hotel.)

1940   Age 47   Edward Warren Everett dies in January at the age of 67 in Hartford, Connecticut.

1941   Age 49   September 18. Ruth's mother, Clara Fuller, dies at age 78. Buried at Bronswood Cemetery in Oak Brook, Illinois.

1941   Ruth purchases and renovates brownstone at 124 E. 65th Street, New York, as apartment for her and home for Sokei-an and Sokei-an's zendo.

1941   Age 50   December 6. Sokei-an's new quarters at 124 E. 65th Street, named the Buddhist Society of America, open the day before attack on Pearl Harbor.

1942		Sokei-an taken to Ellis Island on June 15, and then interned at Fort Meade, Maryland, on October 2.
1943	Age 51	August 17. Sokei-an released. Buddhist Society of America changes its name to First Zen Institute (FZI) at Sokei-an's request.
1944	Age 52	Sokei-an goes to Little Rock, Arkansas, to get a divorce from wife, Tome. They had been separated for years.
1944		July 10. Ruth and Sokei-an get married in Hot Springs, Arkansas.
1945	Age 53	May 17. Sokei-an dies at age 63 (1882–1945). His ashes are buried at Woodlawn Cemetery in the Bronx.
1947	Age 55	Under Ruth's editorship, *Cat's Yawn* is published by the First Zen Institute.
1948	Age 56	Walter Nowick joins the First Zen Institute as a member.
1949	Age 57	Daughter Eleanor and Alan Watts end their marriage.
1949		Ruth returns to Kyoto in October, finds a house, and starts studying with Goto Zuigan Roshi at Daitoku-ji. Stays four months.
1949	Age 58	December 17. Haru ("Penny") Yoshida begins work as secretary for Ruth.
1950		Walter Nowick arrives in Kyoto and begins study with Goto Roshi.

1950		August 4. Eleanor marries Carlton Gamer, a musicologist whom she had met when she was with Alan Watts at Northwestern University.
1950		Ruth returns to Kyoto. Haru Yoshida goes to Kyoto for eight months.
		Ruth, living in house at Daitoku-ji, resumes study with Goto Roshi.
1951	Age 59	Burton Watson arrives in Kyoto.
1952	Age 60	March 1. Washino Akiko begins working for Ruth as personal assistant in Kyoto.
1953	Age 61	Lindley Williams Hubbell moves from New York to Kyoto. Helps Ruth with typing and setting up a library collection.
1954	Age 62	Philip Yampolsky arrives in Kyoto.
1954	Age 63	November 28. Ruth's only sibling, brother David Fuller, dies November 28 at age 59.
1955		Ruth, Washino, and Miura Isshu Roshi tour the southwest of the U.S. with Eleanor, Carlton, and son Michael. First trip to U.S. for Miura Roshi. Meet with Gary Snyder in San Francisco.
1956	Age 64	Ruth establishes the Kyoto branch of the First Zen Institute of America in Japan and starts gathering scholars for work on projects.
1956		Gary Snyder arrives in Kyoto. Ruth serves as his sponsor.
1956		Miura Roshi invited to become Zen teacher at FZI and initially accepts.

1957 Age 65 Miura Roshi declines to become Zen teacher for FZI.

1957 Ruth's granddaughter, Joan Watts, spends the year in Kyoto with Ruth; meets and marries Joseph Sudlow. Ruth arranges Kyoto wedding.

1957 Philip Yampolsky hired by Ruth to be librarian and member of the First Zen Institute in Japan research team. Members of the research team include Iriya Yoshitaka, Yanagida Seizan, Kanaseki Hisao, Burton Watson, Philip Yampolsky, and Gary Snyder.

1958 Age 66 May 7. Nyogen Senzaki dies.

1958 May 17. Ruth ordained a priest and given name of "Jokei," (or Jyokei) sponsored by Oda Sesso Roshi. Installed as abbot of the restored Ryosen-an, ceremony held to name Sokei-an Founder of the Restored Ryosen-an, and Ruth ordained as jushoku.

1958 Janwillem van de Wetering starts as student at Daitoku-ji with Oda Roshi.

1958 Age 67 November 25. Ruth gives a talk to students at Massachusetts Institute of Technology, written up in *Zen Notes*, then expanded for *Zen: A Method of Religious Awakening*.

1958–1963 Publication by the First Zen Institute of small pamphlets:

    1958, 1963 *Zen: A Religion*
    1959   *Zen: A Method for Religious Awakening*
    1960   *The First Zen Institute of America in Japan*
    1960   *Rinzai Zen Study for Foreigners in Japan*

1959 Gary Snyder returns after a year away.

1959		Relations with Goto Roshi become difficult.
1959		Claude Dalenberg comes for Zen study, stays at Zuiun-ken. Paul Wienpahl comes for the summer. Haru Yoshida visits.
1960	Age 68	February. Joanne Kyger sails for Japan, marries Gary Snyder.
1960		Remodeling of Zuiun-ken for use as a dormitory by Ryosen-an students.
1960		Irmgard Schloegl arrives in Kyoto for Zen study at Ryosen-an, 1961–1964.
1961		July 13. Philip Yampolsky dismissed by Ruth over a misunderstanding. Burton Watson and Gary Snyder resign in protest.
1961	Age 69	*Wooden Fish* published by FZI, translated by Gary Snyder, with Gutetsu as advisor.
1963	Age 71	Miura Roshi separates from First Zen Institute and sets up his home and zendo on 72nd Street. Invites a few students to join him. (Miura Roshi dies December 10, 1978.)
1965	Age 72	April. Goto Zuigan Roshi dies.
1965	Age 73	*Zen Koan* published by the First Zen Institute of America in Japan, later by Harcourt.
1966		*Zen Dust* published first in Japan, later in New York by Harcourt.
1966		July 12. D. T. Suzuki dies (1870–1966).
1966		September 16. Oda Sesso Roshi dies.

1967	Age 74	October 24. Ruth dies suddenly of a heart attack at Ryosen-an one week before her 75th birthday. Half of her ashes buried at Ryosen-an, half buried at Woodlawn Cemetery in the Bronx with Sokei-an's ashes.

1971   Publication of *The Recorded Sayings of Layman P'ang*.

1975   Publication of *The Recorded Sayings of Ch'an Master Lin-chi Hui-chao of Chen Prefecture* (Kyoto: Institute for Zen Studies).

Endnotes

Chapter 1: The Chicago Years, 1892–1929

Page

3   "One of the few surviving anecdotes": Gary Snyder, in discussion with the author, June 2003.

3   "wealth in the Chicago grain stock market": Gary Snyder, in discussion with the author, June 2003, and Carlton Gamer, in discussion with the author, November 1997.

4   "junior and senior years" and "Ruth took piano lessons . . . from Rudolf Ganz": Carlton Gamer, in discussion with the author, November 1997.

5   "occasionally giving recitals": Women's Club Notes, Miss Ruth Fuller's piano recital, the *Doings* (Hinsdale), Saturday, December 18, 1909.

5   "Ruth married Edward Warren Everett": marriage of Ruth Fuller to Edward Warren Everett, *Chicago Tribune*, April 7, 1917.

5   "Edward gave Ruth a yellow Stutz Bearcat . . . for a wedding present": Gary Snyder, e-mail to author, November 2005.

6   Eleanor's early childhood recollections: Carlton Gamer, in discussion with author, November 1997.

7   Pierre Arnold Bernard: Paul G. Hackett, "Life and Works of Theos Bernard," http://C250.columbia.edu/c250_celebrates/remarkable_columbians/theos_bernard_scholar.html. "Pierre Bernard, 'Oom the Omnipotent,' Promoter and Self-styled Swami, Dies,"

New York Times, September 28, 1955. Hugh B. Urban, "Pierre Bernard," http://www.esoteric.msu.edu/Volume III/HTML/Oom.html. "Blanche De Vries Bernard," Rockland County *Journal-News*, September 5, 1984.

8   "both Ruth and Edward gave lectures": *Life at the Clarkstown Country Club* (Nyack, NY: The Club, 1935), pp. 127–129.

8   "Ida Rolf" obituary, Rolf Institute of Structural Integration, http:// www.rolf.org/about/yoga.htm.

8   architecture of Swan House: Sandy Williams (from Hinsdale Historical Society Archives), e-mail to author, February 2, 2005.

9   "A neighbor said Ruth's bedroom was": Mrs. Ann Grube, phone interview with the author, February 1998.

9   "the house was rented to Boss Ketering": Mr. William Regnery (son of William F. Regnery), phone interview with the author, January 15, 1998.

9   "Ruth . . . had to do her Sanskrit": Gary Snyder, discussion with the author, July 2004.

CHAPTER 2: FIRST TRIPS TO ASIA, 1930–1940

Page

11   Edward Warren Everett, *Far East for Ninety Days: Narrative of a Trip to Japan and China in 1930*. "Read before Law Club of Chicago and Published in Central Manufacturing District Magazine" (privately published, n.d., 23 pp.).

14   "Ruth later described this first visit with D. T. Suzuki": Ruth F. Sasaki, "To Dr. Daisetsu Teitaro Suzuki: An American Appreciation." *The Young East* 1: 1 (1952): 11–16.

15   Ruth and Nanzen-ji, Kamo River house: Ruth Fuller Everett, "Another Buddhist Interlude" (typed manuscript for a talk in Chicago, 1933, 28 pp.), pp. 14–15.

15   Nanzen-ji details described: Ibid., pp. 15–16.

18   "Decades later Ruth would refer to this extended period": Gary Snyder, Taped interviews with Ruth Fuller Sasaki, 1966. Tape 1, p. 24 of transcript. Unpublished, Snyder personal archives.

20   "In March 1933, Goddard wrote to Ruth": letter from Dwight Goddard to Ruth Everett in Michael Hotz, ed., *Holding the Lotus to the Rock* (New York: Four Walls Eight Windows, 2003), p. 249.

21   "Ruth wrote to Sokei-an in early April 1933": Gary Snyder, Taped interviews with Ruth Fuller Sasaki, 1966. Tape 6, p. 8 of transcript.

23   Ruth and Eleanor sail for Kyoto: *Chicago Tribune*, October 8, 1933.

23   "Ruth returned to Kyoto in the autumn of 1933": Gary Snyder, Taped interviews with Ruth Fuller Sasaki, 1966. Tape 1.

23   "she gave each of the monks a copy": Gary Snyder, Taped interviews with Ruth Fuller Sasaki, 1966. Tape 1, p. 23 of transcript.

24   Nanshinken Roshi and Western food: Gary Snyder, Taped interviews with Ruth Fuller Sasaki, 1966. Tape 2, p. 23 of transcript.

25   Hakuin Ekaku (1689–1769), considered the father of modern Rinzai Zen.

25   "when Mrs. Suzuki would think of introducing": Gary Snyder, Taped interviews with Ruth Fuller Sasaki, 1966. Tape 1, p. 25 of transcript.

26   "meeting with minister of war General Hayashi Senjuro": "Japanese War Chief Honors Chicago Man and His Wife," *Chicago Tribune*, May 26, 1934.

26   visit to Manchuria: "E. W. Everett Family Home," *Chicago Tribune*, July 31, 1934.

26   Ruth's return trip on the *Asahi*: *Chicago Tribune*, July 27 and 31, 1934.

27   gems stolen from the Everetts' Bermuda vacation home: *Chicago Tribune*, April 20, 1936.

28   Eleanor taking care of her father: Carlton Gamer, in discussion with author, November 1997.

28   "He had been very active": "E. W. Everett, 67, Former Chicago Attorney, Dies," *Chicago Tribune*, January 21, 1940.

28   sanitarium in Hartford, Connecticut: Edward was most likely a resident of the Hartford Retreat, a well-established sanitarium for mentally ill patients catering to the upper middle class. The grounds were landscaped by Frederick Law Olmsted (who landscaped Central Park in New York).

28   death of Edward Everett: Obituary, *Chicago Tribune*, January 21, 1940.

29   Ruth took credit for encouraging zazen for Sokei-an's students: Ibid., Tape 3, p. 1 of transcript.

29   "He gave teisho twice a week": Gary Snyder, Taped interviews with Ruth Fuller Sasaki, 1966. Tape 3, pp. 12–13 of transcript.

30   "He was giving koans in English": Ibid., pp. 12–13.

31   "Sokei-an seemed so different to Ruth": Ibid., p. 23.

31   "Sokei-an's father began teaching him Chinese": Ibid., 35–38.

33   "Sokei-an and his wife had a son, Shintaro": Ibid., p. 41.

33   "he spent a summer in the Columbia River valley": Ibid.

34   "Sokei-an tried unsuccessfully to enlist in the U.S. Army": Ibid., pp. 11–12.

34   "he knew reams of Rongo": Ibid., p. 46.

35   "Sokatsu gave him his inka": Ibid., p. 48.

35   "He returned again to New York, now as a roshi": Ibid., p. 48.

35   "Miya also was instrumental": Ibid., pp. 16–17.

36   "She was by this time the vice president": Ibid., Tape 6, p. 9 of transcript.

36   "her mother had been very domineering": Richard P. Leavitt, letter to author, January 10, 2006.

CHAPTER 3: NEW YORK, 1941–1948

Page

37   "Buddhist Society of America opened the doors": Gary Snyder, Taped interviews with Ruth F. Sasaki, 1966. Tape 6, p. 9 of transcript.

37   taken to Fort Meade: Michael Hotz, ed., *Holding the Lotus to the Rock*, pp. 208–209.

37   woodcarving by Sokei-an for army officers: Ibid. (quoting letters of Sokei-an from summer 1943).

39   Sokei-an's "parole" conditions: Gary Snyder, Taped interviews with Ruth F. Sasaki, 1966. Tape 6, p. 10 of transcript.

39   "Sokei-an's health was unstable": Ibid., p. 11 of transcript.

39   events surrounding Ruth's marriage to Sokei-an: Gary Snyder, Taped interviews with Ruth Fuller Sasaki, 1966. Tape 6, pp. 10–16 of transcript.

40   Sokei-an's desire for Ruth to continue studying: Ibid., p. 12 of transcript.

40   "Sokei-an went to Little Rock, Arkansas": Ibid., p. 13 of transcript.

40   problems obtaining marriage license: Ibid., pp. 14–15 of transcript.

41   Sokei-an's declining health: Ibid., pp. 15–16 of transcript.

41   "changed its name to the First Zen Institute of America": Michael Hotz, ed., *Holding the Lotus to the Rock*, p. 18.

41   death of Sokei-an: Obituary in *New York Times*, May 19, 1945, 19:5.

42   "Ruth and Mary Farkas corresponded with Goto Zuigan Roshi": Mary Farkas to Goto Zuigan, June 1, 1949, and Ruth F. Sasaki to Goto Roshi, June 1, 1949 (Yoshida personal archives).

42   "next step was to get permission from Goto Roshi for Ruth to go to Japan": Mary Farkas to Goto Zuigan, June 1, 1949 (Yoshida personal archives).

43   "started to work with Goto Roshi on translation projects": Ruth F. Sasaki to Haru Yoshida, November 30, 1949 (Yoshida personal archives).

43   daily routines at Daitoku-ji: Ibid.

43   "tell Walter . . . my sitting": Ibid.

44   house search in Kyoto: Ibid.

44   visit to Ibuka: Gary Snyder, Taped interviews with Ruth F. Sasaki, 1966. Tape 5, p. 6 of transcript.

44   Ruth's visit to Ibuka: Ruth F. Sasaki, "Talk presented to First Zen Institute, June 1, 1950" (taped and transcribed by Haru Yoshida, unpublished). Also in Gary Snyder, Taped interviews with Ruth Fuller Sasaki, 1966, Tape 5, p. 6 of transcript.

CHAPTER 4: KYOTO BEGINNINGS, 1949–1955

Page

50   Ruth's talks on the stories of the roshis: Ruth F. Sasaki, typed copies of talks presented at the First Zen Institute (taped and transcribed, Yoshida personal archives). Also reprinted in subsequent issues of *Zen Notes*: April 5, April 12, June 1, June 28, and July 5, 1950.

51   Ruth urging Goto Roshi to find a Zen teacher for Sokei-an's former students: Ruth F. Sasaki, letter to Goto Roshi, July 31, 1950 (Yoshida personal archives).

53   Goto Roshi and the naming of Ryosen-an: "Hermitage of the Dragon Spring," Ruth F. Sasaki, "Letter from Kyoto: Dear Everyone," June 3, 1956, *Zen Notes* III, No. 7.

53   Daitoku-ji: Jon Covell and Abbot Yamada Sobin, *Zen at Daitoku-ji* (Tokyo: Kodansha, 1974), p. 28. Rinzai-Obaku Zen: The Official Site of the Joint Council for Japanese Rinzai and Obaku Zen. http://zen.rinnou.net/head_temples/07/daitoku.html. Daitoku-ji history: Daio Kokushi (1235–1309); his pupil Daito Kokushi (1282–1337). Various dates are given for the founding, including 1315 and 1319, and also a date of official dedication of December 8, 1326.

57   D. T. Suzuki's visit: Ruth F. Sasaki, "Dear Everyone" letter, July 5, 1951, to members of the First Zen Institute. Unpublished (Yoshida personal archives).

60   Nyogen Senzaki's visit: Haru Yoshida to Ruth Fuller Sasaki, November 3, 1952 (Yoshida personal archives).

60   Ruth's personal and household staff: Jessie Duff-McLaurin, e-mail to author, January 25, 2000. Jessie's parents worked for Ruth in Hinsdale in the late 1930s.

61   Lindley Hubbell's arrival: Walter Ristow to Ursula Smith (sent on to Gary Snyder by Yoko Danno). Walter Ristow was at the New York Public Library with Hubbell. Also, "An Interview at Kunishima Hospital, Kyoto, January 31, 1994," in *Autumn Stone in the Woods: A Tribute to Lindley Williams Hubbell*, edited by Yoko Danno (Middletown Springs, Vt.: P.S.A. Press, 1997), pp. 59–60.

62   Lindley Hubbell's photograph of the Showa Emperor: Gary Snyder, e-mail to author, February 17, 2006.

63   temple politics and Hosshun-in: Ruth F. Sasaki to Haru Yoshida, September 11, 1952 (Yoshida personal archives).

63   "I wonder what they'll say about the *Ho Koji*": Ruth F. Sasaki to Haru Yoshida, January 28, 1955 (Yoshida personal archives).

63   "lucky to have found Professor Iriya": Ruth F. Sasaki to Haru Yoshida, June 23, 1954 (Yoshida personal archives).

64   D. T. Suzuki's letter with questions for Goto Roshi: D. T. Suzuki to Ruth Fuller Sasaki (copy), January 14, 1954 (Yoshida personal archives).

67   Miura Roshi's remarks about Hakuin: Ruth Fuller Sasaki to Mary Farkas, August 13, 1954 (Yoshida personal archives).

Chapter 5: Rebuilding Ryosen-an, 1955–1960

Page

72   Daio Kokushi (1235–1309) was the teacher of Daito Kokushi (1282–1337) and considered the founder of Daitoku-ji.

85   "Ryosen-an would build a separate zendo": Ruth F. Sasaki to Haru Yoshida, February 13, 1957 (Yoshida personal archives).

87   resignation of Miura Roshi: Ruth F. Sasaki to George Fowler, Sam Reiser, and Mary Farkas, June 10, 1957 (Yoshida personal archives).

91   "Dr. Iriya led the weekly seminars": Burton Watson, "Memories of a Friend," in *Iriya Yoshitaka Sensei tsuito-bunshu* (Tokyo: Kyuko Shoin, 2000), pp. 3–7.

92   Philip Yampolsky: Ruth F. Sasaki to Haru Yoshida, June 15, 1957 (Yoshida personal archives).

93   "Professor Iriya also loved hiking": Gary Snyder, e-mail to the author, February 17, 2006.

95   "all the boys are working hard in the library": Ruth F. Sasaki to Gary Snyder, February 28, 1958 (Ryosen-an archives).

95   "honor of being the jushoku": Ruth F. Sasaki to Haru Yoshida, April 2, 1958 (Yoshida personal archives).

96   "in our conference with Fukutomi Roshi": Ruth F. Sasaki to Kobori Sohaku, March 21, 1958 (Ryosen-an archives).

96   "in a fourteen-page memorandum": Ruth F. Sasaki, "Memorandum," April 10, 1958 (Ryosen-an archives).

97   "Ruth was photographed": "The Zen Priest," *Time Magazine*, May 26, 1958, p. 65.

100   special issue of the *Chicago Review* on Zen: *Chicago Review* 12: 2 (Summer 1958). Issue was coordinated by John Fles, former managing editor of the *Chicago Review*, and included articles by Ruth Fuller Sasaki, Alan Watts, D. T. Suzuki, Jack Kerouac, Philip Whalen, Gary Snyder, and many others. Gary Snyder told Ruth that it was the best-selling issue *Chicago Review* had ever had.

100   "We still miss you": Ruth F. Sasaki to Gary Snyder, August 19, 1958 (Ryosen-an archives).

100   "Janwillem van de Wetering later went on to write": Janwillem van de Wetering, "A Latter Day Kwannon," unpublished essay sent to author with permission to use, October 1997.

101   "Jack Kerouac's book": Ruth F. Sasaki to Gary Snyder, November 13, 1958 (Ryosen-an archives).

102   "I will be glad to talk to your friend Claude Dalenberg": Ruth F. Sasaki to Gary Snyder, March 16, 1959.

102   "Ruth read widely": Gary Snyder, e-mail to author, February 17, 2006.

102   "Frustration was growing among the research team": Philip Yampolsky, "Kyoto, Zen, Snyder," in *Gary Snyder: Dimensions of a Life*, edited by Jon Halper (San Francisco: Sierra Club, 1991), p. 68.

105   Letter to Ruth from Gary Snyder, July 31, 1964 (Ryosen-an archives): "it would be a pleasure to revise and expand—as you suggest—*The Wooden Fish*. The demand for it at City Lights (San Francisco bookstore) is surprising, and steady." *Wooden Fish* sold in Japan for 150 yen, or approximately $0.40, in 1964.

106   "Ruth felt that it was Walter's problem": Ruth F. Sasaki to Haru Yoshida, January 12, 1960.

106   "It was suggested by Phil Yampolsky": Philip Yampolsky, "Kyoto, Zen, Snyder," pp. 67–68.

106   Ruth's visit to Goto Roshi: Ruth F. Sasaki to Haru Yoshida, January 31, 1961 (Yoshida personal archives).

107   "Ruth was reaching a troubled time": Ruth F. Sasaki to Haru Yoshida, December 27, 1961 (Yoshida personal archives).

CHAPTER 6: RESEARCH AND TRANSLATION, 1960–1967

Page

110   Ruth praised *Anthology of Zen* by William Briggs: Ruth F. Sasaki to Haru Yoshida, December 28, 1961. "it is an unpretentious work, but by far the best so far, that is for having a real Zen flavor."

111   perspective of Joanne Kyger on Ryosen-an: discussion with the author, December 15, 2001.

112   perspective of Al Klyce: discussion with the author, May 4, 2002.

112   Ruth's visit to Tokyo: Ruth F. Sasaki, "Dear Everyone," January 23, 1960, *Zen Notes* VII, No. 3, March 1960.

113   Zuiun-ken: Ruth F. Sasaki, "Dear Everyone," August 6, 1960, *Zen Notes* VII, No. 9, September 1960.

115   Professor George Kennedy: Ruth F. Sasaki, "Dear Everyone," May 10, 1960, *Zen Notes* VII, No. 6, June 1960. Professor Kennedy left Kyoto by ship in early August 1960 and died at sea on August 15 from a heart attack: Ruth F. Sasaki, "Dear Everyone," September 3, 1960, *Zen Notes* VII, No. 10, 1960.

115   Philip Yampolsky's paper: "Some Problems in the Translation of Chinese Zen Material," given at the Tokyo conference, *Zen Notes* VII, Nos. 10 and 11, October and November 1960.

116   "Ruth's perception edged into the realm of paranoia": Gary Snyder, discussions with the author, November 2005; and Gary Snyder, e-mail to author, February 23, 2006.

116   Philip Yampolsky's dismissal: Gary Snyder, discussion with author, July 2004.

118   "Ruth described the process of working on the manuscript": Ruth F. Sasaki to Haru Yoshida, December 27, 1961 (Yoshida personal archives).

118   "It makes one wild, especially at my age": Ruth F. Sasaki to Haru Yoshida, December 27, 1961.

118   Miura Roshi's visit to Ryosen-an: Ruth F. Sasaki to Haru Yoshida, November 2 and December 28, 1961 (Yoshida personal archives).

119   Miura Roshi and Mary Farkas: Haru Yoshida to Ruth Fuller Sasaki, August 11, 1963 (Yoshida personal archives).

119   "Miura Roshi returned to New York and moved": Haru Yoshida to Ruth Fuller Sasaki, December 5, 1963 (Yoshida personal archives).

119   "notes for the first half of *Zen Dust*": Ruth F. Sasaki to Haru Yoshida, July 17, 1962 (Yoshida personal archives).

120   "*Zen Dust* was almost finished except for the index": Ruth F. Sasaki to Haru Yoshida, February 13, 1965 (Yoshida personal archives).

120   "amazed at how big the book had become": Ruth F. Sasaki to Haru Yoshida, June 27, 1963 (Yoshida personal archives). "just to give you another idea of what it means to get out a book like *Zen Dust*, I have made over 3000 cards for checking names, etc. for the texts and notes,

and bibliography. . . . I anticipate over 5000 new cards will have to be made."

121 Ruth's dinner with Gary Snyder and Allen Ginsberg: Gary Snyder, e-mail to author, February 2, 2006.

121 "Ruth was in good spirits": Ruth F. Sasaki to Haru Yoshida, June 27, 1963 (Yoshida personal archives).

122 Ruth's health problems: Ruth F. Sasaki to Haru Yoshida, January 15, 1963 (Yoshida personal archives).

122 dinner with Fukutomi Roshi and Kobori: Ruth F. Sasaki to Haru Yoshida, September 20, 1964 (Yoshida personal archives).

124 "after having dinner with Professor Demiéville of Paris": Ruth F. Sasaki to Haru Yoshida, March 1, 1966 (Yoshida personal archives).

124 "the last period to the Index for *Zen Dust*": Ruth F. Sasaki to Haru Yoshida, June 28, 1965 (Yoshida personal archives).

125 Ruth's visit to Amsterdam: Ruth F. Sasaki postcard to Haru Yoshida, April 18, 1966.

125 Ruth's visit in Paris: Ruth F. Sasaki to Haru Yoshida, May 1, 1966 (Yoshida personal archives).

125 Ruth's collapse at Ryosen-an: Richard Leavitt to Haru Yoshida, September 18, 1966 (Yoshida personal archives).

126 "She informed Daitoku-ji": Ruth F. Sasaski to Haru Yoshida, August 23, 1966 (Yoshida personal archives).

126 "Fukutomi Roshi was elected chief secretary": Ruth F. Sasaki to Haru Yoshida, February 14 and May 1, 1967 (Yoshida personal archives).

127 "By June, Harcourt had sold all of its copies": Ruth F. Sasaski to Haru Yoshida, June 29, 1967.

127 trip to Colorado Springs: Ruth F. Sasaki to Haru Yoshida, August 31, 1967 (Yoshida personal archives).

128 Ruth's death: Eleanor Gamer to Carlton Gamer, October [n.d.] and November 6, 1967 (Gamer personal archives). "Walter [Nowick] was here this A.M. and together we went thru [sic] stacks of papers and found all her private koan notebooks which we burned—also Sokei-an's private koan book which we will return to his dharma-brother as is proper."

128   cremation details: Eleanor Gamer to Carlton Gamer, November [n.d.] 1967 (Gamer personal archives).

129   Ruth's obituary in *Mainichi Daily News*, October 26, 1967.

129   "She was very fair in all her dealings": Richard P. Leavitt, letter to author, May 2, 2001.

Glossary

butsudan	altar
dharma	the Buddhist Universal Law or Principle
eko	memorial sutra reading
gassho	formal bow, with palms placed together
gatha	verse passages in sutras
hondo	main hall
honzan	headquarters
inka	legitimate seal of confirmation of authentic enlightenment from the Zen master to the disciple
jakugo	capping phrase for answering koans
jushoku	abbot
kancho	head abbot and Zen master
karma	deed, following the universal law of cause and effect
kesa	shoulder cloth for Buddhist priests and Zen masters

koan	formal question/riddle used by the Zen master to deepen knowledge of the student/disciple
koro	incense burner
koromo	priest's robe
kura	small building used as a storehouse
matsu-ji	subtemple
Noh	Japanese performance dramas combining dance, drama, music, poetry, and masks, dating from the fourteenth and fifteenth centuries
nyoi	carved wooden scepterlike stick used by the Zen master
rakusu	rectangular piece of patched fabric worn on a cord around the neck
rohatsu	year's most intensive sesshin, in commemoration of Buddha's enlightenment, usually held December 1–8
roshi	Zen master
sanzen	personal instruction with a Zen master
seiza	kneeling meditation
sesshin	intensive formally structured days of zazen and sanzen. Also Osesshin
sodo	Zen Buddhist monastery (and meditation hall)
sutra	primary Buddhist text
tan	raised platform bench where cushions (zabuton, zafu) are placed for zazen meditation

tansu	traditional Japanese storage chest
teisho	talk given by a Zen master
tokonoma	decorative alcove
tokudo	ordaining or initiating a Buddhist monk or a layperson
zabuton	large square cushion fitting underneath zafu for zazen practice
zafu	smaller round cushion for zazen practice
zazen	Zen meditation practice
zendo	a hall or room for the practice of Zen meditation

Bibliography

A Note on Sources

THE HARU YOSHIDA PERSONAL ARCHIVES contain copies of personal correspondence and personal papers of the years that she worked for Ruth Fuller Sasaki. Her work was personal and not institutional. Official correspondence of Ruth Fuller Sasaki is located at the First Zen Institute in New York. At the present time the personal archives of Haru Yoshida are not available to researchers. Permission was granted to the author for gathering information from this material.

The Carlton Gamer archives contain written timelines and notes of his former wife, Eleanor Everett (Watts) Gamer, and some personal correspondence. Permission was granted to the author for citing material from these archives.

The Gary Snyder papers are currently housed at the University of California, Davis, and permission to view these materials can be obtained from the special collections department. Additional materials relating to Ruth Fuller Sasaki, such as the taped transcripts of interviews Gary Snyder had with Ruth Fuller Sasaki, were provided directly to the author with permission to use them for the book.

Official papers relating to the First Zen Institute are privately held at the First Zen Institute in New York, and their availability is limited. Permission was granted to the author to view a small portion of these materials, but none of the material was subsequently used in the book.

Official papers relating to the First Zen Institute of America in Japan (at Ryosen-an) are privately held at Ryosen-an, Daitoku-ji, and their availability is limited. Permission was granted to the author for searching and quoting from these materials.

WRITINGS OF RUTH FULLER SASAKI

Books

Dumoulin, Heinrich. *The Development of Chinese Zen After the Sixth Patriarch in the Light of Mumonkan*. Translated by Ruth Fuller Sasaki. New York: The First Zen Institute of America, 1953.

Sasaki, Ruth Fuller. *Zen: A Religion*. Kyoto, Japan: The First Zen Institute of America in Japan, 1958, 1963. 38 pp.

Sasaki, Ruth Fuller. *Zen: A Method of Religious Awakening*. Kyoto, Japan: The First Zen Institute of America in Japan, 1959. 28 pp.

Sasaki, Ruth Fuller. *The First Zen Institute of America in Japan: Ryosen-an, Daitoku-ji*. Kyoto, Japan: The First Zen Institute of America in Japan, 1960. 26 pp. Photos.

Sasaki, Ruth Fuller. *Rinzai Zen Study for Foreigners in Japan*. Illustrations by Donatienne Lebovich. Kyoto, Japan: The First Zen Institute of America in Japan, 1960.

Miura Isshu and Ruth Fuller Sasaki. *The Zen Koan: Its History and Use in Rinzai Zen*. New York: Harcourt, 1965.

Miura Isshu and Ruth Fuller Sasaki. *Zen Dust: The History of the Koan and Koan Study in Rinzai (Lin-chi) Zen*. New York: Harcourt, 1966.

P'ang, Layman. *The Recorded Sayings of Layman P'ang: A Ninth-Century Zen Classic*. Translated by Ruth Fuller Sasaki, Iriya Yoshitaka, and Dana Fraser. New York: Weatherhill, 1971.

Lin-chi Hui-chao. *The Recorded Sayings of Ch'an Master Lin-chi Hui-chao of Chen Prefecture*. Translated by Ruth Fuller Sasaki. Kyoto, Japan: Institute for Zen Studies, 1975. 35 pp.

Selected Essays and Translations

Everett, Ruth Fuller. "Another Buddhist Interlude." 28 pp. Unpublished typescript. A brief history of Buddhism and descriptions of Ruth's experiences at Nanzen-ji. 1933.

Everett, Ruth Fuller. "Talk on the Contributions of Buddhism to the Spiritual Wealth of the World." Given at Union Church, Hinsdale, Illinois, March 5, 1933. Unpublished.

Sasaki, Ruth Fuller. "Why Zen Buddhism Appeals to American People: A Talk Given by Ruth F. Sasaki Before the Students of Ryokoku University, Kyoto, Japan, October 31, 1950." *Bukkyogaku-Kenkyu* (No. 5) June 1951: 63–68.

Sasaki, Ruth F. "An American Appreciation: To Dr. Daisetsu Teitaro Suzuki." *The Young East* 1 (January 1952): 11–16.

Sasaki, Ruth Fuller. "Anthology of Zen Poems (translated from the Zenrinkushu)." *Zen Culture* 4 (March 1956): 1–7.

Sasaki, Ruth Fuller "Jokei." "Memorandum: The Establishment of the Restored Matsu-ji of Daitoku-ji, Ryosen-an, and the Incorporation of the First Zen Institute of America in Japan (Nichibei Daiichi Zen Kyokai)." April 10, 1958. Unpublished. 14 pp.

Kita, Reikichi, and Kiichi Nagaya. "How Altruism Is Cultivated in Zen." Translated by Ruth Fuller Sasaki. In *Anthology of Zen*. Edited by William Briggs. New York: Grove Press, 1961, pp. 45–69. Other essays in this volume include "Zen: A Religion," pp. 111–21, and "Why Zen Buddhism Appeals to American People," pp. 218–24.

"Dear Everyone" Letters

Note: Ruth's "Letter from Kyoto: Dear Everyone" letters were included as inserts with many issues of *Zen Notes*, 1955–1963, and signed RFS, Ruth F. Sasaki, or Eryu.

July 1955 (no day specified). Description of trip with Miura Roshi and Washino through New Mexico and Colorado after being in New York, with stops in San Francisco and Honolulu on their return journey. *Zen Notes* II, No. 9, September 1955.

August 4, 1955. RFS resumed sanzen with Goto Roshi; Joseph Campbell visit along with Lindley Hubbell and RFS to see Goto Roshi, Oda Roshi; many other brief visitors. *Zen Notes* II, No. 10, October 1955.

September 25, 1955. Descriptions of earlier visit to Mudo-ji with Walter Nowick hermitage of Kanshu-ji; walking practice. *Zen Notes* II, No. 11, November 1955.

October 1, 1955. O Bon, picnics. *Zen Notes* II, No. 12, December 1955.

October 22, 1955. Goto Roshi's 77th birthday party. *Zen Notes* III, No. 1, December 1955.

November 11, 1955. News: Oda Roshi elected Kancho of Daitoku-ji; Walter Nowick now at Rinko-in, Sokoku-ji; Walter's recital and dinner with Nakagawa Soen Roshi, Nyogen Senzaki, and Mrs. Padelford. *Zen Notes* III, No. 2, February 1956.

February 13, 1956. Mary Farkas itinerary, November 18–December 19. *Zen Notes* III, No. 3, March 1956.

March 1, 1956. Mary's [Farkas] Japanese Tour, December 20–January 13. *Zen Notes* III, No. 4, April 1956.

May 1956. Mary's [Farkas] Japanese Tour, January 22–February 12, diary outline. *Zen Notes* III, No. 5, May 1956.

May 3, 1956. Spring in Kyoto. *Zen Notes* III, No. 6, June 1956.

June 3, 1956. Descriptions of temple buildings, Mother Temples, Dai-toku-ji (250 acres). *Zen Notes* III, No. 7, July 1956.

July 1, 1956. Brief history of Ryosen-an: founder Yojo Sojo Zenji, b. 1429, founded Ryosen-an between 1492 and 1500. Became the 70th kancho of Daitoku-ji in 1504, died in 1511. *Zen Notes* III, No. 8, August 1956.

August 1, 1956. Continues story of Ryosen-an. *Zen Notes* III, No. 9, September 1956.

September 4, 1956. Granddaughter Joan Watts comes for a year's visit; descriptions of places they visit. *Zen Notes* III, No. 10, October 1956.

October 9, 1956. Continuing the story of Ryosen-an and Ruth's part in its history and development. *Zen Notes* III, No. 11, November 1956.

November 5, 1956. News of Walter, studying with Goto Roshi since 1950; news of Gary Snyder's arrival in the spring; Vanessa Coward, Henry Platov. *Zen Notes* III, No. 12, December 1956.

December 1, 1956. Holiday preparations, rocks for the garden. *Zen Notes* IV, No. 1, January 1957.

January 1957 (no day). (Holiday news; began moving books into the new library. *Zen Notes* IV, No. 2, February 1957.

February 5, 1957. Advice for foreigners about Zen in Japan. *Zen Notes* IV, No. 3, March 1957.

March 4, 1957. "We have decided to build a zendo"; advice for places to stay in Kyoto for those who will come. *Zen Notes* IV, No. 4, April 1957.

April 7, 1957. Advice on challenges of Zen study in Japan. *Zen Notes* IV, No. 5, May 1957.

May 2, 1957. Construction of the new zendo begun April 26; advice for foreigners coming to Japan to study Zen. *Zen Notes* IV, No. 6, June 1957.

June 5, 1957. Advice for foreign students, continued. *Zen Notes* IV, No. 7, July 1957.

July 7, 1957. Advice for foreigners, continued. *Zen Notes* IV, No. 8, August 1957.

August 3, 1957. Summer news; stopping sanzen "as my koan study is gradually reaching its conclusion." *Zen Notes* IV, No. 9, September 1957.

September 1957 (no day). Continuation of advice on Zen study in Japan. *Zen Notes* IV, No. 10, 1957.

October 5, 1957. Ruth's reflection on her two promises to Sokei-an and her progress. *Zen Notes* IV, No. 11, November 1957.

November 5, 1957. Literary activities, progress, current and future projects. *Zen Notes* IV, No. 12, December 1957.

December 4, 1957. Description of the literary library staff: Goto Roshi, advisor Prof. Iriya Yoshitaka, Prof. Yokoi [Yanagida] Seizan, Philip Yampolsky, Dr. Burton Watson, assistant Miss Manzoji Yoko, printer Mr. Saito Kikutaro; also description of current projects. *Zen Notes* V, No. 1, January 1958.

December 26, 1957. Gratitude, home altars. *Zen Notes* V, No. 2, February 1958.

February 4, 1958. Japanese Shinto wedding, Masao's wedding. *Zen Notes* V, No. 3, March 1958.

March 3, 1958. Japanese Shinto wedding ceremonies, continued; Kanaseki Hisao. *Zen Notes* V, No. 4, April 1958.

April 1, 1958. Letters of Walter Nowick to Goto Roshi of Walter's trip to Jerusalem for his piano teacher Henriette Michelson's 75th birthday, printed with permission of Goto Roshi. *Zen Notes* V, No. 5, May 1958.

May 9, 1958. Peony viewing party at Daiko-in. *Zen Notes* V, No. 6, June 1958.

June 3, 1958. Restored Ryosen-an events in detail. *Zen Notes* Vol. V, No. 7, July 1958.

July 4, 1958. Continues description of Ryoko-in history, art; compares Mokkei's Persimmons to Soami's Ryoan-ji rock garden. *Zen Notes* V, Nos. 8 and 9, August–September 1958.

September 1958 (no day). General news; favorable review of *Sources of Japanese Tradition*, ed. by Wm. Theodore de Bary; notice of upcoming travel by Ruth to Europe, New York. *Zen Notes* V, No. 10, October 1958.

October 1958 (no day). Written from New York about trip to Europe. *Zen Notes* V, No. 11, November 1958.

December 1958 (no day). First installment of a talk given by Ruth F. Sasaki before a group of students of the Massachusetts Institute of Technology, Cambridge, Mass., on November 25, 1958: "Zen: A Method of Religious Awakening." *Zen Notes* V, No. 12, December 1958.

December 1958 (no day). Second installment of a talk given by Ruth F. Sasaki before a group of students of the Massachusetts Institute of Technology, Cambridge, Mass., on November 25, 1958. *Zen Notes* VI, No. 1, January 1959.

January 1959 (no day). Third installment of above. *Zen Notes* VI, No. 2, February 1959.

February 1959 (no day). Last installment of above. *Zen Notes* VI, No. 3, March 1959.

March 1959 (no day). Excerpts from letter Ruth was sending to Buddhist group in England in response to their letter on Zen in Japan and the West. *Zen Notes* VI, No. 4, April 1959.

April 14, 1959. Continued from the previous letter, mentions *Dharma Bums*, describes problems of Zen for the West. *Zen Notes* VI, No. 5, May 1959.

May 1959 (no day). Homecoming back to Ryosen-an after six-month trip to Europe and the U.S. *Zen Notes* VI, No. 6, June 1959.

June 4, 1959. Sanzen with Goto Roshi on *Mumonkan* koans; koan translation work; study group for *The Record of Rinzai*—with Yanagida, Iriya, Nowick, Watson, Yampolsky, Snyder, Ruth. *Zen Notes* VI, No. 7, July 1959.

July 4, 1959. List of translations of Zen texts in English, French, and German, to be continued. *Zen Notes* VI, No. 8, August 1959.

July 4, 1959. List of translations continued. *Zen Notes* VI, No. 9, September 1959.

September 2, 1959. Notes of long- and short-term visitors; visit of Haru Yoshida. *Zen Notes* VI, No. 10, October 1959.

October 4, 1959. Description of Gary Snyder's Moon Festival party. *Zen Notes* VI, No. 11, November 1959.

November 4, 1959. Description of Donatienne Lebovich's interest in Goethe, art. *Zen Notes* VI, No. 12, December 1959.

January 1, 1960. Description of visit Ruth and Washino made to see the fire walking ceremony November 15 by *yamabushi* (mountain monks) at the temple Gumonjido, Miyajima, near the summit of Mount Misen, on island in the Inland Sea. *Zen Notes* VII, No. 1, January 1960.

January 8, 1960. Review of *The Practice of Zen* by Chang Chen-chi and a subsequent *Zen Notes* in April, VII, No. 4, includes a response by Professor Chang, "An Open Letter to Mrs. Ruth F. Sasaki." *Zen Notes*, VII, No. 2, February 1960.

January 23, 1960. Train trip to Tokyo to with Donatienne Lebovich, Vanessa Coward, Washino, and Ruth to view paintings as possible illustrations for *Zen Dust*; visited Kamakura to visit with Dr. Suzuki. *Zen Notes* VII, No. 3, March 1960.

March 8, 1960. Daitoku-ji wedding of Gary Snyder and Joanne Kyger. *Zen Notes* VII, No. 4, April 1960.

March 31, 1960. Further descriptions of visit to Beijing in 1934, increase in cars; visits with Dr. Hu Shih, dean of literature, at the university; visit with D. T. Suzuki at the Peking City Library to study Dunhuang manuscripts/sutras. Ruth and Dr. Suzuki also visited two Buddhist temples together. *Zen Notes* VII, May 1960.

May 10, 1960. Spring events and ceremonies, including the installation of the new kancho of Nanzen-ji, Shibayama Zenkei Roshi, on May 3. *Zen Notes* VII, No. 6, June 1960.

June 7, 1960. Description of Ruth's 1934 visit to Beijing with Edward W. Everett. *Zen Notes* VII, No. 7, July 1960.

July 5, 1960. Continuation of Ruth's 1934 visit to China. *Zen Notes* VII, No. 8, August 1960.

August 6, 1960. Picnics, summer events, miscellaneous notes of people visiting Ryosen-an. *Zen Notes* VII, No. 9, September 1960.

September 3, 1960. Includes full talk of Philip Yampolsky at a conference, "Some Problems in the Translation of Chinese Zen Materials." *Zen Notes* VII, No. 10, October 1960.

October 3, 1960. Continues Yampolsky's talk; description of Empuku-ji history. *Zen Notes* VII, No. 11, November 1960.

November 4, 1960. Ruth's opinions/discussion of vegetarianism vs. eating meat. *Zen Notes* VII, No. 12, December 1960.

December 11, 1960. Zuiun-ken, Bollingen awards, publications of *Ryosen-an Zendo Practice* and *The Wooden Fish*, by Gary Snyder and Gutetsu; Rohatsu held at Ryosen-an. *Zen Notes* VIII, No. 1, January 1961.

January 1, 1961. Review of Alan Watts's *This Is IT*. *Zen Notes* VIII, No. 2, February 1961.

February 7, 1961. Part of the introduction for *Zen Dust*, in progress. *Zen Notes* VIII, No. 3, March 1961.

March 2, 1961. Continuation of previous letter on satori in Zen. *Zen Notes* VIII, No. 4, April 1961.

April 4, 1961. Some material being prepared for *Zen Dust* footnotes on Lin-chi. *Zen Notes* VIII, No. 5, May 1961.

May 6, 1961. Essay on Zen and the Nembutsu (to think about the Buddha). *Zen Notes* VIII, No. 6, June 1961.

June 7, 1961. Car trip with Ruth's friends the Iwasas to Joruri-ji, Ikkyu-ji, and Kaiho-ji. *Zen Notes* VIII, No. 7, July 1961.

July 8, 1961. Essay on what kind of Buddhism is suitable for the West. *Zen Notes* VIII, No. 8, August 1961.

August 6, 1961. Summertime in Kyoto. *Zen Notes* VIII, No. 9, September 1961.

September 7, 1961. Description of O Bon festival and history; also a note on the end of the Mount Fuji climbing season with an estimate of 174,523 climbers for the eight-week season. *Zen Notes* VIII, No. 10, October 1961.

October 6, 1961. Continuation of O Bon ceremony. *Zen Notes* VIII, No. 11, November 1961.

January 4, 1962. Description of Kyoto holiday activities, Christmas, New Year's. *Zen Notes* IX, No. 2, February 1962.

December 5, 1962. Continued from previous letter, memories of sesshin at Nanzen-ji in early 1930s. *Zen Notes* X, No. 1, January 1963.

January 14, 1963. Ryosen-an reflections, eight students in residence; Eleanor, Carlton, and son Michael staying at Zuiun-ken since the fall, details of their visits. *Zen Notes* X, No. 2, February 1963.

February 10, 1963. Extremely cold winter; biography excerpt on Sekito Kisen being prepared for *Zen Dust*. *Zen Notes* X, No. 3, March 1963.

March 9, 1963. Essay on the four Universal Vows, *Sixth Patriarch's Sutra*. *Zen Notes* X, No. 4, April 1963.

April 8, 1963. Essay on long-term students at Ryosen-an vs. brief visitors; notes on Bill Laws leaving for Myoshin-ji. *Zen Notes* X, No. 5, May 1963.

May 7, 1963. Review and discussion of *Christianity and World Religions* by Dr. Copeland, and his inclusion of some of Ruth's *Zen: A Method for Religious Awakening* as well as the concerns of Baptists over the growing popularity of Zen. *Zen Notes* X, No. 6, June 1963.

June 13, 1963. Continuation of previous letter's topic; review of Dumoulin's *History of Zen Buddhism* (favorable); review of *Zen Catholicism*, by Dom Aelred Graham (unfavorable). *Zen Notes* X, No. 7, July 1963.

August 10, 1963. Modernizing Kyoto; annual picnic at Arashiyama. *Zen Notes* X, No. 11, November 1963.

September 7, 1963. Description of Empuku-ji and the Foreigner's Zendo of the early 1930s with Kozuki Tesshu Roshi. *Zen Notes* X, No. 9, September 1963.

November 15, 1963. Trip in late October to Kurama for the Fire Festival (Hi-matsuri). *Zen Notes* X, No. 12, December 1963.

Works Cited

Abe, Masao, editor. *A Zen Life: D. T. Suzuki Remembered*. New York: Weatherhill, 1986.

Aitken, Robert. *Encouraging Words: Zen Buddhist Teachings for Western Students*. New York: Pantheon, 1993.

App, Urs. "Linji's Evergreens" (review article). *Japanese Journal of Religious Studies* 21 (4): 425–36. 1994. Compares translations of Watson, Iriya, Yanagida, Sasaki, Schloegl, and Demiéville.

Austin, James H. *Zen and the Brain: Toward an Understanding of Meditation and Consciousness*. Cambridge, Mass.: MIT Press, 1998.

Briggs, William A. *Anthology of Zen*. New York: Grove Press, 1961.

Chicago Review. Summer 1958 12(2): 1–110. The "On Zen" section is 72 pages with articles by eleven people: Alan Watts, D. T. Suzuki, Jack Kerouac, Shinichi Hisamatsu, Philip Whalen, Ruth F. Sasaki,

Nyogen Senzaki, Gary Snyder, Harold McCarthy, Akihisa Kondo, and Paul Wienpahl.

Chicago Tribune. "Marriage of Ruth Fuller to Edward Warren Everett." April 7, 1917.

Chicago Tribune. Ruth and Eleanor sail for Kyoto. October 8, 1933.

Chicago Tribune. "Japanese War Chief Honors Chicago Man and His Wife." May 26, 1934.

Chicago Tribune. Ruth's return trip on the *Asahi.* July 27 and 31, 1934.

Chicago Tribune. "E. W. Everett Family Home." July 31, 1934.

Chicago Tribune. Gems stolen from the Everetts' Bermuda vacation home. April 20, 1936.

Chicago Tribune. "E. W. Everett, 67, Former Chicago Attorney, Dies." January 21, 1940.

Clarkstown Country Club. *Life at the Clarkstown Country Club, Nyack, N.Y.* Nyack, N.Y.: The Club, 1935.

Covell, Jon, and Yamada Sobin. *Zen at Daitoku-ji.* Tokyo: Kodansha, 1974.

Danno, Yoko, editor. *Autumn Stone in the Woods: A Tribute to Lindley Williams Hubbell.* Middletown Springs, Vt.: P. S. A. Press, 1997.

Doings (Hinsdale). "Miss Ruth Fuller's piano recital," Women's Club Notes. Saturday, December 18, 1909.

Dower, John W. *Embracing Defeat: Japan in the Wake of World War II.* New York: Norton, 1999.

Dumoulin, Heinrich. *The Development of Chinese Zen After the Sixth Patriarch in the Light of Mumonkan.* Translated by Ruth Fuller Sasaki. New York: The First Zen Institute of America, 1953.

Dumoulin, Heinrich. *Zen Buddhism in the 20th Century*. New York: Weatherhill, 1992.

Eidmann, Philipp Karl, translator. *The Sutra of the Teachings Left by the Buddha*. Osaka: Koyota Yamamoto, 1927.

Everett, Edward Warren. *Far East for Ninety Days: Narrative of a Trip to Japan and China in 1930*. "Read before Law Club of Chicago and Published in Central Manufacturing District Magazine." Privately published, n.d., 23 pp.

Fields, Rick. *How the Swans Came to the Lake: A Narrative History of Buddhism in America*. Boulder, Colo: Shambhala, 1981.

Furlong, Monica. *Zen Effects: The Life of Alan Watts*. Boston, Mass.: Houghton Mifflin, 1986.

Guy, David. "Ancestors: Dragon Wisdom: The Life of Ruth Fuller Sasaki." *Tricycle* IV (2): 16–21. 1994.

Halper, Jon. *Gary Snyder: Dimensions of a Life*. San Francisco: Sierra Club Books, 1991. Includes essays by Kanaseki Hisao, Burton Watson, and Philip Yampolsky.

Hori, Victor Sogen, compiler, translator, and annotator. *Zen Sand: The Book of Capping Phrases for Koan Practice*. Honolulu, Hawaii: University of Hawai'i Press, 2003.

Hotz, Michael, compiler. *Holding the Lotus to the Rock: Autobiography of Sokei-an Sasaki*. New York: Four Walls Eight Windows, 2003.

Kapleau, Philip, compiler and editor. *The Three Pillars of Zen*. Boston: Beacon, 1965.

Kyger, Joanne. *The Japan and India Journals, 1960–1964*. Bolinas, Calif.: Tombouctou, 1981.

Lancaster, Lewis. "*Zen Dust*. By Isshu Miura and Ruth Fuller Sasaki." Book review in *Journal of the American Oriental Society* 88 (3): 621–22. 1968.

Layman, Emma McCloy. *Buddhism in America*. Chicago: Nelson-Hall, 1976.

New York Times. Obituary of Sokei-an. May 19, 1945.

Randall, Monica. *Phantoms of the Hudson Valley*. Woodstock, N.Y.: Overlook Press, 1995.

Richie, Donald. *Zen Inklings: Some Stories, Fables, Parables, Sermons, and Prints, with Notes and Commentaries*. New York: Weatherhill, 1982.

Ross, Nancy Wilson, compiler and editor. *The World of Zen: An East–West Anthology*. New York: Vintage Books, 1960.

Ross, Nancy Wilson. *Buddhism: A Way of Life and Thought*. New York: Knopf, 1980.

Roth, Martin, and John Stevens. *Zen Guide: Where to Meditate in Japan*. New York: Weatherhill, 1985.

Sasaki, Sokei-an. *Cat's Yawn: The Thirteen Numbers* (published 1940–1941). Compiled by Ruth Fuller Sasaki. New York: The First Zen Institute of America, 1947.

Sasaki, Sokei-an. *The Zen Eye: A Collection of Zen Talks by Sokei-an Sasaki*. Edited by Mary Farkas. New York: Weatherhill, 1993.

Sasaki, Sokei-an. *Zen Pivots: Lectures on Buddhism and Zen by Sokei-an Sasaki*. Edited by Mary Farkas and Robert Lopez. New York: Weatherhill, 1998.

Schloegl, Irmgard. "My Memory of Ruth Fuller Sasaki." *The Eastern Buddhist* II (2): 129–30. 1969.

Schloegl, Irmgard. *The Wisdom of the Zen Masters*. New York: New Directions, 1975.

Snyder, Gary. "On Rinzai Masters and Western Students in Japan." *Wind Bell* 8 (1–2): 23–28. 1969.

Snyder, Gary, and Gutetsu Kanetsuki. *The Wooden Fish: Basic Sutras and Gathas of Rinzai Zen*. Kyoto: The First Zen Institute of America in Japan, 1961. 56 pp.

Suzuki, D. T. *Essays in Zen Buddhism*. First Series. London: Rider & Co. for the Buddhist Society, 1949, 1958.

Watson, Burton. "Memories of a Friend." In *Iriya Yoshitaka Sensei tsuito-bunshu*. Tokyo: Kyuko Shoin, 2000, pp. 3–7.

Watts, Alan. *Zen*. Stanford, Calif.: James Ladd Delkin, 1948. "Dedicated to Ruth Fuller Sasaki."

Watts, Alan. *In My Own Way: An Autobiography, 1915–1965*. New York: Pantheon, 1972.

Wind Bell. Zen Center of San Francisco, Vol. VIII, Nos. 1–2 (Fall 1969), 55 pp. Entire issue devoted to articles relating to Ruth Fuller Sasaki, including pieces by Gary Snyder.

Index

Alice in Wonderland, 31
American Oriental Society, 15
Anthology of Zen, 110
Analects, 34
"Another Buddhist Interlude",
    18
Araki Eichi, 76
Asahina Roshi, 66, 76
Autumn Stone in the Woods, 62
Awano Roshi, 42

Beck, Lily Adams, 14, 19
Bernard, Pierre Arnold, 6–7
Blyth, R. H., 76
Bodenheim, Max, 34
Bollingen Foundation, 115
Briggs, William, 110
Brill, 124
A Buddhist Bible, 20
Buddhism in England
    (magazine), 18
Buddhist Lodge, 27
Buddhist Lodge (magazine), 20
Buddhist Society (London), 27,
    113
Buddhist Society of America, 28,
    36, 37, 41
Bukkyogaku Kenkyu
    (magazine), 56

Calchas, 13
California Institute of Art, 33
Campbell, Joseph, 73, 110
Cat's Yawn (book), 41, 49
Cat's Yawn (magazine), 36
Chang Hsueh Liang (Zhang Xue
    Liang), 13
Chicago Review, 100
Chikudo Ohasama Roshi, 21
Chuo Koron, 34–35
Chotoku-in, 59, 67
City Lights Bookstore (San
    Francisco), 106
Clarkstown Country Club, 6–8,
    10, 18
Coward, Vanessa, 68, 81–82,
    84–85, 112
Craig, Albert, 58

Daishu-in, 48, 74, 81, 88
Dalenberg, Claude, 102, 113
Das Gupta, Kedernath, 22
Daio Kokushi (teacher), 72, 98
Daito Kokushi, (pupil,
    Founder), 53
Daitoku-ji, 15, 42, 44, 53, 98
"Dear Everyone" letters, 53, 57,
    65, 72–73, 78, 80,
Demiéville, Paul, 124

Denenshitsu Roshi, 44, 54
Development of Chinese Zen, 59, 62–63, 68, 123
de Vries, Blanche, 7
Dhammapada, 23
Dharma Bums, 101–102
Doshisha University, 52, 62, 78, 81
Duff, Jessie, 15
Dumoulin, Heinrich, Father, 59, 76

Early T'ang Colloquial Grammar, 64
Eidmann, Philipp Karl, 59
Eizan (monk at Nanzen-ji), 17
Eizan Tatsuta Roshi, 21, 66, 76
Empuku-ji, 113
Engaku-ji, 20, 21
Enryaku-ji, 67
"Eryu" ("dragon wisdom" Ruth's Buddhist name from Sokei-an Roshi), 35, 130
Essays in Zen Buddhism: (first series) 14; (third series) 26
Everett, Edward Warren, 5, 11, 26–28
Everett, Eleanor (later Eleanor Watts, later Eleanor Gamer), 5–6, 23, 27, 47, 52

"*Far East for Ninety Days; Narrative of a trip to Japan and China in 1930*", 11
Farkas, Mary, 41, 42, 56–57, 64–66, 75–77, 119
The First Zen Institute of America (formerly Buddhist Society of America), 24, 41, 71
The First Zen Institute of America in Japan, 79, 103–104
Forman, Georgia, 19
Fort Meade Internment Camp, 37

Fowler, George, 41, 77
Fuller, Clara Elizabeth, 3, 36
Fuller, David, 3, 51, 69
Fuller, George E., 3
Fraser, Dana, 109, 126
Fukutomi Isei, 122–123, 126, 129–130, 132
Fukutomi (Settei) Roshi, 132
Furuta Kazuhiro, 109, 122, 127
Furuta Shokin, 76

Gamer, Carlton, 52, 73, 78, 113
Gandavyuha, 59
Ganz, Rudolf, 4
Ginsberg, Allen, 82, 121
Goddard, Dwight, 19, 20, 23
Goto Zuigan Roshi, 21, 42, 47–49, 72, 88, 106–107

Hara, Maya, xxii
Harada Roshi, 80
Hayashi, Senjuro, General, 26
Hayashi, Suseki (Lindley Williams Hubbell), 38, 61–62
Hekigan (*Blue Cliff Record*), 64
Herrigel, Eugen, 19
Ho Koji, 63, 123
Hofuku-ji, 25
Hokubei Shinpo (Seattle), 33–34
Hori, Victor Sogen, xiv, xxii, 132
Hoshun-in, 63, 78, 126
Hosshin-ji, 80, 112
Hubbell, Lindley Williams, 38, 61–62
Humphreys, Christmas (Toby), xvii, 27
Hurvitz, Leon, 65–66, 121

Ikeda, 15, 26
Imperial Academy of Arts, 32

In My Own Way, 39
Iriya Yoshitaka, 63, 88, 91–93, 102, 129

jakugo, 30
Japan Club, 22, 35
Japanese Exclusion Clause of the Immigration Act, 26
Jokei (Ruth F. Sasaki's priest ordination name), 94

Kajiura Itsugai Roshi, 44–45
Kanaseki Hisao, 52, 62, 66, 74, 91, 92, 118, 125
Kapleau, Philip (and wife deLancey), 112
Kato, 24, 52
Keitoku dento roku (Record of the Transmission of the Lamp), 66, 115
Keene, Donald, 125
Kennedy, George, 115
Kerouac, Jack, 82, 101
Kido Osho, 72. *See* Xutang
Kinkaku-ji, 62, 128
Kirchner, Tom, 132
Klyce, Al, 112
Koon-ji, 24, 77, 87, 118
Kobori Sohaku, 58, 95, 98, 114, 122–123
koro (incense burner), 56
Kosen Imakita Roshi, 20
Koto-in, 15
Kozuki Tesshu Roshi, 14
Kuge (Ruth's Buddhist name from Nanshinken Roshi), 23, 35
Kyger, Joanne, 93, 110, 111–112, 121
Kyoto Women's University, 81

Lampadion, 4
Laws, Bill and Judith, 113
Leavitt, Richard, 36, 109, 122, 125, 127–129
Lebovich, Donatienne, 73, 103, 112
Life at the Clarkstown Country Club, 8

Mainichi Daily News, 129
Manjusri, 96, 99
Manzoji, Yoko, 88, 91
March, Arthur C., 18
Marshall, Benjamin H., 8
Maspero, Henri, 64
Matsunami Taiun Osho , xxii, 131
May, Jacques, 113
McGovern, William T., 14, 56
Mei Lang Fang, 13
Miura Isshu Roshi: at Nanzen-ji, 23–24; biographical story, 66; separates from First Zen Institute, 118–119;visits New York, 71, 77; Western students, 66–67; Woodlawn Cemetery visit, 130; *Zen Dust* from teisho, 89
Miya (Mr.), 22, 35
Miyako Hotel, 12
Mudo-ji, 67
Mumonkan, 16, 64, 89
Myoshin-ji, 18, 49–50

Nakagawa Soen Roshi, 75
Nanshinken (Kono Mukai) Roshi, 15–17, 23–25
Nanzen-ji, 15–18, 23
Newell, Isaac N., Colonel, 13
Nichibei Daiichi Zen Kyokai, 79

Nowick, Walter, 43, 47–48, 65, 67, 75, 85
nyoi, 25, 30

Oda Sesso Roshi, 44, 50, 74, 97, 25–126
Ogata Sohaku, 18–19, 42, 59, 66, 81, 114
Orientalia Bookstore (New York City), 35
Otani University, 18, 58
Oyamazaki Roshi, 25

Partington, Richard, 33
Philips, Bernard, 112
Platov, Henry, 69
Platov, Mariquita, 28
Pollock, Hugo, 38, 40
Pu-yi, Emperor, 26

Record of Rinzai (Rinzai roku, Lin-chi lu), 55, 89, 91, 94, 102, 123
The Recorded Sayings of Ch'an Master Lin-chi Hui-chao of Chen Prefecture, 129
The Recorded Sayings of Layman P'ang, 129
Regnery, William F., 9
Reiser, Sam, 77
Rinko-in, 75, 81, 83, 106
Rinzai Zen Study for Foreigners in Japan, 103
Rokusu dankyo, 90
Rolf, Ida, 8
Ross, Nancy Wilson, 110
Russell, Ida, 76
Ryomo Kyokai ("The Society for Abandonment of Subjectivity and Objectivity"), 20, 35

Ryoko-in, 58, 76
Ryosen-an, 53–55, 85, 104
Ryosen-an Zendo Practice, 105
Ryokoku University, 14, 56

Sasaki Seiko, 33, 38
Sasaki Shigetsu (Sokei-an) Roshi: childhood upbringing, 31; inka, 35; interned and released, 37–38; Manchurian war, 32; married Ruth F. Everett, 39–40; meets Ruth F. Everett, 20–22; named Founder of Restored Ryosen-an, 94, 99
Sasaki Shintaro, 33, 38
Sasaki, Tome, 33, 34, 40
Schillinberg, Fielder, 53, 77
Schloegl, Irmgard (Venerable Myokyo-ni of the Zen Centre of London), 75, 113, 126, 134
Seigo Hogaku, 77
Senko-an, 16
Senzaki Nyogen, 42, 60, 75
Shapiro, Secki, 77
Shively, Donald, 67
Shokoku-ji, 25, 81
"Shounso" Pine Cloud Villa, 15
Smith, Huston, xx, 103, 110
Snyder, Gary, 60, 67, 78, 82–83, 116
Sokatsu Shaku Roshi, 20, 21, 32, 43, 65
Soyen Shaku Roshi, 20, 76
The Spirit of Zen, 27
Suzuki, Beatrice Lane, 14, 25–26, 58
Suzuki, Daisetz T.: 14–15, 31, 42, 57, 64, 125
Swan House, 9–10, 23

takuhatsu, 60
Takamura Koun, 32
"*Talk on the contributions of
    Buddhism to the Spiritual Wealth
    of the World*", Union Church,
    Hinsdale, Illinois, 18
Time, 84, 97
Tokai-an, 49

Ueno Naozo, 62

van de Wetering, Janwillem, 75,
    100–101

Washino Akiko, 61, 112, 117
Walden, Ken, 113, 120, 122
Watson, Burton, 65, 91–93, 116
Watts, Alan, 19, 27, 39, 100, 124,
    134
Watts, Ann (Andrews), 27
Watts, Joan, 27, 80, 87–88
Wienpahl, Paul, 106, 110
Winston, Strawn, & Shaw, 28
*The Wooden Fish: Basic Sutras and
    Gathas of Rinzai Zen*, 105–106
Woodlawn Cemetery, New York
    City, 41, 60, 129–130
Woodhouse, George, 27

World Fellowship of Faiths, 22

Xutang (Hsu-t'ang), 72
    (Kido Osho)

Yanagida Seizan (formerly Yokoi
    Seizan), 78, 93
Yampolsky, Philip, 83, 91–92, 106,
    115–116
Yasutani Roshi, 112
Yen Hsi-shan, General, 13
Yoshida, Haru, 43, 51–52, 55, 61,
    68, 130
Young East, 58

*Zen: A Method for Religious Awaken-
    ing*, 103
Zen: A Religion, 97
Zen Dust, 24, 88–89, 95, 127
ZEN Hermitage, 19
ZEN Magazine, 19
Zen Koan, 119, 124
Zen Notes (newsletter), 53, 57–58,
    64, 71, 97
Zengyu Kunmoku, 72
Zenrin Kushu, 30–31, 89
Zen Sand, xiv, 132
Zuiun-ken, 113–114, 122